'Faced with what some describe ⸺ y
dares to say this is no time to de⸺ ⸺ e
as a developmental economist, h⸺ ⸺ ⸺ trying to tick on each
problem as it comes along is doomed to failure. Part history, part
manifesto, *Sustainable Futures* calls for an integrated approach
which brings together the resources of government and the power of
the people. Those who want to avoid the mistakes of the past and
re-make our future should read this book.'

George Alagiah, BBC Journalist and Author

'Dedicated to "all the grandchildren", *Sustainable Futures* is written
in the hope of contributing to a pathway out of the current dreadful
state of our world and into a sustainable future for them. Kaplinsky
provides a theoretical and conceptual framework to better understand the current crises and to extract lessons for the future from
epochal moments in history and sets out an ambitious agenda for
change. He has indeed provided a compelling and hopeful message
"for the grandchildren".'

Keith Bezanson, former President of Canada's International
Development Research Centre

'A most inspirational and enlightening book by a leading development scholar and thinker, analysing courses and actions to build
an economically, socially and environmentally sustainable future.
A book with historical and analytical depth as well as a global and
forward vision which is much needed at a moment when the world
is at crossroads.'

Xiaolan Fu, Professor of Technology and International
Development, University of Oxford

'A compelling read, brilliantly written and bubbling with thought-
provoking ideas, experience and outlines for the future.'

Sir Richard Jolly, former Assistant Secretary-General of the UN

'Read this book! It's tightly argued, packed with an astonishing depth
and range of evidence on our current crises, and yet is ultimately
equally full of hope and practical inspiration, ambitiously laying out
a sweeping agenda for change. Kaplinsky combines the big vision of

how society must come to grips with innovation together with the mechanics of driving change.'

Harriet Lamb, CEO of Ashden and former CEO of Fairtrade International

'As the pandemic continues to grip the world, we are facing increasing demands for a more resilient and sustainable socio-economic system. Taking a Schumpeterian perspective, this book offers an effective clue to a way out of the current crisis. While it still sees a window of opportunity in the potentials of information communication technologies, it also sets outs a blueprint for collective action by us. It is a must read for all of us, who should participate in this joint effort.'

Keun Lee, Winner of the Schumpeter Prize, 2014, and Professor of Economics, Seoul National University

'This work is a tour de force by a mature and insightful social scientist, worth reading by anybody concerned with how to tackle simultaneously challenges such as global warming and growing inequality. It explains how the world got into its current unsustainable state and it comes with brave and radical ideas for how to move it back towards sustainability.'

Bengt-Åke Lundvall, Emeritus Professor of Economics, Aalborg University

'There are many critics of the current capitalist system. And equally many others who profess how to organize it better. What is often missing is a link between the two. That is, an understanding of how we got into the mess we have, and using this understanding to analyse what is required to do better. Kaplinsky's book does just that, bringing together historical, political and economic research in a way that allows us to both learn from history, and to have a more prosperous and sustainable future.'

Mariana Mazzucato, Founding Director of the UCL Institute for Innovation and Public Purpose, and author of *Mission Economy: A Moonshot Guide to Changing Capitalism*

'Kaplinsky has laid out with clarity, historical perspective and illuminating supporting data just how the current economic picture indicates a turning point in advanced capitalism. Kaplinsky's driving and compelling historical narrative undergirds an ambitious case for political change that is both grounded and hopeful, touching on income equality, environmental resilience and economic development. *Sustainable Futures* is a serious and highly readable account of our recent economic history and our potential path forward. Informative, insightful and inspiring.'

William Milberg, Dean and Professor of Economics, The New School for Social Research, New York

'A timely and must-read book as the world ponders how to build better. It shows that the age of mass production, with endless harnessing of energy and matter, has resulted in multiple crises of declining growth, the rise of plutocracies and populism, and the ravaging of the environment. Kaplinsky argues that the power of the financial sector and the plutocracy needs to be overcome, in order to realize the potential of the ICT-based techno-economic paradigm to build a more sustainable and environment-friendly system of production.'

Dev Nathan, Visiting Professor at the Institute for Human Development, New Delhi, and Director of GenDev Centre for Research and Innovation, India

'Kaplinsky illustrates the depth of the crises of the twenty-first century. *Sustainable Futures* distinguishes itself in its interdisciplinary, pluralist, and historical approach coupled with an emphasis on the broader techno-economic paradigm: technological drive, economic development, environmental sustainability, social change and political structure. This timely book is extremely relevant to policymakers and researchers of both the industrialized and developing world.'

Arkebe Oqubay, Senior Minister and Special Adviser to the Prime Minister of Ethiopia, and Distinguished Fellow of the Overseas Development Institute

'If you want to understand today's world and how to fix it, this is the book to read. Kaplinsky shows a formidable capacity to encompass the whole spectrum of today's global problems and provides realistic – though ambitious – solutions. Indispensable reading!'

Carlota Perez, author of *Technological Revolutions and Financial Capital: The Dynamics of Bubbles and Golden Ages*

'Engagingly written and spanning economic, social and environmental agendas in an exemplary way, *Sustainable Futures* places Information and Communication Technology at the heart of a compelling argument, but never as a technology fix. On the contrary, the book argues convincingly for a wide range of social and political solutions that should provide a much-needed and powerful directionality to the opportunities offered by these technologies.'

Johan W. Schot, Professor of Global History and Sustainability,
Utrecht University

'This work provides a careful, historically based, tough-minded but ultimately optimistic agenda for action that could rise to the challenges of the rapidly deteriorating climate and environment, threats to social cohesion, predatory elites, and destructive nationalism. We really can go beyond the fragile and destructive models and paths that we have followed, towards a much better economy, society and way of living. But we must decide and decide now; as the book's final sentence states, drawing on Sartre, "to choose not to act, is to choose".'

Lord Nicholas Stern, co-chair of the Global Commission on
the Economy and Climate, Professor of Economics at the
London School of Economics and Political Science, and former
Chief Economist of the World Bank

'*Sustainable Futures* is a triumph. Drawing on all the social sciences, it demonstrates how bulldozer trends of our time can be understood as fuelled by the declining phase of the Mass Production "techno-economic paradigm". The book ends with a vision of what an ICT-enabled, more sustainable world could look like. Anybody interested in the future of human – and non-human – society should debate it.'

Robert H. Wade, Professor of Global Political Economy,
London School of Economics and Political Science

'The journey from the world's current multiple crises to a sustainable future looks almost impossibly difficult. But in Raphael Kaplinsky we have a guide who inspires confidence. He is that rare thing: an economist who combines a real understanding of society and politics with a seasoned idealism, and in this book he gives us what is perhaps our best chance.'

Richard Wilkinson, co-author of *The Spirit Level* and co-founder of
The Equality Trust

Sustainable Futures

Sustainable Futures

An Agenda for Action

Raphael Kaplinsky

polity

First published in 2021 by Polity Press

Polity Press
65 Bridge Street
Cambridge CB2 1UR, UK

Polity Press
101 Station Landing
Suite 300
Medford, MA 02155, USA

ISBN-13: 978-1-5095-4782-1
ISBN-13: 978-1-5095-4783-8 (pb)

A catalogue record for this book is available from the British Library.

Library of Congress Cataloging-in-Publication Data
Names: Kaplinsky, Raphael, author.
Title: Sustainable futures : an agenda for action / Raphael Kaplinsky.
Description: Cambridge, UK ; Medford, MA : Polity Press, 2021. | Includes
    bibliographical references and index. | Summary: "How to steer the
    economy and society to a more sustainable future"-- Provided by
    publisher.
Identifiers: LCCN 2020053493 (print) | LCCN 2020053494 (ebook) | ISBN
    9781509547821 (hardback) | ISBN 9781509547838 (paperback) | ISBN
    9781509547845 (epub) | ISBN 9781509548439 (pdf)
Subjects: LCSH: Sustainable development.
Classification: LCC HC79.E5 K3644 2021 (print) | LCC HC79.E5 (ebook) |
    DDC 338.9/27--dc23
LC record available at https://lccn.loc.gov/2020053493
LC ebook record available at https://lccn.loc.gov/2020053494

Typeset in 10.5 on 12.5 Sabon
by Fakenham Prepress Solutions, Fakenham, Norfolk NR21 8NL
Printed and bound in Great Britain by TJ Books Limited

For further information on Polity, visit our website:
politybooks.com

To my grandchildren (Arlo, Kika, Eva and Cam), to my children and their partners (Natasha, Ben, Justin and Nichole) who made them for us, to my godson (Kian) and, of course, to all the grandchildren of the world

In memory of my parents, Morris and Becky, with love and gratitude for building the platform on which our family stands, and to Cecil, who left us too early

Contents

Figures   page xii
Tables   xiv
Preface   xv
Acknowledgements   xvi

1   A Fork in the Road   1
2   The Rise and Fall of the Mass Production Economy   6
3   The Bumpy Ride to Social Decay   34
4   The Collapse of Environmental Sustainability   65
5   Mass Production Runs Out of Steam   95
6   Information and Communication Technologies: The Motor
    of the New Techno-Economic Paradigm   121
7   Transformative Change in Practice   144
8   What's To Be Done?   174
9   Who Will Do It? Making Change Happen   203

Notes   226
Index   235

Figures

2.1 The expansion of Gross Domestic Product, 1961–2018:
World, US and Europe (% per annum)   9

2.2 Share of investment in equipment and other physical
assets (Gross Capital Formation) in GDP   12

2.3 Annual growth of labour productivity, 1951–2019   13

2.4 Balance of payments: largest debtor and surplus
economies, 1998–2019 ($m)   16

2.5 Corporate tax rate: France, Germany, US, UK, Japan and
Sweden, 1981–2019 (%)   19

3.1 Top 1% personal wealth share in emerging and rich
countries, 1913–2015   38

3.2 Changes in global inequality, 1980–2016   41

3.3 Share of labour in total national income, high-income
economies, 1960–2012   42

3.4a Life-expectancy and inequality, 22 OECD economies   45

3.4b Life-expectancy and inequality, 50 US States   46

3.5 Health and social problems and degree of inequality,
inter-country differences   47

3.6 Index of status inequality and degree of inequality   48

3.7 Index of social participation and degree of inequality   49

3.8 Index of civic participation and degree of inequality   50

3.9 Belief in conspiracy theories, US and UK   55

3.10 Inflows of migrants, selected high-income economies,
2006–2016 (millions)   60

3.11 Immigrant share of population and far-right voting   62

4.1 The Holocene in historical perspective: not just warm
temperatures but stable temperatures   67
4.2 The Great Acceleration   70
4.3 Take, Make, Use and Waste   72
4.4 Energy equivalent global output of different energy
forms, 1800–2019 (terawatt hours)   76
4.5 The growth in global total resource supply, 1970–2010
(million tonnes)   77
4.6 Index of energy efficiency in the EU, 1990–2014 (1990 =
100)   78
4.7 Variation of CO_2 emissions from transport in the EU,
1990 and 2010 (million tonnes energy equivalent)   79
4.8 US advertising expenditure, 1990–2017 ($m)   86
4.9 Rising frequency of natural disasters, 1980–2007   94
5.1 Six phases of techno-economic paradigms   98
5.2 US corporate profitability as share of domestic income,
1951–1966 and 1966–1990 (post-tax profits as a share
of domestic income, %)   108
5.3 US corporate profitability as share of domestic income,
1990–2007 (post-tax profits as a share of domestic
income, %)   111
6.1 Six phases of techno-economic paradigms   123
7.1 Broadband connections per 100 inhabitants, 2005–2018 146
7.2 The global share of different energy sources, 1971–2014 151
7.3 Frequency and cost escalation of electricity infrastructure
projects (based on analysis of 411 projects)   152
7.4 The Zambezi river basin   156
7.5 Global average annual net capacity additions by energy
source   160
7.6 Wheat and barley crop yields in UK agriculture,
1948–2017 (tonnes/hectare)   163
7.7 Sources of productivity growth in UK agriculture,
1973–2017 (1973 = 100)   163
7.8 'Tom' gathering data on soil and weeds   170
8.1 Levels of circularity: the 10 Rs   187
8.2 Total UK tax receipts, 2018–2019 (£bn)   190

Tables

2.1 Average annual economic growth rates: World, US and
Europe (%)   10

3.1 Extent and character of migrant inflows in ten high-
income economies   60

4.1 Range of approximate CO_2 emissions per unit of
electricity produced, different sources of energy
(grammes CO_2/kWh)   75

4.2 Projected impacts of global warming at increase of 1.5 °C
and 2 °C   91

5.1 Post-tax wages in global economies, March 2009 ($)   112

Preface

I decided to write this book after returning from a wonderful family summer vacation in September 2018.

Looming over the warm afterglow of the holiday was the spectre of a damaged and increasingly unsustainable world. Donald Trump was two years into his malign disruptive Administration, threatening safety and livelihoods not just in the US, but across the world. It was increasingly clear that the UK was descending into a narrow tunnel in which delusions of past imperial grandeur, coupled with rising xenophobia, fuelled an insular and destructive nationalism. In my country of origin, South Africa, 'state capture' had led to the looting of state coffers by a predatory and opportunistic new elite. In Brazil, President Bolsonaro was following in the footsteps of his mentor, Donald Trump, and in the slums of the Philippines, police were encouraged to shoot on sight. If that wasn't enough, climate change and global warming were accelerating at an alarming rate.

Out of my post-holiday depression was born a desire to contribute in some small way to finding a solution to these societal ills. This book is an attempt to identify a path which might help us to get out of the mess in which we find ourselves. Learning from history, it is not inevitable that our worlds collapse into increasing unsustainability. To the contrary, there are credible reasons for optimism, and this is the furrow which I plough in this book.

Out of crisis comes opportunity. It is possible to rebuild a more sustainable world by taking advantage of the potential offered by a new socio-economic paradigm. The lives of all of our grandchildren – to whom this book is dedicated – demand that we do so.

Acknowledgements

During the course of my professional life, I have been privileged to work with three truly inspirational colleagues. Their contributions play a central role in the ideas advanced in this book.

The late Chris Freeman mentored my early career development and alerted me to the centrality of innovation in the unfolding of history.[1] Chris was resolute in his belief that technologies are socially created, and are hence malleable. Thus, he argued, we have a choice about the nature and trajectory of the society we live in. This choice, however, is frequently obscured by disciplinary silos and a belief in technological determinism. In the early 1980s, Chris pioneered the theory of 'long waves', which is the analytical structure I have drawn on and extended in order to analyse our contemporary crises in sustainability.

I worked with the late Robin Murray for more than two decades. Robin was an inspirational teacher and a visionary colleague.[2] Amongst the imprints he left on me was the understanding that distributed power, robust communities and civic participation are the foundations of a more socially and environmentally sustainable world. Robin helped me to realize that more inclusive societies not only are normatively desirable, but can also be more 'efficient' and are, hence, feasible. He was a pioneer in the development of ideas about the Circular Economy and the urgent need to take action to avoid a looming environmental crisis.

More recently, I have had the pleasure and privilege of working closely with Carlota Perez.[3] Carlota collaborated with Chris Freeman in extending long wave theory from its preoccupation with economic trajectories to an analysis of the co-evolution of technology, economy and society. Subsequently, she elaborated this framework to take account of the role which finance plays in the unfolding rise and atrophy of techno-economic paradigms. Drawing on insights gained from an understanding of the evolution of past techno-economic paradigms, Carlota provides us with a vision of what a more sustainable world might look like as the new Information and Communications techno-economic paradigm is deployed. But, she argues, this can only be achieved through purposeful action, particularly by visionary and effective governments. Carlota has stood by my side throughout the drafting and redrafting of this book. We have put on weight during our long lunches, and she has read (and sometimes reread) my draft chapters.

Although I have leant heavily on the contributions of these three colleagues, I take responsibility for the views expressed in this book.

My editor at Polity, Jonathan Skerrett, has been exceptional. He helped me to sharpen my focus and to make my material less inaccessible to a non-specialized audience. Shan Vahidy provided an invaluable and highly professional read of an earlier draft, Stevie Holland was my constant foil as an intelligent general reader, and Keith Bezanson provided insightful comments on the complete draft. Annie James (in Delhi) and Courtney Barnes and Chris Grant (both in Cape Town) assisted me with excellence in the processing of some of my data. Leigh Mueller assisted with a close copy-editing of the text. And, of course, the wonderful Wikipedia – how did we manage without it?

A number of colleagues and friends provided data and comments on individual chapters. The list is long. What surfaces as the work of an individual author is always a compilation of the views of others, sometimes absorbed explicitly and at other times seeping into the author's unconscious through the ether. So here are the culprits (in alphabetical order):

Andreas Antoniades (Chapter 2), Mike Boulter (Chapter 4), Tim Foxon (Chapter 4), Stephany Griffiths Jones (Chapter 2), James Hampshire (Chapter 3), Tim Jackson (Chapter 4), Richard Jolly (Chapters 2 and 3), Giorgos Kallis (Chapter 4), David Kaplan (Chapter 2), Bill Lazonick (Chapter 2), Rasmus Lema (Chapter 7), Paul Lewis (Chapter 3), Mathew Lockwood (Chapter 4), Mariana Mazzucato (Chapter 2), Erik Millstone (Chapter 4), Mike Morris

(Chapters 3, 7, 8 and 9), Dev Nathan (Chapter 4), Hubert Schmitz (Chapter 2), Benjamin Sovacool (extensive assistance with Chapters 4 and 7), Mark Stroud (Chapter 7), Nikos Vernardakis (Chapter 2), Sam Watson-Jones (Chapter 7), Richard Wilkinson (Chapter 3) and Martin Wolf (Chapter 2).

I apologize to my family, Hugh Fowler, Jenny Higgo, Jim Roby, Karen Fowler, Kate Springford, Leslye Orloff and Penny Leach for spoiling your meals during the development of my ideas. I owe you all a drink (or two).

And finally, my wife, Cathy. Like most authors, I have been a grumpy and distracted companion as I ploughed my way through drafts and redrafts. Cathy has been an insightful intellectual companion, not only encouraging me to avoid beginning sentences with 'But' and 'And' and to reduce sentence length, but, more importantly, with the development and elaboration of my ideas. She is too tactful to say so, but I am sure she is even more relieved than I am that the book has eventually been completed. I cannot measure her generous assistance.

1
A Fork in the Road

We live in perilous times.

Not just have we damaged our environment, but our environment is now damaging us. Our economies no longer function effectively – economic growth has been uneven, has slowed and is increasingly precarious. Our politics and social fabric are in trouble – societies have become more unequal, citizens feel a loss of agency, and populist leaders flourish. Most recently, we have been overcome by the Covid-19 pandemic, which has highlighted the underlying structural problems in our societies. It is evident that, once (if?) we overcome the pandemic, we cannot return to 'normal', since 'normal' was clearly the problem in the first place.

What will it take to return us to a semblance of a more sustainable world? The distinctive feature of this book is that it sets out an integrated programme which spans economic, social and environmental agendas requiring action not just by governments, but also by a range of societal stakeholders.

The central argument of this book is that the integrated systemic response required to provide a more sustainable world is built on an appreciation of the character of humankind's economic and social progress over the past three centuries. This has been marked by a series of surges in economic growth that I will refer to as techno-economic paradigms. Each of these paradigms involves a *synergy* between economic structures and social and political relations, and each has had characteristic environmental footprints. After a period of roughly five to six decades, each surge has decayed and been super-seded by a new dominant paradigm. This book will show how the interrelated economic, social and environmental crises which are now overwhelming us result from the atrophy of the most recent paradigm (Mass Production).

But there is hope, in the form of the new techno-economic paradigm which is unfolding – the Information and Communications Technology (ICT) paradigm. This offers the potential for a more sustainable trajectory of economic growth and a more equal, cohesive and inclusive society and polity. However, the emerging ICT paradigm is malleable. It has a 'dark side', seen in the growing asymmetry of power and income, the development and diffusion of alarming and frightening autonomous military technologies and the erosion of privacy. So, what measures are required to allow the 'bright side' to triumph? These policy responses are set out in Chapter 8, and the key stakeholders required to achieve progress are analysed in Chapter 9.

Clearly, before we can get to these policy issues, we need to step back and understand the historical trajectory which has resulted in the confluence of connected economic, social and environmental crises. We begin in Chapter 2 with what I believe is the most technical chapter for non-specialized readers. This charts the rise and fall of Mass Production as an economic system. It evidences the unprecedented 'Golden Age' after World War 2 when economic growth proceeded at historically unprecedented rates, not just in the richer northern economies but in almost every country of the globe. But, after roughly three decades, the 'Golden Age' of Mass Production began to atrophy. Not only did the rate of economic growth slow in all of the major high-income economies, but, as the millennium approached and advanced, the underlying fundamentals of growth became increasingly uncertain. A high-tech financial bubble in the late 1990s was followed by the prolonged Great Recession after 2008. The Covid-19 pandemic in 2020 raised the stakes in economic fragility, exposing underlying structural weaknesses which have been unfolding for some decades.

As in each of the previous post-Industrial Revolution surges, the Mass Production techno-economic paradigm was supported by patterns of social and political organization, by lifestyles and by societal norms and values. In the 'Golden Age', this saw the extension of liberal democratic political systems, mass consumption, suburbanization and, despite periods of turmoil, a generalized sense of common social and political purpose. Despite differences, there was a widespread sense that 'We are all in it together.' But, just as the economic system of Mass Production began to atrophy from the mid-1970s, so too did the social compact which supported Mass Production. In Chapter 3, I describe the evolution of these social and political developments which, since the early 1980s, have resulted in increasing inequality, increasing social discontent and the rise of populist politics.

Whilst the link between the economic, the social and the political can be seen as involving a 'close synergistic fit' between 1950 and the late 1970s, and then their interrelated decay after the early 1980s, the unfolding environmental crisis has much deeper roots. Although the origins of the environmental crisis go back at least until the Industrial Revolution in the early eighteenth century, after 1950 the biosphere witnessed a sharp increase in the forces driving climate change and environmental unsustainability. This has come to be termed 'The Great Acceleration'. Although the Great Acceleration and its increasingly severe impact on the environment is in large part a consequence of sheer numbers (of people and consumption), in some important respects it also flows from the specific character of the Mass Production techno-economic paradigm. These developments are described in Chapter 4.

Chapter 5 explores the character of these interlinkages between the economic, the social, the political and the environment through the lens of what is referred to as 'socio-technical systems' – that is, the body of theory which I use to analyse the rise and fall of the Mass Production techno-economic paradigm. Working with this framework, I analyse and explore the nature of these interactions during the Golden Age, and then the linked crises in sustainability after the late 1970s.

Chapters 6 and 7 turn to the future. Chapter 6 recounts the development and evolution of the ICT techno-economic paradigm. It illustrates the 'revolutionary' and disruptive nature of this new technology, seen though the historical lens of five previous techno-economic paradigms. Each of the previous paradigms was driven by a core 'heartland technology' – that is, a technology which has ubiquitous use through the terrain of economic and social activity, which offers major reductions in cost and the possibility of new products, and which not only is characterized by declining cost but has no physical limits to its supply. Information and Communications technologies exhibit all of these attributes. In Chapter 7, I present three case-studies which not only evidence these 'heartland technology' characteristics, but also show the synergy between the economic, the social and the political, and their capacity to strengthen environmental sustainability. They set the scene for the development of a synergistic systemic policy agenda simultaneously tackling the remaking of economic, social and environmental sustainability.

A five-point programme to provide a sustainable trajectory to the deployment of the ICT paradigm is outlined in Chapter 8. Although the diffusion of electronic technologies lies at the heart of the new paradigm, achieving a more sustainable world cannot be achieved through a technical fix. The systemic nature of techno-economic paradigms requires complementary changes in social and political organization and in lifestyles, values and norms. Chapter 9 concludes the book by discussing agency – *who* must do *what*, and *when*, if a sustainable trajectory is to be achieved?

A word of caution is needed from the outset. The terrain of discussion in this meta-analysis of crisis and response is vast. The interpretation of history in Chapter 5 and the theory of techno-economic paradigms are subject to disputation among historians. There are many uncertainties in the impact of particular policies, and there are many reactionary forces resisting progressive change. However, a nihilistic rejection of the ideas in this book has its own dangers. It is abundantly clear that existing policy proposals are not adequately addressing the challenges to the environment, to our economies and to the social and political fabric. In large part, this is because they do not recognize the need for a holistic response to the crises in sustainability and because they fail to learn from history.

This book is a plea for agency and activism. It sets out an agenda for action. But action must be purposefully guided to achieve more sustainable societies. The character of the new paradigm is malleable. What emerges will depend on how individuals and groups of individuals react to the challenge. If we really care about the state of our world, then we cannot remain neutral observers. We must exercise our individual agency to help to shape the direction of change. Only if enough of us work in concert can we avoid the dark side of paradigm change and facilitate the transition to a new more economically, socially and environmentally sustainable (dare I say 'civilized'?) world.

This book focuses on the experience of the dominant high-income economies in North America, Europe and Japan. Their growth trajectories dictated the shape of the global economy and global politics, at least until the end of the twentieth century. Despite the recent rapid growth of China, India and other emerging countries, the high-income economies continue to dominate the world and to determine the trajectory of global economic, social and environmental sustainability. Clearly, there is an urgent need to explore the potential of the ICT paradigm to promote sustainable development in low- and middle-income countries as well. This is a herculean but crucial task, but requires separate exploration.

2

The Rise and Fall of the Mass Production Economy

The Covid-19 pandemic crashed the global economy.

In the first half of 2020, the UK economy declined at the fastest rate since the beginning of the Industrial Revolution three centuries ago. In the US, the unemployment rate mushroomed to 25 per cent of the labour force. Germany, long the lead economy in Europe, fell into recession. The economic car-crash was not confined to the high-income countries, but affected the global economy. For the first time since its growth spurt began in the 1980s, China decided not to produce a target for its rate of economic growth. The collapse in world trade (more than 30 per cent in the first half of 2020) was the largest on record. But not all citizens suffered equally. Despite government programmes to support employment and production, as a general rule the poor were hit more by the economic collapse than were the rich. And that was as true for distributional impacts within countries as between high- and low-income economies. A simple indicator of the scale of this challenge can be seen in the cost to governments of trying to arrest the rate of economic decline. In April and May 2020, high-income countries injected $17tn into their economies. This raised an already high average government-debt/GDP (Gross Domestic Product) ratio of 109 per cent in mid-February 2020 to 137 per cent in May.

Governments and citizenry alike ponder how the economy will recover after the pandemic? Will it be a V-shaped recovery – rapid growth following rapid decline? Or might the recovery be W-shaped – rapid growth, followed by a second collapse, and then recovery? Perhaps a U-shape – rapid decline and a period of prolonged stagnation before revival? How about a K-shaped recovery – with the rich getting richer and the poor getting poorer? Each of these scenarios assumes that a recovery is inevitable, that the shape of global economic growth will not take the form of the 'dreaded L' – a sharp decline and no recovery. Underlying most of this speculative frenzy is the belief that it was Covid-19 that disrupted 'normality'. As if what existed before the pandemic was sustainable. As if the Great Recession which followed the Financial Crisis of 2008 was a temporary blip which could be managed with a modicum of tinkering to economic policy.

This optimism about the prospects for renewed future economic growth – a return to 'normality' – is misguided. The global economy witnessed historically unprecedented rates of economic growth after the Great Acceleration in 1950. But this growth surge began to taper off after the mid-1970s. The fundamentals had turned. Deep structural flaws which undermined sustained economic growth had begun to emerge. Their impact was delayed by the expansion of globalization from the mid-1980s. But the relief was temporary. The structural weaknesses in the Mass Production growth paradigm poked their heads above the surface in the burst high-tech bubble in 1998–9. After a brief respite, they then re-emerged frontally in the global Financial Crisis in 2008 which resulted in the greatest economic decline since the 1930s. Again, the impact of these structural problems was temporarily masked, with the reflationary economic policies failing to address underlying structural problems, particularly with regard to the size and character of the financial system.

This is the story which is described in this chapter. In documenting this growing spectre of economic unsustainability, I will begin by reviewing the rise and then the slowdown in the rate of economic growth after World War 2. I will show how this slowdown resulted from a decline in investment- and productivity-growth. Two sets of related factors explain this fall in the underlying drivers of growth. The first was the exhaustion of the productivity gains delivered by the Mass Production techno-economic paradigm. I will discuss this phenomenon in Chapter 5. The second – the subject matter of this chapter – was the economic policies adopted after the triumph of neo-liberalism in the early 1980s. These not only resulted in an increasingly unequal society but also decisively shifted the political economy of growth in favour of the financial sector and (as I will show in the next chapter) the interests of the plutocracy. The post-1980s neo-liberal era was characterized by a decline in investment in long-term innovation and growth, intensifying financial speculation, deindustrialization, rising debt, increasing economic volatility and the adoption of austerity economic policies. The chapter concludes by highlighting a number of developments intrinsic to the evolution of the Mass Production economy which threaten the sustainability of the global economy. These developments made sustainable economic growth unlikely, even before the economic collapse resulting from the Covid-19 pandemic.

2.1 The Rise and Fall of Economic Growth, 1950–2018

The dawn of the new decade in 1950 followed twenty years of global turmoil, particularly in Europe and North America. The 1930s had been dominated by the Great Depression, with falling living standards and millions of people thrown out of work. The decade saw the rise of Nazism in Germany, and fascism in many other European countries. If the Depression was not bad enough, 20 million soldiers and 40 million civilians were killed during World War 2. Much of the productive capacity of European economies was destroyed, and Europe's infrastructure was in tatters.

It was on these shaky foundations that the world transitioned to two decades of unparalleled rapid economic expansion after World War 2, and not just in the high-income industrialized economies. Economic historians characterize this era as the 'Golden Age'. This economic expansion was based on a reconstruction boom, with very large investments going into repairing the damages of war, massive house-building programmes and creating the infrastructure for a new age of mass consumption, automobilization and suburbanization. This sustained economic progress was made possible by the productivity gains generated by the deployment of the Mass Production techno-economic paradigm.

However, the benefits of these stimulants to growth began to tail off. After the early 1970s, the global economic growth rate and the rate of growth in the two major economic regions (the USA and Europe) declined steadily. Figure 2.1 provides a pictorial snapshot of these post-war growth trends for the world, for the US and for those economies currently members of the European Union. The data

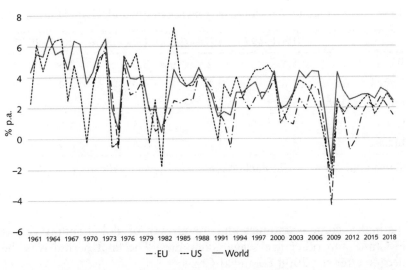

Figure 2.1 The expansion of Gross Domestic Product, 1961–2018: World, US and Europe (% per annum)
Source: data from World Bank World Development Indicators

reflect the simple average of individual economies' growth rates, and take no account of the relative size of their economies. Eyeballing this graphical representation, three trends are clear. First, there was considerable variation between years. Second, the average growth rates of the world, the US and Europe broadly followed similar trends. Third, after 1973 the trend rates of growth declined. Given population growth this means that in recent years – on average and not taking account of the distribution of growth – there was barely any increase in per capita incomes. (In fact, as I will show in the following chapter, most of the gains from growth were reaped by the already rich. In the US, for example, real wages for the low- and middle-skilled workforce stagnated after 1979.)

Table 2.1 decomposes these broad trends into four periods. The first reflects the high-growth phase between 1961 and 1973, the Golden Age. (In fact, the boom began during the 1950s, but a consistent database is unavailable to illustrate this.) The second period – 1974 to 1985 – was dominated by the recovery from the two oil-price shocks of 1973 and 1979. The third phase (1986–2006) was one of deepening globalization, coinciding with China's policy of 'Opening Out' in 1985. This led to the unbundling of production in

Table 2.1 Average annual economic growth rates: World, US and Europe (%)

	1961–1973	1974–1985	1986–2006	2007–2017
World	5.5	3.2	3.0	2.6
United States	4.6	3.1	3.0	1.4
European Union	5.0	2.3	2.4	1.0
China	5.2	8.9	9.4	8.8
India	3.5	4.9	5.6	6.9

Source: data from World Bank World Development Indicators

the high-income economies and the growth of global supply chains in China and other low-wage economies. The final period was the decade after the 2008 Financial Crisis.

These data evidence a steady decline in economic growth rates in the US and European economies which dominated the global economy. During the Golden Age first phase, their average annual growth rates exceeded 4.5 per cent. Thereafter, they declined steadily to an annual average of around 3 per cent until 2006. After the Financial Crisis in 2008, the rate of economic growth in both the US and Europe did not even match the rate of population growth. By contrast, some developing countries, including very large economies such as China and India, experienced sustained and high rates of growth over this long time period, exceeding 8 per cent in China and 5 per cent in India for more than two decades.

2.2 What Accounts for the Fall in the Rate of Economic Growth?

Broadly speaking, economic growth arises from four sets of factors. The first is more and increasingly skilled labour; the second is more physical investment ('capital'); the third is increased productivity as a result of improvements in equipment and in the organization of production; and the fourth is improvements in the infrastructure supporting the use of these inputs. I will predominantly focus on the first three of these growth-drivers in this chapter, but will revisit the role played by infrastructure in post-war growth in Chapter 5.

Was it a consequence of a shortage of labour?

The shortage of labour contributed little to the declining rate of economic growth after the early 1970s. There were, of course, skills shortages in particular sectors and economies. But, in general, the quantity of labour available to support investment remained in relatively abundant supply. When labour shortages did occur in the high-income industrial countries during the post-war boom, labour was imported from the developing world. For example, the UK actively encouraged both unskilled workers and skilled migrants from the Caribbean and South Asia during the 1950s and 1960s. In Western and Northern Europe, millions of migrants were drawn from North Africa and Turkey, and after the turn of the millennium both skilled and unskilled labour were sourced from Central and Eastern Europe. Further, access to labour in the high-income economies was not limited to migration. At the world level, labour was in abundant supply. The deepening of globalization after the mid-1980s took advantage of this global labour force and outsourced millions of jobs in manufacturing and services, from the high-income economies to China and other low- and middle-income economies. This enabled the corporate sector to draw on a vast global pool of cheap unskilled, and increasingly also semi-skilled, workers.

What about the contribution of investment to the growth slowdown?

In contrast to the availability of labour, the amount of new capital investment and its productivity were critically important in explaining this declining growth performance. Since 1970 (unfortunately, consistent data is not available to consider investment trends before that date), there has been a steady fall in the share of investment in all of the major high-income economies (measured as the share of new investment in Gross Domestic Product, GDP – Figure 2.2). This was particularly the case for the US. However, similar trends can be observed across the board in the major economies, especially Italy and the UK.

At the world level, considering the average of all economies irrespective of size, the share of new investment in GDP fell between 1970 and 1990, and stabilized thereafter. It is worth noting that much investment takes the form of replacing worn-out 'depreciated' productive capacity, buildings and infrastructure. In general, it is only when investment exceeds 15–16 per cent of GDP that it can be said that investment provides for additional productive capacity. As can be seen from Figure 2.2, the investment rate in the US and the Euro area after the 2008 Financial Crisis was perilously close to this depreciation rate.

As in the case of declining growth trends (Figure 2.1), China has been a very significant outlier to this pattern of global slowdown in investment. Not only has the share of investment in its GDP been on a rising trend since 1970, but the size of this share is significantly higher than that for the major global economies and for the world economy as a whole. Compare China and the USA, for example. The investment-share in the US fell from its high point of 24 per cent between 1978 and 1980 to less than 20 per cent after 2010. In China, this share was more than 40 per cent throughout the 1990s and after the millennium, and reached 46 per cent in 2013. That means that China was devoting almost half of its total annual production to new capital investment.

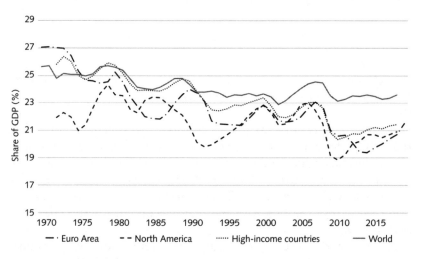

Figure 2.2 Share of investment in equipment and other physical assets (Gross Capital Formation) in GDP

Source: data from World Bank World Development Indicators

And what about the productivity of investment?

The quantity of investment does not necessarily translate into increased output: it all depends on the quality – that is the productivity – of investment. There is a widespread belief that productivity was enhanced by the diffusion of computing across a range of industries after the invention of the microprocessor in 1971. Surely, it was argued, the availability of equipment capable of speeding up data-processing, providing greater accuracy in production and communicating with similar electronically controlled equipment would facilitate the substitution of machines for human endeavour – in other words, speed up labour productivity growth? And surely, electronically controlled machinery would be more productive than mechanically controlled equipment? Surprisingly, the evidence does not support this assertion. This led the Nobel Prize-winner Robert Solow to remark in 1987 that 'You can see the computer age everywhere but in the productivity statistics.'

As can be seen from Figure 2.3, with the exception of a

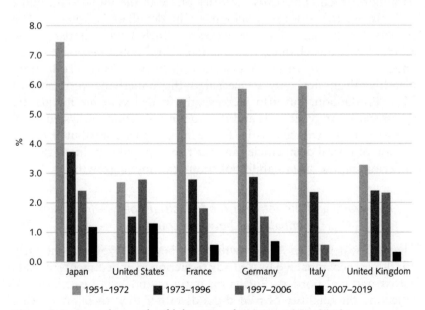

Figure 2.3 Annual growth of labour productivity, 1951–2019
Source: data from The Conference Board (www.conference-board.org)

productivity-growth decade in the US after 1997, resulting from the
initial deployment of ICTs, all of the major economies witnessed a
declining trend in their growth of productivity (in this case, labour
productivity) after World War 2. This fall in the rate of productivity
growth was accentuated after the 2008 Financial Crisis. The productivity growth rates in the most recent decade (1 per cent, 0.9 per cent,
0.9 per cent, 0.6 per cent, 0.4 per cent and – 0.4 per cent for the US,
Japan, Germany, France, UK and Italy, respectively) were significantly below those for the whole period between 1951 and 2017 (1.9
per cent, 4.1 per cent, 3.4 per cent, 3.1 per cent, 2.3 per cent and 2.6
per cent, respectively).

2.3 Neo-liberalism and the Decline in Growth, Investment and Productivity

Two factors explain the decline in the rates of productivity growth,
economic growth and investment. As I have already observed, the first
is that these outcomes result from the atrophy of the Mass Production
paradigm which entered its maturity phase in the mid-1970s, and I
will discuss this critical development in detail in Chapter 5. The
second determinant of the slowdown, which I will discuss in the
remainder of this chapter, was the neo-liberal policy response to the
underlying slowdown in the growth trajectory of Mass Production.
Neo-liberalism not only exacerbated the underlying problems of
Mass Production, but also increasingly fuelled systemic inequality,
the precarity of livelihoods and the fragility of economic systems. All
of these, as we will see in the following chapter, contributed to the
erosion of liberal democracies and the rise of populist politics, further
undermining the sustainability of future economic growth.

Free trade and the retreat from Industrial Policy – increasing imbalances between countries

The post-war Golden Age growth boom between 1950 and the early
1970s was accompanied by a steady reduction in impediments to trade
across national borders. Tariffs on imports and 'non-tariff barriers'
(affecting the quantity of traded goods rather than their price) were
steadily reduced in most of the high-income economies. After the
mid-1970s and until the second decade of the twenty-first century,

the pace of trade liberalization intensified. It also spread throughout the global economy to low- and middle-income economies, as well as to the formerly heavily protected communist countries in Eastern Europe. Even China, which continued to maintain many formal and informal restrictions on imports, opened many of its markets to imports.

The neo-liberal commitment to free trade was premised on the belief that market-based trade relations would promote growth much more effectively than controls introduced by governments on trade with other countries. This commitment to free trade and 'open borders' was complemented by the withdrawal of government support for 'Industrial Policy' (a term loosely used to describe policies directed at all activities in the productive sector). Government support for industry – 'picking winners' (promoting particular sectors and 'national champion' firms) – and financial support for innovation and other determinants of long-term growth were seen as raising the tax burden and reducing the efficiency of resource allocation, and thus being harmful to economic growth.

The consequence of this dual neo-liberal policy agenda was a hollowing-out of manufacturing in those high-income countries pursuing the neo-liberal agenda most vigorously, particularly the US and the UK. It resulted in the growth of high levels of unemployment in the rust-belt regions which had formerly been centres of industrial activity, for example in cities such as Michigan in the US Midwest, and Birmingham and Sunderland in the Midlands and the North-East in the UK. (I will discuss the social and political consequences of this deindustrialization in the next chapter.) It also led to a shift in the geography of investment by many of the major global corporations. There was a massive outflow of investment from the home economy and other high-income economies to economies in the developing world, particularly China. Much of this investment was directed to shifting supply chains to low-wage developing economies. The share of global direct foreign investment directed to developing economies rose from 17 per cent in 1990 to 44 per cent in 2019.[1]

These developments resulted in the growth of trade imbalances between economies. That is, they consistently imported more from other countries than they exported. The level of this deficit was particularly high for the world's largest economy, the US, and for the UK (Figure 2.4). By contrast, countries such as China, Korea and Germany, which had pursued dirigiste policies to support industry,

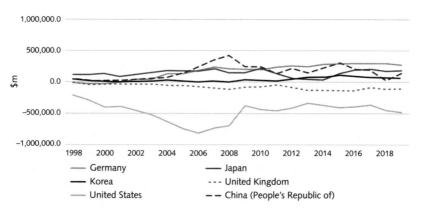

Figure 2.4 Balance of payments: largest debtor and surplus economies, 1998–2019 ($m)

Source: data from Organisation for Economic Co-operation and Development (OECD)

had growing trade surpluses, accompanied by relatively high rates of economic growth.

This toxic combination of deindustrialization and free trade undermined the incentive to invest and reduced the rate of productivity and economic growth in the economies pursuing neo-liberal policy agendas. But, as we will see in the following chapter, it also contributed to growing inequality, the precarity of livelihoods and the rise of populist political leaders.

The crisis in macroeconomic policy – matching demand with supply

Building factories and infrastructure requires a variety of inputs, including labour, material supplies and services. The production of these inputs generates incomes. Workers earn wages and salaries, and this cascades along the supply chain as suppliers require their own suppliers. But does this economic activity add up to the balancing of supply and demand? Are the incomes generated in all of the supply chains sufficient to consume what is being produced in the economy?

'Say's Law' in economic theory posits that supply (investment and production) creates an equivalent level of demand (incomes and consumption). In other words, the making of things produces the incomes required to consume what is made. Thus, it is believed, one problem which should not concern policy makers is the need to help consumers to mop up all the goods and services which the economy can produce. However, history shows that this key tenet in economic theory is fallacious. At its core, capitalism has consistently experienced periods in which demand is unable to keep up with productive capacity. This is not surprising. New technologies produce more products with less labour. Thus, unless wage growth or consumption by the owners of productive capital outstrip productivity growth, it stands to reason that the incomes generated in production will not be sufficient to consume the products churned out by new, more efficient production lines. Moreover, in periods when consumer confidence is low, consumers may prefer to hold back, to save their incomes for a rainy day.

Both of these factors were at play during the Great Depression in the 1930s. The Great Crash in the stock markets in 1929 plunged many consumers into debt. Unemployment grew rapidly, partly – as we will see in Chapter 5 – as a result of the introduction of labour-saving mass production technologies. And consumer confidence plummeted. Moreover, income inequality had grown rapidly during the 1920s and there were limits to how many luxury yachts, gold-plated watches and designer clothes an individual could consume. The combination of these developments resulted in a downward spiral in the major economies. As consumption fell, firms reduced their output or went out of business. This led to a reduction in the incomes required to consume what was being produced. Consumer confidence fell, further dampening the demand for the goods. And thus, the economy spiralled downwards.

These problems, and the resultant policy responses, were addressed by Keynes during the 1930s. He argued that, since there was a periodic tendency in capitalism towards under-consumption, public policy had to intervene to support demand. Tackling the crisis in confidence during his inauguration in 1932, President Roosevelt famously declared, 'The only thing we have to fear is fear itself.' He then rolled out his New Deal Program which increased government expenditure and helped to grow the US economy out of its deep depression. The New Deal provided relief to the unemployed. It created 250,000 jobs for young men to work in projects in rural areas, and promoted very large investments in infrastructure, skills development, schools and other public facilities. Although in itself the New Deal did not solve the problem of economic stagnation (it was the 'boom' created by the mass production of arms during World War 2 which proved to be the decisive stimulant to growth), these government-led investment programmes played an important role in economic revival.

The challenge of managing consumption to balance production remained a critically important component of public and economic policy throughout the twentieth century, and has endured during the first two decades of the twenty-first century. As we will see in subsequent chapters, after World War 2, government expenditure played an important role in sustaining consumer demand. In the US, and then in Europe, there were massive investments in housing and in the infrastructure required to promote the growth of automobilization and suburbanization. In Europe, welfare programmes played a complementary role in sustaining consumption. Although these post-war welfare programmes were not rationalized in terms of their contribution to economic stability and growth, both directly (though benefit payments) and indirectly (as jobs were created in the public sector delivering welfare benefits) they played a critical role in bolstering consumption.

But from the beginning of the 1980s, these well-tried structures for matching demand and supply in the economy were undermined by the introduction of neo-liberal economic policies. These were pioneered in the UK and the US – the Thatcher–Reagan revolution – and then replicated across the globe, sometimes as a result of national choice and, in other cases (notably in the developing world), as a result of pressure exerted by the US, the UK and the EU. Neo-liberalism sought to reduce the role of government and to reduce the 'tax burden'. It promoted lower tax rates on higher incomes in order to 'remove the disincentive to entrepreneurship and investment'. Simultaneously, the neo-liberal agenda attacked welfare payments on the basis that social security promoted the growth of a 'work-shy' labour force living off welfare. (The irony in this agenda was that, whilst it was argued that welfare support reduced the incentive of the poor to work, it was simultaneously argued that tax reduction would increase the incentive of the rich to work even harder!)

Corporate tax rates were progressively reduced in an attempt to encourage investment and to bid investments away from competitor countries through a 'war of incentives'. Figure 2.5 shows the trajectory of corporate profit taxes in major high-income economies. In some cases – notably the UK and Sweden – these have fallen by

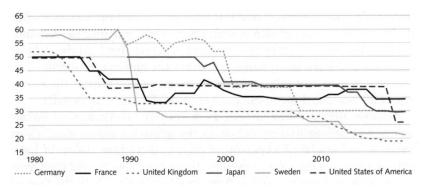

Figure 2.5 Corporate tax rate: France, Germany, US, UK, Japan and Sweden, 1981–2019 (%)
Source: data from OECD

two-thirds since the neo-liberal tax revolution in the early 1980s. The evidence to support the investment-promoting function of these tax-reducing reforms is weak. For example, in the UK corporate taxes were reduced from 27 per cent in 2010 to 19 per cent in 2017 (with a commitment to a further reduction to 17 per cent in 2020). This had no impact on the rate of corporate investment, which stagnated between 2010 and 2018. In the US, as we will see below, swingeing cuts to corporate tax rates were mostly used to reward shareholders. As I will show in the chapter which follows, this fall in corporate tax rates was matched by a large decline in personal tax rates.

This neo-liberal agenda undermined the capacity of governments to fund investments in infrastructure. Consequently, over the subsequent decades the deficit in infrastructure spending mushroomed in the high-income economies, particularly in the US and the UK. In the US, between 2003 and 2017, public expenditure on roads, bridges, water systems and other infrastructure fell by 8 per cent. In 1930 (even before Roosevelt's New Deal Program investments in roads and dams), infrastructure investments were 4.2 per cent of GDP. In 2016, this ratio had fallen to 2.5 per cent. The American Society of Civil Engineers estimated that underinvestment in infrastructure between 2016 and 2025 would exceed 2 trillion dollars.[2] The UK is in an even more parlous state with the share of infrastructure spending in GDP being even lower than that in the US.[3]

The falling rate of investment in infrastructure had an adverse impact on economic productivity as it increased the logistical costs of moving goods, services and information around the economy. But it also had the effect of dampening the growth in aggregate demand. This is because investments in infrastructure tend to be labour intensive and have many linkages within the national economy. The greater the extent of infrastructural expansion, the greater the multiplier effect on local incomes, and hence on aggregate demand.

Additionally, at the same time as the rate of infrastructural investments was falling, the reduction in the growth (and in some cases the absolute levels) of expenditure on social welfare also held back what had been a major underwriter of consumption during the Great Depression and in the Golden Age after World War 2. In the face of these two dampeners to consumption, what measures did neo-liberal governments adopt to prop up aggregate demand?

Sustaining demand through Quantitative Easing

Faced with stagnant – and, in some cases, falling – demand, governments in the high-income economies sought to stimulate consumption through the introduction of Quantitative Easing programmes (QE). QE involves governments pumping money into the economy using a variety of instruments to buy securities, such as bonds, from the private sector. It had been pioneered during the Great Depression in the US, but in recent years it was the government of Japan which first resorted to QE. Following a decade of low growth, in 2001 the Japanese government began a programme which pumped liquidity into the economy. As the Global Financial Crisis unfolded after 2008, the Japanese initiative was copied by the US Federal Reserve Bank, the Bank of England and the European Central Bank. They each injected very large sums into their economies, designed to promote investment and thereby, indirectly, to promote demand. In the US, QE added more than $2 trillion to the money supply. The UK's QE programme injected £79 billion of liquidity into the economy between 2009 and 2012. The European Central Bank provided €2.5 trillion to Eurozone economies between the beginning of the Financial Crisis and the end of 2018.

The critical feature of these QE monetary-stimulus programmes is that, although they were intended to promote investment in productive assets, in reality, outside of China (where money was directed to promote infrastructure), they were undirected. As a result, the money pumped into the economy was largely used to finance speculation. As we will see below, this speculative boom also led to an increase in consumer borrowings and spiralling debt. Speculation has taken a number of forms. At the relatively trivial end of the speculative spectrum, a Da Vinci painting was sold for $450m in 2017, a Cezanne for $272m in 2011 and a Gauguin for $217m in 2014. But the most significant arena for speculation has been in housing. In the US, house prices doubled between 2000 and 2007. They fell sharply during the 2008 Financial Crisis, but then resumed their upward trend. By 2018, they were 50 per cent greater than they were in 2012, and 70 per cent higher than in 2002. In the UK, residential house prices grew by more than 230 per cent between 2002 and 2018. In Germany, house prices grew by more than 40 per cent between 2011 and 2018. This speculation in property was not confined to the high-income economies. In India, property prices increased by more than 250 per cent between 2011 and 2018. In Shanghai, the price index for second-hand homes grew by 300 per cent between 2004 and 2017.[4]

Growing financialization fuelled short-termism and dulled innovation

The neo-liberal policies adopted after the early 1980s fostered the growth of what has come to be termed financialization, particularly in the US, the UK and other high-income countries. Financialization describes a structure in which the financial sector grows very much more rapidly than the productive sector producing goods and services for sale to consumers. And where there is a conflict of interests between the productive and financial sector, the interests of finance triumph. As we will see, financialization has had adverse consequences for economic growth, income distribution, innovation, investment and other drivers of economic and social wellbeing.

The roots to financialization can be traced back to the neo-liberal policy agenda and the changes in tax legislation in the US in the early 1980s. This provided companies with the facility to repurchase their shares and, in so doing, to distribute profits to shareholders. The mantra for these changes was that of 'maximizing shareholder value'. The argument was that economic growth would be fostered if corporations were run in the interests of their shareholders rather than their workforces, society at large or a combination of these stakeholders.

These changes in the tax regime had a major impact on corporate governance. The new incentives for stock repurchases led to senior executives receiving their remuneration in the form of shares as well as salaries. This meant that, being both 'owners' and managers, corporate managers had a triple-dip into the cash generated by their enterprises – their salaries, the rewards they received through dividends on the shares they held, and cash repurchases of shares.

There were two major related consequences of this change in incentives to corporate managers. The first was their impact on innovation and investment. Providing management with the incentive to pay themselves with shares meant that they had an overwhelming interest in driving up the value of their company's stocks. Share prices increasingly responded to short-term profit trends – usually reported at quarterly and half-yearly intervals. Investments in research and development, innovation and costly equipment required to deliver productivity change and growth in the medium and long term reduced profits in the short term and so were neglected. This led to a frenzied focus on the capacity of managers to deliver immediate profits at the cost of long-term growth and had perverse outcomes. New managers would sweep into a company, cut investments in innovation and costly equipment and produce sparkling profits. Share prices would consequently rise and management would cash in their shares. They would then move on as 'heroes' (because of their amazing impact on profitability) to the next company, which would be hollowed out in similar fashion. Ironically, their 'hero status' would be enhanced by the collapse of profitability in the firms which they had previously 'rescued' after they left, with scant recognition that this decline in profitability was a direct result of their 'heroic' management. As Bill Lazonick has shown, all of this led to a sharp decline in investment in innovation and other drivers of longer-term productivity growth.[5]

A second and related consequence of this change in tax incentives was a process of widespread and systematic 'looting' of company coffers by senior executives and shareholders. Not only did senior management gain from their appreciating share options but, instead of using profits to invest in the future, profits were distributed to shareholders, which of course included the very same executives who made the decisions on what to do with profits. Mariana Mazzucato refers to this as a transition from 'value addition' to 'value extraction'.[6]

The outcome of these developments can be seen in the changing face of stock markets. Stock markets are in theory supposed to provide the finance for new productive investments. Companies which require funds to invest in expansion and product development can raise resources by issuing shares to investors. During the 1950s and 1960s, the stock markets in the US had served this function. They provided substantial investment finance for the non-financial corporate sector, averaging more than 0.5 per cent of GDP. But the changes in tax legislation introduced in the early 1980s by Ronald Reagan changed the direction of financial flows. The flow of funds shifted from investors providing funds to the corporate sector via the stock market, to the corporate sector shifting funds to shareholders, again via the stock market. In the decade before, during and after the 2008 Financial Crisis, the accumulated flow of funds from the corporate sector to the stock markets was an astonishing $4.46tn, equivalent to 2.7 per cent of total US GDP over the period.[7]

The neo-liberal tax reforms introduced by the Trump Administration in 2017 (the Tax Cuts and Jobs Act) provided a further bonanza to shareholders. Sixteen US corporations which had held financial assets of more than $1 trillion outside the US had been waiting for the day in which they could repatriate these funds to the US at reduced tax rates. They argued that punitively high corporate taxes of 35 per cent inhibited them from returning global profits to invest in the US. The value of these external assets for the five major companies was $269bn for Apple, $143bn for Microsoft, $107bn for Alphabet, $76bn for Cisco and $71bn for Oracle. Following intense lobbying from these major corporations, the 2017 tax reforms reduced the tax paid on these repatriated funds from 35 per cent to 16.5 per cent. In the first nine months of 2018, the five largest tech firms utilized only $19.3bn of this windfall for capital investment. They distributed the bulk ($115bn) to shareholders in the form of share buybacks. So much for tax reduction inducing investment and growth!

The consequences of financialization are not limited to undermining long-term investments in the corporate sector and the looting of corporate funds. It has also led to the development of a component of the financial sector which is detached from the economically useful function of transferring money from savers to productive investors. Fuelled in part by the liquidity injected into economies by QE programmes, massive quantities of money have been directed into arbitrage, that is buying and selling to gain from price differentials. This was one of the factors driving up the prices of raw materials during the commodities boom between 2003 and 2014. Growing demand for raw materials from China and other countries led to an increase in their price. Anticipating this growing demand for commodities, financial speculators bought primary commodities in the expectation that their prices would continue to rise. In so doing, they accentuated the growth in commodity prices.[8] Financial speculation for arbitrage was not limited to physical commodities. For example, investors took advantage of the low interest rates in their home economies to speculate on changing currency rates. Large sums of money were borrowed and transferred to bank accounts in other countries which had very slightly higher interest rates. The differential in interest rates was often minute and short-lived, but, since they applied to very large money transfers, profits were substantial.

As we saw above in the discussion of Quantitative Easing, another avenue for financial speculation was the housing market, particularly in the US. During the 1990s, and especially after the turn of the millennium, many poor and middle-income householders were aggressively sold mortgages to buy their own homes. The attraction to borrowers was that house prices were growing at 10 per cent per annum. Moreover, they were offered enticing terms. These loans often began with near-zero interest rates, which then escalated after a few years to unaffordable levels. Irresponsible lenders paid little attention to the valuation of the properties or to the capacity of borrowers to meet their monthly repayments. They were only interested in the commissions they earned on arranging these loans. Risky loans were bundled together with more secure mortgages in Collateralized Debt Obligations (CDOs). These CDOs had very low levels of transparency and were sold and resold as if they were secure assets. Each round of sale, of course, earned commissions for the financiers involved in the transactions. But, ultimately, the pack of cards in these schemes collapsed, triggering the 2008 Financial Crisis. Mortgage defaults led to a sharp fall in house prices and widespread personal bankruptcy, with devastating welfare impacts. As I will show in the following chapter, the numbers of homeless families in the US ballooned, as did the incidence of poverty and ill health. After decades of improvement, life-expectancy began to fall.

So, what is the relevance of the post-1980s neo-liberal policy regime to the rise and fall of the Mass Production paradigm from the end of World War 2 to the present day? As we have seen above, these policies exacerbated the underlying decline in rates of productivity growth, investment and economic growth. Changes in the tax regime and the inability to direct QE money into productive investments fuelled a climate of short-termism and a reluctance to invest in innovation for the long term. The combination of free-trade policies and the retreat from industrial policies destroyed large swathes of manufacturing and led to the growth of depressed rust-belt societies. It also resulted in unsustainable unevenness in global trade, with the US in particular sinking into ever deeper international trade deficits.

2.4 Can the Mass Production Paradigm Be Reinvigorated?

So much for the past seventy years. But what are the prospects for the Mass Production growth trajectory being sustainable in the future? Leaving aside the challenge of recovering from the economic damage of Covid-19, can Mass Production's growth trajectory be reinvigorated? In what follows in the concluding sections of this chapter, I discuss a number of structural features intrinsic to the Mass Production paradigm which undermine the prospects for sustainable economic growth.

The Great Recession of 2007–2018 – the sticking plaster wears off

The twentieth century ended with a collapse in stock markets, particularly in the US, and particularly in the share values of the high-tech sector. More than 100 million people globally were plunged below the $1-per-day absolute poverty line as a consequence of this burst high-tech stock bubble. This economic crisis was relatively short lived. But it was succeeded by a much more severe and persistent economic crash which began to unfold in late 2007. As we have seen, the trigger for this severe economic disruption was a crisis in the US housing market.

The domino effect of this real estate crash spread rapidly through the US economy. In short order, 176 banks failed in 2009. Unemployment doubled from 4.9% in 2007 to more than 10% in 2009. The Dow Jones stock exchange index fell 54% in 17 months. Two of America's largest automobile companies – Ford and Chrysler – had to be rescued with government funding. It is estimated that the total level of support provided by the Federal Government to the financial sector was more than $4tn. Although much of this was repaid, this nevertheless led to a long-term burden on taxpayers of more than $1.2tn.

Contagion from the crisis in the housing market was not confined to the US economy. The International Monetary Fund calculated that only one of the thirty-three high-income OECD economies (Australia) avoided the fallout. In Iceland, the three largest banks failed. Greece, Ireland and Spain were pushed to the edge of default. Between January 2008 and January 2009, industrial output fell by 31% in Japan, 26% in Korea, 16% in Russia, 15% in Brazil, 14% in Italy and 12% in Germany. More than 20 million jobs were lost worldwide, predominantly in the construction, services and automobile sectors. Stock markets throughout the world became increasingly volatile, with values on a declining trend. In 2008, share prices fell by almost a third in Europe and the Asia-Pacific region. In wealthy European countries, an increasing number of people were living on the streets and begging for handouts, and the number of foodbanks mushroomed. The list goes on.

Recovery from the Great Recession took some time. It was only in 2016 that average real living standards in Europe returned to their pre-Recession levels. Countries such as the UK and Greece which adopted austerity policies took much longer to recover than those such as the US, where governments took active steps to revive demand and stimulate economic activity. But, as we saw earlier, the primary vehicle used to stoke recovery – Quantitative Easing – ratcheted up the very financialization of the economy which had led to the Great Recession in the first place. Moreover, despite much protestation, most of the financial sector which had engaged in irresponsible lending and non-productive speculation was left untouched. Most of the key economic architects appointed by incoming President Obama were Wall Street bankers who had been key players in the financial sector which caused the crisis in the first place. Thus, the 'rescue' did not address the major systemic flaws in the economic system. It was merely poor-quality sticking plaster, ready to peel off under the slightest abrasion. Quantitative Easing programmes were renewed, and by 2019 the pyramid of speculative finance which had led the financial system to collapse in 2007 had regrown to pre-Great Recession levels. Global debt is at a historically high level, and spans the spectrum of borrowers – governments, households and, despite record profits, the corporate sector as well.

Debt continues to spiral

Debt has spiralled across the global economy. In early 2020, before the Covid-19 pandemic, the ratio of global debt to global GDP doubled from 160 per cent in 2000 to 330 per cent. In the high-income countries, much of the undirected QE was used to underwrite debt-driven consumption. In the UK, according to the National Audit Office, in 2018 8.3 million people were unable to pay off their personal debt or to cover their household bills. In the US, household debt rose from $13.65tn in 2008 to $14.15tn in 2019.[9] US corporate debt rose from $439bn in 1980 to $3.1tn in 2007, before the Great Recession. Thereafter, it mushroomed to reach $14.15tn in 2019.[10] US Federal Government debt also grew rapidly, from $879bn in 1980 to $9.5tn before the Great Recession, and to $22.8tn in 2019. US Federal debt owed to international and foreign parties rose from £492bn in 1990 to $2.4tn in 2007, and to $6.9tn in 2019.[11] All of this spiralling debt, of course, predated the Covid-19 epidemic which hit the global economy in 2020, exacerbating each of these growing debt piles.

These spiralling levels of household, corporate and government debt reflect the underwriting of consumption in the US, the UK and other high-income countries. For, as we saw above, the levels of investment in productive assets remained stagnant (Figure 2.2). Growing debt thus took the place of investments in infrastructure and productive capacity in the balancing of aggregate demand with aggregate production capacity. But debt is a tax on the future – it has to be repaid. When interest rates are extremely low, as in the era of the Covid pandemic, growing debt is a relatively minor problem. But these low interest rates depend on a depressed economy. If growth were to revive, the repayment schedules would place a heavy burden on sustainable future growth.

Added to this problem of domestic debt in the US, the UK and other high-income economies, is the spectre of sovereign debt – that is, money borrowed by governments. This, too, represents a time-bomb at the base of revived economic growth. For a while, it seemed as though Greece (with sovereign debts of $353bn, equivalent to 182 per cent of its GDP in 2018) was a prime candidate for sovereign default. When the Financial Crisis struck in 2008, virtually all of this debt was owed to the commercial banking system, particularly to banks in Germany and France. Had Greece defaulted at that time, the blow to the interconnected global banking system would surely have thrown the global economy into a substantial crisis. Yiannis Varoufakis, Greece's then Minister of Finance, has chronicled the manner in which these sovereign debts were transferred from the commercial banking system to European governments. This reduced the systemic risk of a potential default, and added muscle to the arm of Greece's creditors. In the subsequent decade, Greece implemented a traumatic austerity programme. (Because this led to a 25 per cent fall in the size of the economy, this perversely led to an increase in its debt-to-GDP ratio.) Whilst inflicting enormous costs on its suffering population, it has (at least hitherto) saved the global financial system from a financial meltdown.

Whilst Greece's experience illustrates the power of creditors to contain disruptive defaults, however, it would be wise not to be too sanguine about the dangers to sustained global growth arising from sovereign defaults. The Council on Economic Affairs expressed its concern about the potentially contagious impact of an Italian default.[12] Italy's debt of $3.6tn in 2018 was 131 per cent of GDP, twice the levels permitted by the EU. Italy is the third biggest economy in the EU and an Italian default would hit banks across Europe. If Italy decided to leave the euro currency and return to the lira, this would cause massive losses to investors, triggering another financial crisis.

And then there is the problem of debt in the emerging economies. Between 2000 and 2017, the value of their dollar debts trebled from less than $1tn to more than $3tn. Their Euro debts more than doubled from around €200tn to more than €550tn. The vulnerability of these emerging-economy debts is not just due to their absolute size and the share of debt in their domestic economies. It is also because much of this debt was transacted in foreign currencies and by the private sector. If a debtor economy willingly or unwillingly devalues its currency, this magnifies the burden on debtors whose earnings are in local currency. A default by a large emerging economy (say Brazil), or perhaps a default by more than one emerging economy (Brazil and Argentina and Indonesia) may have serious repercussions for the sustainability of growth in the global economy. If these debts are contracted to the commercial banking system or to the private corporate sector, these dangers will be magnified.

Volatility and fragility in the financial sector threaten the likelihood of a new stock market crash

There are a number of structural characteristics within the financial system which have the potential to spill over into a systemic crisis. One potential source of instability in these markets is the fragility of automated trading systems.[13] Automated trading is increasingly used to drive investments in stocks. Programmable buy–sell computer-driven systems allow for automated transactions based on algorithms designed by the programmers. This is referred to as 'black box high frequency trading'. The share of automated trading transactions in the US rose from 15 per cent of total market volume in 2003 to 85 per cent in 2012. During the 2008 Financial Crisis, it was not uncommon for market prices to fall/rise by 5–10 per cent in a single day, largely driven by algorithmic trading. These algorithms have the potential to produce what is referred to as a 'flash crash'. On 6 May 2010, the US Dow Jones Industrial Index fell by 9 per cent in the space of 15 minutes. This is widely believed to have resulted from unregulated automatic algorithmic trading. It is believed that the growing use of Artificial Intelligence in these systems may reduce the possibility of a flash-trading crash. Perhaps they will. However, the growing sophistication of these algorithms makes them less transparent to external intervention. If only one of these algorithms is incorrectly designed, the financial sector may easily tip into crisis.

Another possible source of disruption which is internal to the financial system is the market in cryptocurrencies such as Bitcoins. These are essentially Ponzi schemes (which are often referred to graphically as pyramid schemes). These schemes generate returns for early investors by bringing in new investors who fund the gains reaped by early entrants. However, the more investors there are in the scheme, the greater the number of new investors required to keep the system growing and to maintain the stability of the pyramid. Thus, Ponzis are inherently unstable. Moreover, because of their need for exponential growth (an ever-growing number of new investors are required to service existing investors), they have a limited life.

Unlike national currencies which are guaranteed by governments, the only value which cryptocurrencies possess is the *belief* that they are valuable. Their appreciation in value depends on more and more investors sharing this belief. They have no guardians, and once belief in their future value is eroded, the edifice may crumble very rapidly.

Take the case of Bitcoins. The value of Bitcoin 'currency' has grown at an extraordinarily rapid rate – between October 2016 and October 2017 by more than 5,000 per cent. In December 2017, a Bitcoin was valued at $19,703. But its value was unstable. In early January 2019, its value had dropped to $4,057, including a fall of $1,000 in a 24-hour period. On 9 March 2020, fears of a spreading Covid-19 pandemic led to a fall of $26bn in the value of cryptocurrencies. In February 2021, the value of a Bitcoin soared to $52,000. As the financial journal *Forbes* warned readers, 'Investing in cryptocoins or tokens is highly speculative and the market is largely unregulated. Anyone considering it should be prepared to lose their entire investment.'[14] If the Bitcoin market was small, this crazed speculation would be of little significance. In 2016, cryptocurrencies totalled less than $18bn. This rose to $129bn in 2018, and $237bn in 2019.

Disruption to global supply chains

As we will see in Chapter 5, deepening globalization after the mid-1980s helped to rescue falling corporate profitability and prolonged the life of the atrophying Mass Production paradigm. However, outsourcing production to low-wage developing economies had important economic and social consequences. In the economic sphere, it resulted in widespread deindustrialization and persistent imbalances in trade for some of the major high-income economies, notably the US and the UK. In the social sphere, in most of the high-income economies it led to the collapse in employment and income in the rust-belt regions which had powered growth in the Mass Production paradigm's heyday.

   In the chapter that follows, I will show how these and other tensions led to the election of populist governments in a number of countries, including in the US. The Trump Administration placed trade imbalances at the forefront of its political agenda. Tariffs were introduced against $50bn of imports from China in 2018, and a further $200bn in 2019. China responded in kind with tariffs against imports of soybeans form the US. In 2019, the US took action to suspend sales of vital technology to Huawei, the Chinese telecommunications firm, and pressured its European 'allies' and Australia to take similar action. The US also imposed tariffs on imports of steel and aluminium from the European Union, which in turn threatened retaliatory actions. Australia's call for an independent inquiry into the origins of the Covid-19 pandemic in China in May 2020 led to the imposition by China of damaging tariffs on Australia's agricultural exports.

These unfolding tensions in trade between the US and its major trading partners have the potential to repeat the 'beggar-thy-neighbour' trade policies widely deployed during the Great Depression. In the 1930s, individual countries tried to protect their domestic industries from import competition. This led to a tit-for-tat response from trading partners and a downward spiral in international trade and economic activity. Coupled with the disruption to global supply chains during the Covid-19 pandemic, this has resulted in the disruption of one of the primary engines of economic growth in recent decades. In the modern global economy where supply chains extend across vast distances, a sharp reversal in the trajectory of global trade poses a severe challenge to the sustainability of economic growth in individual economies and regions such as the EU and North America.

2.5 So What Does the Future Hold?

There are, thus, a variety of points of fragility in the contemporary global economy which make it unlikely that the past trajectory of economic expansion – albeit slow by comparison with the Golden Age – can be sustained. But what event might trigger the collapse of a fundamentally insecure economic system?

The outbreak of World War 1 illustrates how a specific event which triggers a systemic crisis may be unpredictable. Underlying tensions between European powers had grown over the decades preceding the war. Germany was at odds with the two largest colonial powers, Britain and France, over access to raw materials and markets. Russia was witnessing rumbling discontent which would ultimately lead to the Bolshevik Revolution in 1917. There had been a build-up of military expenditures in both Germany and Britain in the preceding decade, and a rise in nationalist fervour throughout the continent. These underlying tensions had led to a number of complex inter-country alliances, notably between Russia and Serbia; Germany and Austria-Hungary; France and Russia; Britain, France and Belgium; and Japan and Britain.

All of these tensions suggested that conflict was likely. But it would have been difficult to anticipate the trigger to this systemic crisis. In 1914, Franz Ferdinand, the Archduke leader of the Austro-Hungarian empire was assassinated by a Serbian nationalist group that sought to detach Bosnia and Herzegovina from the Austrian empire. As a consequence of the interdependency and complex alliances between countries, Austria-Hungary then declared war on Serbia. Russia responded by defending Serbia, and this led Germany to declare war on Russia. In turn, this resulted in France challenging Germany and Austria-Hungary. Germany then attacked France, through Belgium, and this led Britain to enter the fray, supported by its alliance with Japan. Later, as the war unfolded, both Italy and the US joined the conflict.

I have suggested three points of fragility in earlier sections, which might trigger a new and more severe 'Great Recession' – a debt crisis (within leading countries or in sovereign debt), the volatility and fragility of the financial system (a burst stock market bubble, a flash-crash in stock prices resulting from automated trading, a collapse in cryptocurrencies) and a severe disruption to global supply chains. Each of these potential sources of disruption results from the very workings of the Mass Production paradigm. But there are also other sources of fissure which are less tightly linked to Mass Production, such as conflict between China and its regional neighbours (in Taiwan, on the Indian border and in the South China seas), between the US and Iran in the Gulf, and military belligerence by North Korea.

In addition, at the time in which I am writing this book, it is clear that the economic impact of the Covid-19 pandemic will be devastating, and will almost certainly be long lived. Is the Covid-19 pandemic an 'endogenous' disruptor – that is, an event which is a direct consequence of the character of Mass Production? Or is it better seen as an 'exogenous' disruptor, a 'black swan' event which is unrelated to the character of the Mass Production techno-economic paradigm during which it emerged? I will return to this issue in later chapters. In a sense, though, it does not matter. What does matter is that post-pandemic economic recovery, if that is possible, will require a changed economic and political structure, with complex and different impacts on the environment. Seen through the lens of techno-economic paradigms, it is conceivable that Covid-19 not only poses a major economic threat, but also provides the opportunity to transition to a more sustainable world. I will explore these issues in Chapters 8 and 9 when I offer an agenda for turning threat into opportunity.

But one message is clear. As the distinguished *Financial Times* economic journalist Martin Wolf observed, well before the onset of the Covid-19 pandemic, 'These are dangerous times – far more so than many recognize. The IMF's warnings are timely, but predictably understated. Our world is being turned upside down. The idea that the economy will motor on regardless while this happens is a fantasy.'[15]

3

The Bumpy Ride to Social Decay

The rise and fall of the Mass Production economy after World War 2 saw a mirroring transition in the social realm from a relatively cohesive period of liberal democracy to the contemporary era of endemic conflict, culture wars and the rise of populism. In this chapter, I will chart the unfolding decay of social relations and show the organic links between economy and society which are characteristic of techno-economic paradigms.

Margaret Thatcher was a key political driver of the neo-liberal agenda. In 1987 she (in)famously declared 'There is no such thing as society.' Thatcher's statement is, of course, a nonsense. No assembly of people – whether in families, in communities or in countries – can function effectively without individuals cooperating in joint activities and sharing common values. The Wikipedia 'bible' provides a helpful synopsis of the key components of 'the society' so glibly dismissed by Thatcher:

> A society is a group of individuals involved in persistent social interaction, or a large social group sharing the same spatial and social territory, typically subject to some political authority and cultural expectations. Societies are characterized by patterns of relationships (social relations) between individuals who share a distinctive culture and institutions ... Societies construct patterns of behaviour by deeming certain actions or speech acceptable or unacceptable. These patterns of behaviour within a given society are known as societal norms.[1]

Society provides the framework within which economic growth occurs. At a minimum, and to a greater or lesser extent, the exercise of power in society (politics) guarantees property rights and maintains a secure environment. Without these functions, businesses are reluctant to invest in the future, and may even find it difficult to operate in the present. But an effectively functioning economic system requires much more than the sanctity of property and security. The labour force must be healthy and be provided with the skills required by the economy. Moreover, production and distribution require an infrastructure – energy, water, roads – and, because no individual firm can afford the costs of providing this infrastructure, it must necessarily be provided by society at large. Consumer demand has to be managed to provide an incentive for investment.

These examples of collective action which support economic growth are reflected in the institutions which societies develop. Governments collect taxes from the citizenry to finance the activities critical to the economy. These funds then need to be used efficiently, and this requires implementing agencies. But governments have much wider functions than just narrowly supporting economic production. They also need to ensure 'consent' from the citizenry – not just to maintain their own legitimacy, but also to encourage people to participate constructively and willingly in production. The cohesive functioning of a robust society also requires the participation of civil society institutions. These span the size range, from village clubs, reading groups and theatrical associations to national and international non-governmental organizations (NGOs), such as Save the Children and Greenpeace.

The relationship between the economy and society is not a one-way street. That is, it is not just a matter of behaviour and institutions reinforcing economic growth. The pattern of economic growth also determines the nature and structure of institutions, and the norms and values that determine the ways in which work is performed and products are consumed. The economy and society thus co-evolve.

My personal journey took me from political activism in South Africa in the late 1960s to the comfort of graduate study and subsequent professional employment in the UK. I left behind a social system in conflict and in crisis. Metaphorically, the struggle against Apartheid was truly a 'black and white' issue – you were either in favour of the entrenchment of privilege on the basis of colour, or you fought against it. There was no 'in between'. It was not that I found myself living in utopia when I arrived in the UK. Britain in the 1970s, and especially after the Thatcher era in the 1980s, was a divided and increasingly unequal social system. But somehow, despite these class tensions, despite the savage manner in which the coal miners' strikes were put down, there was an acceptance that Britain's complex problems and differences could be aired and discussed in a civilized manner. Rationality and evidence, tolerance and nuance were OK.

Phew! Compare that with the Britain of the last five years. We are now either *for* or *against* Brexit. And if one is *against* Brexit, or *for* treating refugees with compassion, or accept 5G mobile phone masts, then you should not be surprised to be harassed and vilified or to receive death threats. And if you are a Member of Parliament who shares these views (like Jo Cox), then bad luck, your life can be extinguished. This is not just a British phenomenon. Donald Trump both gorged on, and in turn fed, even more pernicious prejudices, intolerances and culture wars in the US. In Brazil, the largest country in Latin America, with half of the continent's total population, President Bolsonaro declared that 'The descendants of slaves do nothing. They are not even good for procreation. I would be incapable of loving a homosexual son – I would prefer my son to die in an accident ... The dictatorship's mistake was to torture but not kill.'[2] The depressing list goes on – in the Philippines and the slums of Brazil, police are encouraged to shoot without questions; neo-Nazi movements are on the rise, not just in Austria, Germany and Hungary, but also in the US and France. Unreason, the denial of scientific evidence and the vilification of expertise now thrive in a swamp of prejudice, ignorance and fake news. They permeate our social and political processes. Increasingly, in many countries, the democratic foundations of politics – in which political power is subject to account and to the constitution – are being eroded.

The resultant collapse of social solidarity and tolerance is worrying enough in welfare terms. But at the same time, as we will see in Chapter 5, it has eroded the institutional framework which has facilitated sustainable economic growth. And it has limited and undermined attempts to rebuild environmental sustainability. Crucially, it has come to threaten the sustainability of democratic governance. It was not that long ago – 1989 in fact – that the American political scientist Francis Fukuyama proclaimed that we were living in an era of the 'end of history'.[3] He argued that, following the collapse of communism, the world had transitioned to an acceptance of market capitalism and liberal democracy. This, he believed, marked the end of ideological conflicts. Barely thirty years later – not a very long period in a context in which the world was supposed to have matured into an uncontestable acceptance of a dominant ideology – a variety of political developments belie Fukuyama's sanguine judgement. The election of Donald Trump in the world's largest economy, the rise of populist demagogic politics in Eastern Europe, the Philippines, Brazil and elsewhere, widespread public disillusion with 'normal politics' and opposition to institutions of global governance such as the European Union, the World Trade Organization and the North American Free Trade Agreement suggest anything but stability. 'Social sustainability' is in a state of crisis in the major global economies.

So let's see how these events have unfolded in the post-World War 2 Mass Production paradigm. I begin by documenting the growth of inequality and absolute poverty in the major high-income economies after the Mass Production economy passed through its heyday in the 1970s. I will show how neo-liberal policies, underwritten by an increasingly powerful plutocracy, were a primary driver in the growth of poverty and inequality. The chapter concludes by describing how right-wing populist leaders have built on social exclusion and discontent and used prejudice against 'the other' – in this case, migrants – to grab control of the political agenda. This populist agenda undermines the capacity to renew economic growth and to transition to a more sustainable ICT techno-economic paradigm.

3.1 The Rise and Rise of Inequality

The growth in inequality since the early 1980s has taken two major forms.[4] The first has been the distribution of wealth – that is, ownership of various forms of assets. The second is the distribution of income – that is, the incomes received by different categories of citizenry. The distributions of wealth and of income are distinct, although related, phenomena. Wealth is inheritable and is an important source of income. But it is not the only source of income.

Changing patterns in the distribution of wealth

Figure 3.1 shows the trend in the changing share of the top 1% of wealth-holders in the USA, France, the UK, China and Russia between 1913 and 2015. Although wealth inequality in 2013 was

Figure 3.1 Top 1% personal wealth share in emerging and rich countries, 1913–2015

Source: World Inequality Report 2018, https://wir2018.wid.world

lower than it was in 1913, there was a marked growth in the degree of inequality in all of these five economies from the early 1980s to 2015. In China and the US (the two largest global economies) and in Russia, the top 1% of the population owns more than 30% of total wealth, and this share is on a rising trend. The top 10% of wealth-holders in these three economies also saw a sharp rise in their share after the early 1980s. In China, the US and Russia, they accounted for more than two-thirds of total national wealth in 2015. The rising inequality was particularly marked in China where the top 10% almost doubled their share, from just over 40% to just under 70%, in a mere twenty years; the top 1% saw a rise from 18% to 30% in the same period.

These trends in wealth inequality provide headline-grabbing sound-bites which influence public opinion. For example, a widely quoted Oxfam Report in 2018 reported that:[5]

- in 2017, there were 2,085 dollar billionaires, 90% of whom were men. Their wealth increased by $762 billion in 2017 alone.
- 82% of the total increase in global wealth in 2017 went to the top 1% of wealth-holders.
- 42 of the world's wealthiest individuals owned as much wealth as the poorest 3.7 billion people worldwide.

- the wealth of the richest 1% of the world's population collectively exceeded that of the rest of humanity.
- in the US, the wealthiest 3 individuals had assets exceeding those of the bottom half of the total population (160 million people).

The list of global billionaires is no longer a preserve of the US and Europe. In 2017, the countries with the largest number of billionaires were China (819), the US (571), India (131), the UK (118), Germany (114), Switzerland (83), Russia (71), France (51) and Brazil and Canada (with 49 each). Even in Africa, the poorest continent in the world, there were 29 billionaires in 2017.

The evidence to support these attention-grabbing claims is not without its problems. For one thing, the dollar value of assets in one country is not the same as in another – that is, these estimates of wealth are not adjusted for Purchasing Power Parity. For another, should these billionaires attempt to realize their wealth quickly or simultaneously, the very act of disposing of their large wealth-holdings would decrease their value. Nevertheless, three important conclusions stand out from this data on individual wealth. First, there is no question that wealth is very unequally distributed amongst the world's population. Second, the degree of wealth concentration grew increasingly rapidly from the end of the Golden Age in the mid-1970s. And third, there is widespread public awareness of these trends and this is one of the factors fuelling the discontent which affects the social and institutional framework in which economies grow and societies function.

Changing patterns in the distribution of income

Wealth involves the ownership of a *stock* of assets. By contrast, income comprises a *flow*, usually calculated on an annual basis. This determines the capacity of recipients to consume (buying today) or to divert present consumption into savings (that is wealth) to enable consumption in the future. Although wealth is a primary source of income for some high-income earners, it is not the major source for the mass of citizenry whose incomes arise from wages, salaries, and earnings from self-employment.

In his widely cited book on historical trends in wealth-holdings, Piketty showed that, both historically and in the contemporary world, wealth is more unequally distributed than is income.[6] Nevertheless, as in the case of wealth, there has been a sharp rise in income inequality since the 1980s. This unequalization takes a number of forms. Since we are concerned with the inter-relationship between distribution, the character of Mass Production and social sustainability, we will focus on three relevant examples. The first is the distribution of income amongst global citizenry. The second is that between classes (capital and labour). The third is that between different sets of skilled workers.

Beginning with the distribution of incomes between individuals around the world, it makes little sense to compare the average levels of per-capita incomes in countries of vastly different population sizes. Instead, the World Inequality Report drew on surveys of household consumption and tax records across the world. They also took account of the differential purchasing power of the dollar in different economies. Using these data, they estimated trends in the share of global income earned by the world's population, irrespective of which country they lived in. Figure 3.2, showing these trends between 1980 and 2016 graphically, needs a little interpretation. On the horizontal axis are shares of the world's total population. Note that, between 0 and 99 per cent, the intervals are essentially the same. Each of the first nine bars (deciles) represent successive 10 per cent increments of the global population. The last four segments on this axis magnify these changes for the highest 10 per cent of income earners. They represent the top 9 per cent, the top 1 per cent, the top one-hundredth and the top one-thousandth per cent of the global population, respectively. The vertical axis shows the growth in the real incomes of these sets of the world's population.

So what can we learn from this picture of the incomes of global citizens? First, there was a rapid increase in incomes in the 2nd-, 3rd- and 4th-bottom deciles of recipients – that is, in those with relatively low incomes globally (but not the very poorest bottom 10 per cent). This is largely the result of very rapid economic growth in China which benefitted from the outsourcing of production from high-income countries. Second, there was a sharp reduction in the rate of growth of incomes in the 5th to 9th deciles. These are the people in the middle of the global income range in high-income economies, whose incomes were eroded as manufactures and services were increasingly imported from low- and middle-income economies such as China. Third, there was an astonishing rise in the growth of incomes in the top decile (and especially at the extreme top) of global income

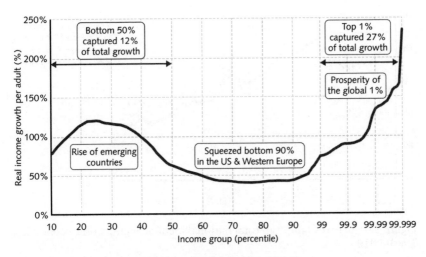

Figure 3.2 Changes in global inequality, 1980–2016
Source: World Inequality Report 2017, https://wir2017.wid.world

recipients. And, finally, the relative winners were located both in the emerging and high-income economies. Those experiencing relative declines were predominantly located in the high-income economies.

So much for the inter-personal distribution of income. But what of the class-distribution of income, which reflects the share of returns from production accruing to two major inputs into production, labour and capital? After three decades of post-war stability, the share of labour in total incomes in the high-income economies began to fall in the 1970s. Between 1990 and 2009, labour's share declined in twenty-six out of thirty high-income economies. Figure 3.3 evidences this declining share of labour for nine major global economies. It shows that, in the space of two decades, it fell from around two-thirds to just over 55 per cent of the total.

But not all workers in the high-income countries met the same fate. Skilled workers benefitted from a growth in real wages. By contrast, unskilled and semi-skilled workers experienced a decline in their real wages. For example, in the US, adjusting for inflation, between 1973 and 2009, the wages of those with greater-than-college-level education more than doubled, and those with college-level education experienced a rise of more than 50 per cent. By contrast, the real average wages of those without any college-level education – most

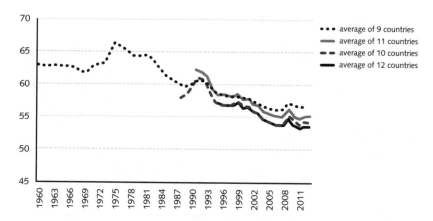

Figure 3.3 Share of labour in total national income, high-income economies, 1960–2012

The 9 countries are Australia, Canada, France, Germany, Italy, Japan, Spain, UK and US. The other series include the Republic of Korea ('10 countries'), Mexico ('11 countries') and Turkey ('12 countries').

Source: ILO–OECD (2015), *The Labour Share in G20 Economies*, Geneva: International Labour Organisation

factory workers and those employed in the retail, agricultural and hospitality sectors – declined.[7] Stripping out inflation, average hourly wages in the US in 2018 ($23.68) had the same purchasing power as those in 1973 ($4.03).[8] The erosion of unskilled wages in the US is mirrored widely in other high-income countries.[9] In the UK, for example, average real wages fell by 10.4 per cent between 2007 and 2015. These trends in the class distribution of income are to a considerable extent a consequence of the era of globalization which emerged in the latter phase of the Mass Production paradigm after the 1980s.

3.2 The Startling Growth of 'Absolute Poverty'

Peter Townsend, the British sociologist who spent much of his life documenting the growth of social exclusion in the UK, distinguished two dimensions of poverty.[10] The first was what he termed 'relative poverty' – that is, the degree of inequality. The second dimension of poverty, Townsend argued, was 'absolute poverty' – that is, the real standard of living. As we have just seen, relative poverty grew rapidly across the board globally after the end of Mass Production's Golden Age. But what about 'absolute poverty'?

Robert Reich, the well-regarded Secretary of Labor in the Clinton Administration during the 1990s, was the author of an influential book published in 1991 entitled *The Work of Nations*.[11] The title, of course, was intended to resonate with that of Adam Smith's classic text, *The Wealth of Nations*, which is often (mistakenly) touted as a celebration of free-market economics. Reacting to the emergence of job insecurity as American jobs were being outsourced to China and other emerging economies, Reich observed the following. America had an upper class; by definition, this, of course, meant that it also had a lower (working) class – but between these extremes lay not a middle class, but an anxious class.

Fast-forward more than two decades, and, at the end of 2015, following visits to rural and Midwest states, Reich wrote a blog which was extensively republished.[12] Entitled *The Revolt of the Anxious Class*, this presciently predicted the election of Donald Trump. Reich observed a number of concerning developments, highlighting the extent to which falling real incomes, rising unemployment and insecure employment were fuelling a rise in insecurity. He noted, for example, that the share of middle-class families in total US income fell from 62% in 1970 to 43% in 2014. Almost two-thirds (62%) of Americans did not have savings of $1,000 or more to cover unexpected job-loss, emergency health expenditures, the need to replace cars, unexpected damages to houses and other life-challenges which characteristically and unexpectedly hit families. (In 2018, a Federal Reserve Board study reported that 40% of Americans would have to borrow or sell something to cover a $400 emergency expense.)[13] The life-span of the American middle class was falling, including as a result of a growing epidemic of opioid and alcohol consumption. Fewer than 25% of Americans had access to unemployment benefits, a figure which had fallen from 75% in 2009.

The Covid-19 crisis in 2020 accentuated these trends. More than a quarter of the US labour force was laid off, and families dipped into their meagre savings and increased household debt in order to survive. Chillingly, the sales of firearms increased by more than 25%. The owner of one of America's largest gun stores ascribed the reasons for this surge in gun sales to 'Financial meltdown, pandemic, crime, politics … you throw it all into a pot and you have one hell of a mess.'

The rise in poverty and employment-related insecurity is not confined to the US. In the UK, the Trades Union Congress estimated the number of insecure jobs in 2017 at 3.2 million.[14] This included a very rapid growth in zero-hours contracts (rising from 70,000 in 2006 to 810,000 in 2016), and the growth in the number of self-employed from 3.8 million in 2006 to 4.8 million in 2016. Of these self-employed in 2016, 1.7 million earned incomes below the government's living wage. In 2020, more than 3 million British children living below the poverty line were in households where at least one parent was in employment. In 2018, a UN Special Rapporteur on Poverty, Philip Alston, spent some weeks visiting large cities, smaller towns and rural areas in the UK to assess the extent of absolute poverty.[15] (Since the UK had promoted such investigations in other countries, it was not in a position to oppose this visit by a UN Special Rapporteur.) Alston was shocked at what he had found. One-fifth of the population were living below the poverty line, and one-third of these were living at less than half of the official poverty level. Homelessness had increased 60 per cent since 2010, and the numbers using foodbanks had increased by four times since 2012. The number of children living in poor households had grown sharply. Because wages had stagnated and work had become more precarious, nearly two-thirds of poor households had at least one working adult. Ethnic-minority households witnessed the largest fall in incomes.

3.3 Growing Inequality and Poverty Undermine Welfare and Social Solidarity

So what impact has this rise in inequality and poverty had on the character of social relations in the latter decades of the Mass Production paradigm?[16] Here we can benefit from the pioneering and illuminating books by two epidemiologists, Richard Wilkinson and Kate Pickett – *The Spirit Level* published in 2009, and *The Inner Level* published in 2018.[17] Their initial interest was the extent to which life-expectancy was associated with standards of living. They observed that, whilst the level of average per-capita income in a country does determine the length of life, this is only true until average living standards are high enough to feed, house and clothe the population. Beyond this level – which, based on comparative analysis, they deemed to be an annual per-capita income of $25,000 – there seemed to be little relationship between life-expectancy and average incomes.

Instead, comparing twenty-two high-income economies, they found a clear and strong link between the length of life and the degree of inequality (Figure 3.4a). In order to assess whether this result was a reflection of national cultural differences, they then undertook the same analysis for the fifty states in the US. That is, they 'held the country constant'. This confirmed the robustness of the relationship between equality and life-expectancy. The higher the degree of inequality within individual states, the lower the level of life-expectancy (Figure 3.4b). (Note that, due to the nature of data availability, the measure of inequality used in these two sets of calculations differs.)

Startled by this graphic link between inequality and life-expectancy, Wilkinson and Pickett turned their attention to a number of other key

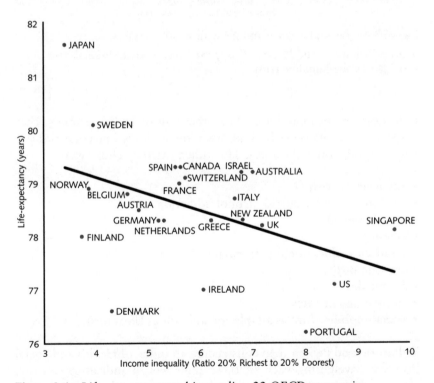

Figure 3.4a Life-expectancy and inequality, 22 OECD economies

Source: Wilkinson and Pickett, *The Spirit Level*; with additional data provided by the Equality Trust

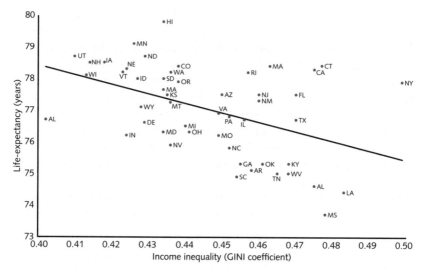

Figure 3.4b Life-expectancy and inequality, 50 US states

Source: Wilkinson and Pickett, *The Spirit Level*; with additional data provided by the Equality Trust

indicators of social welfare. As in the case of life-expectancy, they compared the outcomes both between the high-income countries and between individual US states. The indicators they chose were

- the level of trust
- mental illness, drug and alcohol addiction
- infant mortality
- obesity
- children's educational performance
- teenage births
- homicides
- imprisonment rates
- social mobility (not available for individual US states)

Wilkinson and Pickett then constructed an Index of Health and Social Problems, weighting each of these nine sets of indicators equally. The results are striking. As Figure 3.5 shows clearly, the more unequal the society, the higher the composite Index of Health and Social Problems. As in the case of life-expectancy, the inter-country

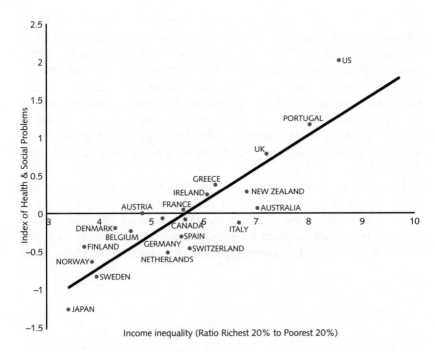

Figure 3.5 Health and social problems and degree of inequality, inter-country differences

Source: Wilkinson and Pickett, *The Spirit Level*; with additional data provided by the Equality Trust

relationship between health and social problems and inequality is replicated in the comparison between different US states.

Wilkinson and Pickett's second book, *The Inner Level*, moves the analysis from the link between income distribution and health and sociological outcomes to that between distribution and the attitudes and behaviour of individuals. Here, the focus is on a diverse set of outcomes such as depression, anxiety, narcissism and road rage. It also extends the earlier analysis on social outcomes to address social mobility, different types of school performance and children's rights. As in the case of *The Spirit Level*, the correlations are strong between these outcomes and distribution, and weak between outcomes and per-capita incomes, both between countries and within the USA.

Two specific conclusions from *The Inner Level* are particularly illuminating. The first is what Wilkinson and Pickett refer to as status anxiety – in other words, the levels of anxiety which are directly associated with comparisons with others. Here, drawing on a variety of psychological studies, they show the extent to which anxiety grows with the degree of social differentiation. For example, in one study respondents were asked to what extent they agreed with the following statement – 'Some people look down on me because of my job situation or income.' Not only are those at the bottom of the income scale more likely to suffer from anxiety, but the extent of status anxiety is closely correlated with the degree of inequality (Figure 3.6).

The pervasiveness of status anxiety and the extent to which this spills over into social conflict can be observed in a whole range of social interaction. One perhaps less-than-obvious but illuminating example is air rage conflicts between passengers. Incidents of air rage amongst economy-class passengers are 3.9 times more likely when

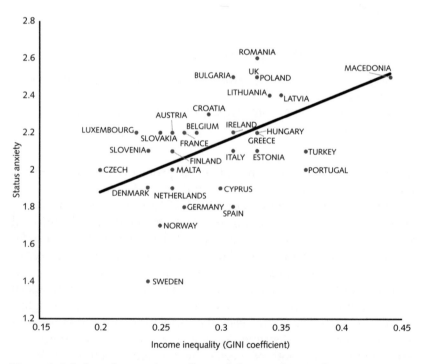

Figure 3.6 Index of status inequality and degree of inequality
Source: data provided by the Equality Trust, courtesy of Richard Wilkinson

the plane has a first-class section. An especially revealing feature of air rage is that, when economy-class passengers entering the plane pass through first class on the way to the back of the plane, the incidence of air rage is much higher than when the different classes of passengers do not cross over. This affects both economy-class passengers (2.18 times more likely to be involved when they pass through the first-class section) and first-class passengers (11.9 times more likely to react with rage).[18] Thus, it is not just the relatively poor whose anger is fuelled by inequality, but also the rich.

A second important finding that Wilkinson and Pickett report relates to social and civic participation. Here they drew on a series of sociological and psychological research studies. For example, they cite a study which found that, in Europe, the greater the degree of income inequality, the lesser the extent to which people, both rich and poor, were prepared to assist neighbours, older people, migrants, the sick and the disabled. Figure 3.7 shows that levels of social participation (defined as the frequency of meeting with friends and relatives) were consistently higher in more equal European countries. There was an

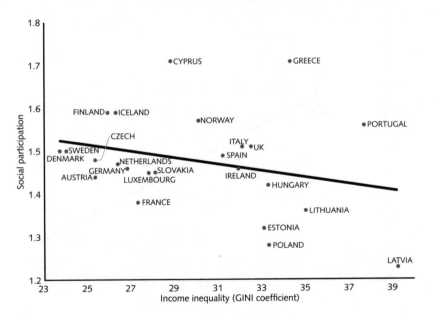

Figure 3.7 Index of social participation and degree of inequality
Source: data provided by the Equality Trust, courtesy of Richard Wilkinson

even stronger relationship for the index of civic participation (defined as participation in civic institutions) (Figure 3.8).

Reviewing a variety of studies on civic participation, Wilkinson and Pickett conclude as follows:

> The single most important reason why participation in community life declines with increased inequality is likely to be the increased social evaluative threat: people withdraw from social life as they find it more stressful. More unequal societies become more fragmented as social distances increase. People become more withdrawn, less neighbourly and more worried about appearances and giving the wrong impression, they prefer to 'keep themselves to themselves'. And *when some people feel excluded or threatened, the same processes which affect so many individual minds and bodies also affect the political process.* [Emphasis added]

To support this final conclusion, Wilkinson and Pickett draw on an analysis from the *Economist* following the US presidential election in 2016. This showed that the higher a combined measure of obesity,

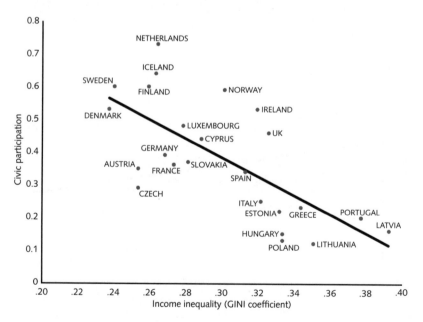

Figure 3.8 Index of civic participation and degree of inequality

Source: data provided by the Equality Trust, courtesy of Richard Wilkinson

diabetes, heavy drinking, lack of physical exercise and low life-expectancy, all of which they argue are made worse by inequality, the greater the electoral swing to Donald Trump. I will elaborate on this link at a later point in this chapter.

3.4 Neo-liberal Austerity Policies and the Power of the Plutocracy Caused Growing Inequality and Absolute Poverty

Three primary factors have driven this rise in inequality and absolute poverty. The first is the character of technological change. Increasingly automated labour-saving technologies have displaced labour and led to higher levels of unemployment. In addition, technologies have required increasingly skilled labour and this, as we observed above, has led to the trend of unequalization in wages within the labour force. The second factor driving inequality and poverty has been the pressure on employment and wages resulting from the expansion of imports as globalization has deepened. I will discuss both of these factors and their relationship to the Mass Production paradigm in later chapters – in Chapter 8 in the case of the labour-saving and skill-intensive character of technological change, and in Chapter 5 in relation to the impact of globalization.

However, there has been a third important driver of inequality and poverty which results from the social character of the Mass Production paradigm. This involves the pursuit of neo-liberal policies and the purposive actions of the plutocracy to steer the policy agenda in favour of the wealthy and high-income earners. As I will show, these two developments (austerity and the power of the plutocracy) are, of course, closely inter-related.

The contribution of neo-liberal austerity policies to rising inequality and poverty

With the exception of the oil-price economic crises of the 1970s, between 1960 and the late 1990s government revenues broadly balanced government expenditures in the high-income countries. But from the late 1990s, and especially in the immediate period following the 2008 global Financial Crisis, governments in many major economies sank into deep fiscal deficits. In most of the high-income economies, political pressures made it difficult for governments to continue running up deficits, even though these were not abnormally high by historical standards. So, how were these fiscal deficits to be filled?

One possible route was to raise money by taxing profits in the corporate sector. But, as we saw in Chapter 2, in many economies corporate taxes were reduced in order to encourage investment and satisfy the demands of the rich. Even then, an increasing number of large global firms developed elaborate schemes to avoid profits by routing payments through a complex web of global affiliates. For example, until 2016, Google's permanent establishment in the United Kingdom (the 'source' of its operations) was supported by its 'residence' in Ireland. In 2012, it paid taxes of £55 million on UK revenue of £5.5 billion, a tax rate of 1 per cent of sales. It rationalized this by arguing that its UK staff were engaged in relatively routine tasks, adding little value to its UK sales. This was despite the fact that average salaries of its staff in the UK exceeded $240,000, more than double the salaries paid to its Irish employees.

Why was Google 'resident' in Ireland? Because of Ireland's tax structure, which was designed to attract tax-avoiding companies such as Google. The taxes it paid in Ireland (14.7 per cent of declared profits in 2017, and 13.8 per cent in 2016) were reduced through the use of a complex tax avoidance scheme referred to as the 'double Irish, Dutch sandwich'.[19] This involves the use of intra-corporate financial transfers between two Irish subsidiaries, the Netherlands and (tax-free) Bermuda.

Google was not alone in the use of complex tax-avoidance schemes. In the decade between 2009 and 2017, Amazon paid a total of only $1bn in US taxes on accumulated pre-tax profits of $27bn – a tax rate of 3 per cent. Its profits in 2018 ($10.8bn) were double those of 2017 ($5.4bn). Notwithstanding these large and growing profits and its low effective tax rate, it managed to engineer a tax rebate of $140m in 2017 and of $130m in 2018. In 2016, the OECD estimated that $240bn was lost annually in corporate tax, as a result of profit-shifting to low-tax jurisdictions.[20]

It was not just corporate tax rates which were reduced in the neo-liberal era. During the 1940s and 1950s, the top rate of tax in the UK exceeded 90 per cent. On assuming power in 1979, Margaret Thatcher attacked the 'disincentives to work' and progressively reduced the highest tax band from 83 per cent to 63 per cent and then to 40 per cent. She reduced the basic tax rate from 33 per cent to 25 per cent, and this was further lowered (by the Labour government) to 20 per cent in 2008. In the US, between 1945 and 1963 the top marginal rate was above, or just below, 90 per cent. This fell gradually to 70 per cent by 1981, to 50 per cent until 1986, and subsequently to its current rate of 32 per cent for the highest income bracket. In addition, so many exceptions were written into the law favouring high-income earners that in 2018 the 400 richest American families had a lower tax rate than the poorest 50 per cent of households.[21]

Given the political pressure forcing reductions in taxes in most of the high-income economies, the shortfall in government revenue was met through a reduction in spending on infrastructure and the introduction of austerity policies. The UK provides a particularly graphic example of the consequences of these austerity policies on inequality and poverty. The Conservative government which assumed power after the 2008 Financial Crisis in the UK took the 'opportunity' offered by this crisis to pursue an ideological agenda to return the level of government expenditure in the economy to that which prevailed during the Great Depression in the 1930s, seemingly oblivious to the fact that the only thing which enabled the UK economy to revive in this decade of depression was the pursuit of deficit spending by government. The austerity policy agenda combined reductions in corporate and personal taxes with massive reductions in state expenditures on welfare and infrastructure.

We have already reported the findings of the UN Special Rapporteur on Poverty's investigation of the impact of austerity policies on increasing absolute poverty in the UK. Reviewing this evidence, Alston commented witheringly that 'Britain is not just a disgrace, but a social calamity and an economic disaster, all rolled into one.' Moreover, he concluded:

> the driving force has not been economic but rather a commitment to achieving radical social re-engineering ... The country's most respected charitable groups, its leading think tanks, its parliamentary committees, independent authorities like the National Audit Office, and many others, have all drawn attention to the dramatic decline in the fortunes of the least well off in this country. But through it all, one actor has stubbornly resisted seeing the situation for what it is. The Government has remained determinedly in a state of denial ... Ministers insisted to me that all is well and running according to plan

... Ministers with whom I met told me that things are going well that they don't see any big problems and they are happy with the way their policies are playing out.

The plutocracy promoted and legitimized austerity policies

Despite the harmful welfare impacts of austerity policies, governments introducing these policies have routinely been re-elected. So how did these welfare-damaging policies survive and thrive? How did the poor come to be blamed for their own plight? The answer lies in the capacity of the very rich elite – the plutocracy – to frame the narrative explaining the descent into inequality and absolute poverty. This control was exercised through their command over opinion-forming media, and two channels in particular – social media and the press.

The recent explosion in disseminated untruths includes a subset of fake news involving lies which are knowingly and deliberately constructed to influence social attitudes and political processes and to promote the introduction of policies favouring the interests of the plutocracy. Donald Trump is perhaps the most prominent proponent of this political tactic, knowingly spreading falsities about his opponents. For example, prior to his election in 2016, the lie was spread by Trump and his allies that President Obama was a Muslim, and that he was not born in the USA. At the time of taking office, Trump twittered extensively that the crowd for his inauguration was larger than that for Obama's inauguration in 2012. After his inauguration, he engaged in an avalanche of daily Twitter posts designed to deny reality. With savage and amoral cunning, he then sought to discredit accurate stories in established media outlets by accusing them of disseminating 'fake news'. This barrage of untruths was predominantly designed to allow him to maintain his hold over the presidency by cultivating his political constituency. But, as we will see below, it also drew on and then reinforced beliefs which challenged the social and political fabric which had supported the neo-liberal policy agenda which emerged in the latter decades of Mass Production.

Similar processes unfolded in other high-income economies. For example, in the UK, the supporters of withdrawal from the EU in the 2016 Brexit Referendum engaged in the deliberate dissemination of lies. They claimed that 'experts' (in fact, the overwhelming proportion of professional economists) could not be trusted above their own demonstrably untruthful claims of 'reality'. They spread untruths such as that withdrawal from the EU would provide a £350 million per week bounty to fund the National Health Service, that the EU was about to be deluged by a massive inflow of migrants from Turkey, and that Britain could, post-Brexit, obtain tariff- and regulation-free access to the EU.

We can see the close association between the dissemination of these sets of fake news in the US and the UK with attitudes that affect political processes and social cohesion. Figure 3.9 illustrates the differences in belief in conspiracies relevant to the sustainability of the liberal democratic social order in the UK and the US in 2016. In the UK, the contrast is between those who voted for Brexit and those who voted to remain in the EU. In the US, the contrast is between those who voted for Trump and those who supported Clinton in the 2016 election. A series of questions were posed reflecting beliefs concerning the role and intentions of Muslim communities, global warming, the truth about vaccines, and plots by global and local power elites to rule the world and the country. The extent of belief in these conspiracies was high.

The results show that there was surprisingly widespread belief that man-made global climate change is a hoax, that governments

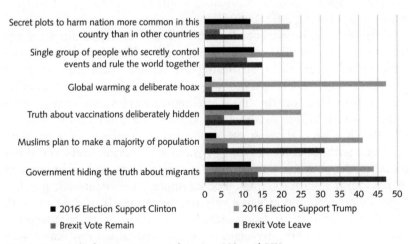

Figure 3.9 Belief in conspiracy theories, US and UK
Source: data from the *Guardian*, 25 November 2018

deliberately conceal the number of immigrants and, perhaps most fancifully, that Muslims have a secret plan to breed rapidly in order to become the dominant ethnic group. There was a clear political orientation to this belief in conspiracies. Political movements that were seeking to sweep away the established social and political order (that is Brexit and Trump supporters) were far more likely to believe in conspiracies than were supporters of the existing social and political order.

If these incidences of fake news were only a manifestation of personal ambition by Donald Trump in the US and politicians such as Boris Johnson and Nigel Farage (the leading Brexiteers) in the UK, the challenges to social and political sustainability would be limited. But there have been darker forces at work providing impetus to these deliberately false agendas designed to disrupt social and political processes. One source of disruption was the involvement of Russia in elections in a number of liberal democracies. In the US, Russia leaked information on Hillary Clinton's private emails, which was instrumental in ensuring Trump's electoral victory. In France, two days before the first round of presidential elections in 2017, tens of thousands of emails, summary notes, photos and invoices were leaked from the Macron campaign, and bundled together with fake news.[22] In Germany, in the 48 hours before elections in 2018, a Russian-linked botnet – automated accounts that can repost online messages rapidly to mass audiences – spread lies that promoted the extreme right-wing AfD party.[23]

Attempts to influence social attitudes and electoral results were not limited to the political establishment, or to Russia. Private parties with vested interests in disrupting established social and political processes and beliefs played a prominent role in disseminating fake news. One of the most telling examples was the contribution of Cambridge Analytica to Trump's electoral victory and the UK Brexit vote. Drawing on sophisticated analyses of meta-data obtained without consent from 87 million Facebook users and other social media sources, Cambridge Analytica developed techniques of 'behavioural microtargeting'. For example, they identified, psychologically profiled and targeted very precise segments of the Facebook population and then disseminated fake news to their Facebook Friends. In each case, messages were directed which resonated with the views of these groups of Facebook users. These softened up the users to be sympathetic to Trump and Brexit, not so much as explicitly political messages, but by reinforcing particular factually inaccurate social attitudes – for example, that there was a flood of Muslims into the US, that Obama was not born in the USA, and that the EU enforced regulations determining the shape of bananas. Cambridge Analytica marketed its services to a variety of countries as a 'general election management agency' and its CEO boasted that it had been involved in forty-four political races in 2014.[24] Cambridge Analytica was partly owned by the billionaire Robert Mercer and his daughter. Mercer provided data-analytic services to Nigel Farage in the UK Brexit campaign, funds to Breitbart News in the US and large-scale funding to organizations sceptical of climate change.

Beyond the Mercer family, Cambridge Analytica and Facebook, there were other intersecting influencers of public opinions, such as those controlled by Rupert Murdoch's News Corp. News Corp has a global reach which includes Fox News and the *Wall Street Journal* in the US; *The Times*, the *Sunday Times* and the *Sun* newspapers and SKY TV in the UK; more than thirty newspapers in Australia; newspapers in Fiji; and a number of global publishing houses. Murdoch has a long history of opposing UK membership of the EU, is a long-term friend of Donald Trump and a substantial contributor to the Republican Party. Steve Bannon is a billionaire who played a central role in establishing Breitbart News before he moved to become Trump's Chief Strategist after the 2016 election.

The Koch brothers are American billionaires. Their wealth is estimated to exceed $120 billion. For more than four decades, they have been engaged in a concerted below-the-radar programme to influence legislation and to shape public opinion. In 1978, Charles Koch declared his intention to establish a 'movement [which] must destroy the prevalent statist paradigm'. It sought to foster legislation to lower taxes and reduce regulations. The latter objective was understandable since Koch Industries paid large fines for oil spills, illegal benzene emissions and ammonia pollution.[25]

Their objectives were pursued through a three-pronged strategy. First, funded university programmes would produce the 'intellectual raw materials'. Then, thinktanks would translate these ideas into 'more practical or usable forms'. Finally, 'citizen activist' groups would 'press for the implementation of policy change'. To achieve these aims, they established a range of implementing institutions including the Mercatus Center at George Mason University, the Cato Institute and the 'citizens' group' Americans for Prosperity. In furthering this agenda, they provided hundreds of millions of dollars to sympathetic institutions in each of these three areas of implementation. This masking by overwhelmingly right-wing sponsors of the funding of apparently citizen-led social movements has come to be referred to as 'astroturfing'.

Interventions by the Koch brothers to influence societal values and norms were not limited to the US. Between 2016 and 2018, they provided more than $170,000 to a fringe magazine called *Spike* in the UK. Ironically, *Spike* had its origins in a far-left activist group (the Revolutionary Communist Movement), but its attraction for the Koch brothers was its support for anti-statist programmes. It railed against the welfare state, government regulation, the Occupy movement, Jeremy Corbyn, George Soros and the #MeToo, 'black privilege' and 'Black Lives Matter' movements. By contrast, it defended figures on the extreme right, including pro-Brexit and UK politicians such as Nigel Farage and Arron Banks, and Viktor Orbán in Hungary. It also ridiculed the idea that air pollution is dangerous to health, and argued that, far from reducing the human ecological footprint, it should be enlarged. A wealthy UK businessman, Arron Banks (who was expelled from two schools, in one case for selling lead stolen from the school buildings) was the major funder of the pro-Brexit Leave.EU campaign. He was also a prime funder of the UK Independence Party.

There was a unifying theme in all of these efforts seeking to mould public opinion in various parts of the world. Some of the initiatives were targeted at specific outcomes, such as tax reduction and the removal of environmental regulation and regulation of labour standards. But others were more insidious, and promoted social attitudes and public opinion questioning the patterns of governance in liberal democracies. This was pursued by fuelling a distrust of politicians, and by challenging the values, norms, patterns of behaviour and unwritten rules underwriting the Golden Age growth trajectory.

These efforts by the plutocracy had concrete payoffs. Robert Reich reported that, in 2016, the richest 1 per cent of Americans – 24,949 people – accounted for 40 per cent of all campaign contributions, and the corporate sector provided $3.4bn to support predominantly Republican candidates in the presidential, state and House election campaigns. This was to good effect. The Pfizer Corporation contributed $16m to the Republican campaign and stands to gain tax savings of £39bn by 2023. General Electric contributed $20m, with an estimated tax payback of $16bn, and Chevron oil invested $13m in expectation of gaining tax advantages of $9bn. The Koch brothers supported the drive for tax cuts with $20m, and the new tax regime saved them and their families between $1bn and $1.4bn a year.[26]

3.5 The Fear of Migration Has Been Used to Fuel Populism

Coterminous with the impact of austerity policies on inequality and poverty, and the targeted intervention by the plutocracy to shape values and political processes, many high-income economies experienced a sharp rise in inward migration. Over the millennia, centuries and decades, the scale of migration has grown. Migrants no longer only move to the next valley, or indeed to the adjacent continent. Relocation horizons have widened as transport technologies and infrastructure have progressed. Recent decades have seen an accumulation of people living in countries which are different from their places of birth. The number of global migrants grew from approximately 75 million people in 1960 to almost 250 million in 2016: nearly 4 per cent of the total global population. The rate of cross-border migration increased in the 1980s as economic globalization deepened, and then again after the 2008 global Financial Crisis.

Figure 3.10 shows the acceleration of migration into a selection of high-income economies after 2010. I have chosen these particular high-income economies – Austria, Czech Republic, France, Germany, Hungary, Italy, Poland, Sweden, the UK and the US – because my focus is on the impact of migration on the character of political systems in the high-income world. They are, of course, not the only high-income economies witnessing substantial migration, and notable omissions (because of lack of comparable data) are Greece and Turkey.

A striking feature emerging from Figure 3.10 is the dominance of two high-income destination countries. The combined share of Germany and the US rose from 70 per cent of total in-migration in 2006 to 74 per cent in 2016. But these aggregate numbers are misleading, since both Germany and the US are heavily populated countries. As Table 3.1 shows, the relative weight of migration paints a somewhat different picture, in three respects. First, as a share of the total population, the proportion of foreign-born residents is highest in Austria and Sweden. Second, the proportion of asylum-seeking migrants is highest in Italy, France and Austria. And third, the rate of increase in migrant inflows between 2006 and 2016 was highest in Germany, Poland, Austria and Sweden.

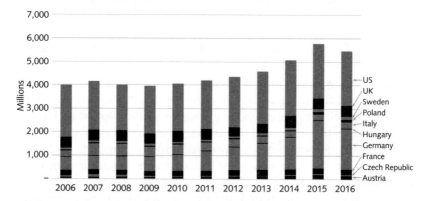

Figure 3.10 Inflows of migrants, selected high-income economies, 2006–2016 (millions)

Source: data drawn from OECD International Migration Outlook 2018, Paris: OECD

Table 3.1 Extent and character of migrant inflows in ten high-income economies

	Foreign-born as % 2016	Increase, 2016:2006 %	New asylum seekers, 2016	
			Number	*% migrants*
Austria	19.0	192	39,880	25.1
Czech R.	7.5	53	1,210	3.5
France	12.7	105	91,070	37.8
Germany	15.5	308	196,260	11.4
Hungary	5.3	101	3,100	13.0
Italy	5.3	103	121,190	46.1
Poland	1.8	313	3,000	2.8
Sweden	18.5	178	22,190	15.5
UK	14.2	101	33,320	7.3
US	13.5	103	329,800	14.2

Source: data from OECD International Migration Outlook 2018

Politicians have used these inflows of migrants to disrupt the political consensus. In the UK, they exploited the growing loss of personal and social agency which I chronicled earlier in this chapter to suggest that migrants were the source of work-insecurity ('taking our jobs'), loss of identity ('foreign values') and pressures on social services ('they overuse the National Health Service'). This was despite the facts that so many of the 'talking head' experts on the TV had non-Anglo-Saxon names, and that the NHS was significantly staffed by migrants. (I, myself, am a migrant – a political refugee in fact – and have a non-Anglo-Saxon surname. Nigel Farage's wife is a German migrant. Are we the cause of unemployment, a stretched health service and an erosion of culture in the UK?) In the US in December 2018, seeking to deflect criticism of his presidency and the links between his campaign and Russia, Trump re-opened the demand for a wall to be built on the US–Mexican border. He based his argument on the extraordinary claim that Central American migrants not only were drug-dealers but also carried contagious diseases. In 2019, he sought funds for the wall he wanted to build on the Mexican border by threatening to declare a State of Emergency, citing the need to protect 'national security'. This would provide the President with the means to over-rule Congress in circumstances in which the US faced acute security challenges. In 2019, he sought to stir a racial divide in American politics by telling four non-Anglo-Saxon Democratic Congresswomen to 'go home', despite the fact that three had been born in the USA.

So, given the capacity of politicians to resort to xenophobic – and often overtly racist – messaging, is it an accident that countries such as Austria and Sweden have seen a rise in right-wing political parties challenging liberal democracy in recent years? Both have disproportionately high shares of foreign-born residents in their population. Both have a large share of asylum seekers in their recent inflows of migrants. Germany's praiseworthy acceptance of Syrian and other humanitarian refugees in recent years – a commitment not without self-interest in an economy with an ageing population and near-full employment – has led to a political backlash with the rise of the openly racist anti-immigrant AfD party. Similarly, in Italy, which because of its coastal proximity to North Africa is unable to easily stem the flow of refugees, the right-wing and anti-migrant xenophobic Northern League came to play a dominant role in government after 2017. Figure 3.11 shows that the higher the share of migrants, the greater the vote-share of these populist parties,

Pr(Rightvote)

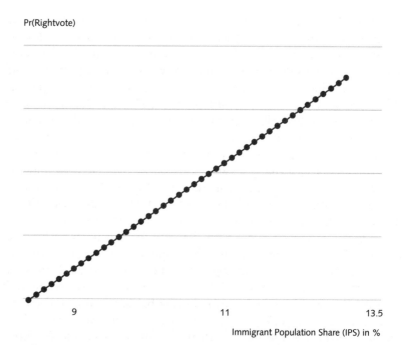

| 9 | 11 | 13.5 |

Immigrant Population Share (IPS) in %

Figure 3.11 Immigrant share of population and far-right voting %
Source: L. Davis and S. S. Deole (2017), 'Immigration and the Rise of
Far-Right Parties in Europe', *ifo DICE Report*, 15, 4 (Winter)

in fourteen European economies (Austria, Belgium, Switzerland,
Germany, Denmark, Finland, France, Great Britain, Hungary, Italy,
the Netherlands, Norway, Portugal and Sweden).

3.6 The Erosion of Liberal Democracy and the Rise of Populism Disrupt the Potential for Sustainable Growth

The benign 'end of history' and the dominance of liberal democracy
forecast by Fukuyama seems a bad joke in the context of the
pervasive rise of populist leaders and nationalism in many parts of
the globe, including in leading high-income economies.

Liberal democratic political systems, with their associated institutions and societal value and norms had developed in the post-war
period as an organic complement to the deployment of the Mass

Production paradigm. They provided the macroeconomic framework to balance supply and demand, a skilled labour force to enable production to expand smoothly and the infrastructure required for mass consumption and access to wider markets. The fruits of growth were 'reasonably distributed' and standards of living rose – in broad terms, there was a measure of consent from the population to the political structure and a recognition of shared norms and values amongst the populace. Rapid economic growth, high levels of employment and confidence in the future encouraged the investment which delivered what seemed to be sustainable growth. An architecture of global governance was constructed which delivered the incentives for growing specialization through international trade. The geo-political environment, whilst tense, appeared to be relatively stable. The relationship between the economy and society thus co-evolved symbiotically.

But, just as the Golden Age ran out of steam after the mid-1970s, so too did liberal democracy and its associated patterns of social intercourse decay. As we have seen in this and in the preceding chapter, macroeconomic policy changed course in the early 1980s in a direction which undermined the fundamentals for growth. Investments in the infrastructure required to support economic expansion were reduced as was the growth in the social expenditure which supported aggregate demand. Instead, the policy agenda shifted in a direction which promoted the interests of the plutocracy. This destabilized demand management policies and undermined the incentives for investment in the productive sector. Globalization 'rescued' the paradigm for a while but increasingly resulted in unemployment, declining real wages, social exclusion and precarious livelihoods.

Each of these developments undermined social cohesion and the stable social and political environment required to encourage investment in the drivers of sustainable growth. Building on this discontent and opportunistically exploiting the fear of 'the other' (that is, migration), populist leaders swept to power in a range of high-income countries, and notably in the US. And even when populist leaders did not rule, their demagogy influenced the currency of social and political debate and the content of economic policies.

The policies introduced by populist leaders in recent years further undermine the potential for sustained future economic growth. However, not only does the domestic policy agenda – macroeconomic demand management, tax policies, welfare expenditures, investments in infrastructure – damage the prospects for sustainable growth, but so too do changes in the management of the global economy. Populist regimes have attacked the fundamental institutions of global governance which supported globalized Mass Production. As we will see in Chapter 5, an open and rules-based trading system was central to the post-World War 2 growth surge. The nationalist and populist Trump Administration in the US attacked this trading system, adopting a beggar-thy-neighbour protectionist mercantilist approach to trade, substituting a bilateral and administered trade regime for an open and rules-based system. Tariffs were introduced on imports, and the operations of the World Trade Organization have been disrupted. It is likely that, even after the end of the Trump era, public support for a liberal and open trading system in the US will have been fatally undermined. These anti-free-trade views in the US were mirrored by European populist movements that cultivated, drew on and exploited anti-EU sentiments. China introduced tit-for-tat protectionism against the US, and there has been a general ground-swell against the further extension of the global supply chains which had delivered economic growth (but not income growth for unskilled and semi-skilled workers) in the high-income countries.

The undermining of global governance by populist regimes was not limited to the economic sphere. Funding of institutions which affected the social sphere – for example, the World Health Organization, the United Nations and aid agencies – was reduced. Moreover, what had been a relatively stable geo-political standoff between the Soviet Union (now Russia) and the Western powers has been disrupted not just by the challenge to their hegemony by rising China, but also by the undermining of NATO. By threatening the stability of the global economy, these populist policy agendas further undermine the incentive for investments in long-term growth.

It is possible that, in a post-Trump era, new incoming regimes in the US, the UK, Poland and other European countries increasingly dominated by populist agendas will overturn some of these economic and social policies which undermine the potential for future sustained economic growth. But these changes, as I showed in the previous chapter, cannot reverse the underlying atrophy of the Mass Production techno-economic paradigm. I will show why this is the case in Chapter 5. But, before we get to this agenda, it is necessary to first focus on the environmental crisis which unfolded with increasing speed and severity during the rise and fall of the Mass Production paradigm.

4

The Collapse of Environmental Sustainability

Humankind has unquestionably damaged the environment. But now the environment is fighting back. This is a challenge so important that it cannot be ignored, or even tolerated. The environmental crisis is out of control and unless effective corrective action is taken, it will overwhelm us. Very literally, it poses an existential threat, not just to humankind but to very many other species as well. It is that important.

In the two previous chapters, we observed the organic and symbiotic co-evolution of the Mass Production economic system and the social and political relations which accompanied its post-war growth surge and subsequent decline. In this chapter, we will focus on the evolution of the environment since the early 1950s. As in the case of economy and society, we can observe a close interaction between the unfolding environmental crisis and the character of Mass Production. However, as we shall see, the environmental crisis has much deeper roots than the development, deployment and decay of the Mass Production paradigm. Its origins stretch back at least until the beginnings of the Industrial Revolution and probably even further, to the development of settled agriculture. Whilst it is possible to see feasible remedies for rebuilding economic and social sustainability, repairing environmental sustainability poses a challenge of a wholly different magnitude.

In what follows we begin by setting the problem in historical context. For this, we need to go back at least 13,000 years to get a full appreciation of how significant current environmental trends are. Next, we must ask: what are the primary drivers of the destructive trajectory of our economic and social system? I will show how many of our environmental problems are a consequence of the character of Mass Production – the manner in which resources are taken from the biosphere, how these resources are used to produce goods and services for mass consumption, how these goods and services are consumed, and how the waste from production and consumption is discharged into the biosphere. We will then see the consequences of the organization of production and consumption in this techno-economic paradigm for the sustainability of the earth's environment.

All of this makes for very painful reading. It certainly made for very painful writing. Hopefully, it might spur us into action but – and this is the central argument of this book – action to create a more sustainable future must be embedded in actions to create a more sustainable economy and a more sustainable society. This requires an appreciation of the character of the atrophying Mass Production paradigm, and the opportunities opened by the Information and Communications Technology techno-economic paradigm for rebuilding a more environmentally sustainable world. But I run ahead of myself – these issues are the subject matter of later chapters. So let us first begin by documenting the character of unravelling environmental sustainability and its links to the Mass Production paradigm.

4.1 From the Dawn of Settled Agriculture to the Great Acceleration

Understanding the character and the speed of development of the current environmental crisis needs a long time-line. The first evidence of photosynthesis goes back to around 3.2 billion years ago (1.2 billion years after the Big Bang origins of the universe). It was only a mere 580 million years back that sufficient levels of oxygen were produced to support the development of different forms of life on earth. The earliest signs of proto-human development were much more recent (2 million years ago) and *Homo sapiens* first emerged some 200,000 years ago. So, human life is a very, very small dot on the earth's time-line.

The conditions which permit the origin and sustenance of life on earth depend on the character of the earth's biosphere. This is comprised of four distinct ecological subsystems. The first is the *atmosphere*, comprising the gases which surround the earth. The *hydrosphere* is the combined mass of water found on, under, and above the surface of a planet. The *cryosphere* is water in frozen form, and the *lithosphere* is the earth's crust. As we will see, the character of each of these subsystems has already been disrupted by the accumulated activities of humankind. Unless radical changes are made to our relationship with the environment, they will be increasingly disrupted in the future, with devastating consequences for environmental, economic and social sustainability.

The end of the last glacial period about 11,700 years ago ushered in a biosphere which was ideal for the development of varied life forms. This is termed the Holocene era. It was characterized not just by warmer temperatures but, critically, by relatively *stable* temperatures (Figure 4.1). The Holocene climate resulted in a massive expansion of different life forms, beginning with single-celled organisms and developing into complex forms of life, including, after many millennia, the human species.

Because of the earth's historically unusual orbit around the sun, earth scientists believe that the Holocene is likely to continue to

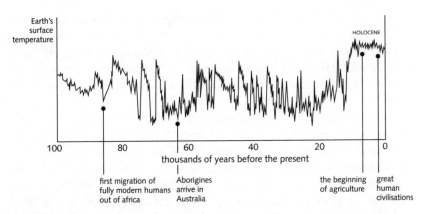

Figure 4.1 The Holocene in historical perspective: not just warm temperatures but stable temperatures

Source: O. R. Young and W. Steffen (2009), 'The Earth System: Sustaining Planetary Life-Support Systems', in I. Chapin, F. S. Kofinas and C. Folke (eds.), *Principles of Ecosystem Stewardship: Resilience-Based Natural Resource Management in a Changing World*, New York: Springer; reproduced with permission from Will Steffen

provide a stable environment for another 50,000 years. However, this stability crucially depends on the absence of shocks to the Holocene biosphere. Two sets of potential shocks can be identified. The first are those which are determined by physical events. These may be either endogenous or exogenous to the earth's biosphere. One exogenous physical threat is that the earth will be struck by a large meteorite, such as the Chicxulub Meteor. This hit Mexico approximately 66 million years ago and was between 11 and 81 kilometres in diameter. It resulted in widespread climate disruption and led to the extinction of many plant and animal species, including non-avian dinosaurs.[1]

The primary potentially climate-disrupting endogenous physical shock – that is, a shock arising within the earth's geophysical system – is a massive volcanic eruption. Volcanoes which are large enough to affect the earth's climate for more than a year inject over 100,000 tonnes of sulphur dioxide into the stratosphere. The sulphur dioxide emissions absorb and scatter solar radiation and create a haze of sulphuric acid surrounding the earth. This has a significant effect on the atmosphere and the climate. For example, the Laki eruption in Iceland in 1783 disrupted the European climate for decades, and the Tambora eruption in Indonesia in 1815 resulted in a global year without summer.[2]

The second class of ecological disruptions, endogenous to the earth's biosphere, are those which are caused by the behavioural practices of one or more of the earth's species. For example, at a relatively trivial local level, an increase in the population of elephants in an ecological zone can lead to the loss of trees; an increase in the number of cattle can lead to overgrazing and the loss of grass-cover in pastures. Both these imbalances may result in regional desertification. However, what we are currently witnessing is a much more profound endogenous behavioural shock to the Holocene era. This results from the impact of the human species on the earth's biosphere.

The first records of this human behavioural shock to the system was the Megafauna extinction of large mammals, between 50,000 and 10,000 years ago. This resulted in the loss of more than 70 per cent of large mammals in North America, more than 80 per cent of large mammals in South America, and nearly 90 per cent of large mammals in Australia. The next significant development in the global ecological impact of humans was the development of settled farming 11,000 years ago in Southwest China, South America and North China, and the domestication of cattle in Southeast Asia. The expansion of extensive farming, particularly the development of rice farming 6,500 years ago in Asia, resulted in growing methane emissions. In addition, settled agriculture led to wear and tear on the soil and the build-up of phosphorous from fertilizers. However, although disruptive to regional micro-ecologies and micro-climates, the early development of non-mechanical settled agriculture had limited extra-regional impacts and had limited consequences for the character of the Holocene biosphere and the climate.

By contrast, the developments which followed the scientific revolution in the sixteenth and seventeenth centuries in Europe initiated a process in which human activity began to have a discernible impact on the biosphere. This impact can be traced through the evolution of a series of energy technologies, each of which enhanced the productivity of human effort. A key invention was the steam engine in the eighteenth century. Steam power exploited the energy stored in coal to drive machinery, and diffused rapidly. The steam engine was followed by the invention of the first electrical motor in 1822, using coal as its primary source of energy. During the second half of the nineteenth century, hydrocarbons (oil, and then gas) entered the scene, and currently dominate global energy supply. These various sources of inanimate energy overlapped, and even today they are all widely used, often in tandem in integrated power-generation systems.

Inanimate energy supplies were not only used to power machinery and light up cities. They also provided the means for extending markets. Natural resources needed to be obtained as inputs for industry and to build infrastructure; food was needed to support growing urban populations. This was made possible by a series of inventions in communications technologies, notably steamships in the late eighteenth century and steam-railways after the 1820s. Transport in the twentieth century was revolutionized by the invention of the internal combustion engine, which powered land, air and sea transport.

These advances in energy generation, and their use in production and transportation, played a transformative role in the development of modern economies. However, they were not the only technological development with widespread economic and social significance. After the middle of the nineteenth century, the chemicals industry began to have a sizeable impact on society. The introduction of synthetic nitrogen in the early twentieth century enabled major advances in agriculture, and the use of chemicals in the pharmaceutical industry has played an important role in improving life-expectancy and livelihoods.

Whilst the Industrial Revolution represented a structural break in the relationship of humans to their physical environment, the decade after World War 2 ushered in a sharp inflexion-point in this inter-relationship. Figure 4.2, summarizing the assessment of a range of scientific disciplines under the aegis of the International Geosphere–Biosphere Programme, draws together an extensive body

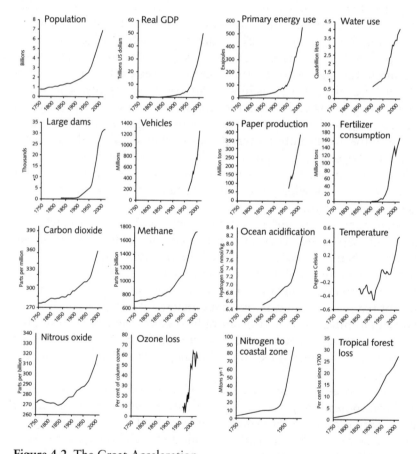

Figure 4.2 The Great Acceleration

Source: compiled by Sam Bliss with data from International Geosphere–Biosphere Programme, https://igbp.net

of evidence on various factors which reflect the impact of humans on the biosphere. The first two are population and the size of economic output (GDP). The other indicators reflect a combination of resource use (energy, water, wood), pollution and environmental impacts (vehicles, fertilizers, paper production) and activities having an impact on the atmosphere (temperature, carbon dioxide, nitrogen, methane, ozone) and on the hydrosphere (acidification of oceans). All of these indicators show a sharp uplift after 1950. This is referred to as the Great Acceleration.

4.2 The Transition to the Anthropocene – Take, Make, Use and Waste

There is now a consensus in the scientific community that, as a consequence of humankind's heavy environmental footprint, the earth's biosphere has transitioned from the Holocene era to the era of the Anthropocene. (The word 'anthropocene' is derived from the Ancient Greek *Anthropos*, ἄνθρωπος, meaning 'human', and *kainos*, Καινός, meaning 'new' or 'recent'.) The Anthropocene epoch is one in which the dominant determinant of the character of the biosphere is no longer the earth's orbit around the sun. The biosphere is now increasingly determined by the activity of a single species on the earth – human beings.

The impact of the human species on the biosphere can be understood in terms of four related sets of activities – 'Take', 'Make', 'Use' and 'Waste' (Figure 4.3). 'Take' refers to the inputs that we use to sustain our livelihoods, the most important of which is energy. These inputs are used to 'Make' a whole range of products and services which stretch existence beyond the bare levels of subsistence. Either during the process of 'making', or after products have been produced, we then 'Use' them – in the present, or after storing them for future consumption. The residues from production and consumption – the 'Waste' – are ejected into the environment.

Each of these four sets of human activities are affected by technologies of production. The application of knowledge, science and technology affects the material efficiency of the cycle. How much of the sun's energy can be usefully harnessed? What is the cost of extracting raw materials? How efficient are the farming and industrial sectors? Do products satisfy 'needs' at lowest cost? What are

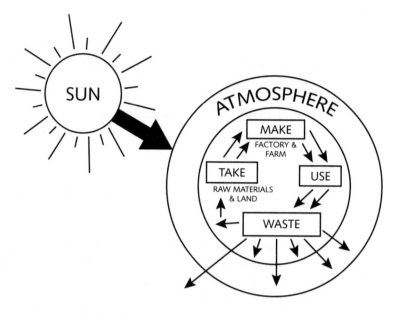

Figure 4.3 Take, Make, Use and Waste

the costs of ejecting, storing and processing waste? However, the character of Take, Make, Use and Waste is not just a reflection of technical and engineering efficiency. It also reflects social technology – that is, the manner in which each of these physical technologies is utilized, and in what broader set of social relations they are embedded. Similarly, the direction of technological change – what innovation challenges are being addressed and what sorts of technologies are being produced – is also determined by the social context in which innovation occurs. To continue knocking the same nail on the head, the environment, the economy and society are indissolubly interlinked.

The range of factors affecting the environment is vast, and it is necessary to be selective in illustrating how Take–Make–Use–Waste determine environmental outcomes. So I will illustrate the 'Take' element in the cycle largely through a focus on the extraction of the key natural resource, energy. The 'Make' phase is seen through the lens of the material intensity of production. 'Use' is considered by focusing on high levels of private consumption and the dominance of throwaway single-use products. 'Waste' is addressed through the growing mountain of discarded plastics, including in the earth's oceans. Since we are ultimately concerned with taking action to remake a more environmentally sustainable world, the focus in what follows will be on the seven decades after World War 2. This is a historical period dominated by the Mass Production techno-economic paradigm.

'Taking' from the biosphere: the example of the energy vector

Energy is essential to the sustenance of life in all of its forms. Without the sun, there would be no life. But the sun and our solar system have a finite life. In 5 billion years (give or take a few hundred millennia), the sun will enter a helium-burning phase. It will turn into a fiercely hot 'red giant' star which will expand and then engulf the earth and other planets. If the Earth, and life on the Earth in one form or another, were to survive that development, life would then expire when the sun eventually dies and becomes a small 'white dwarf'. This time-span is perhaps a little too long to concern us in our analysis of economic, social and environmental sustainability in the twenty-first century.

With two exceptions (nuclear power and geo-thermal power), all of the energy sources available to humankind (and indeed other species on earth) are determined by the sun. One set of solar-based energy supply is 'recurrent'. That is, the power is used at the same time as, or soon after, it is generated. For example, beyond solar power, winds and tidal flows which can be used to generate energy are ultimately a consequence of ongoing solar-driven climatic processes. These recurrent sources of energy are referred to as being 'renewable'. That is, their consumption does not exhaust their capacity to provide energy on an ongoing basis. 'Biofuels' which are sourced from wood and vegetation overlap with true renewables in that the energy provided by these materials can be replaced in a relatively short time period through regrowth.

The second and dominant source of solar-origin energy is fossil fuels. These fuels result from the decomposition of dead organisms buried many millions of years ago. Unlike renewable power sources, which represent an ongoing 'flow' of energy, fossil fuels involve drawing on a 'stock' of energy. Fossil fuels are a very concentrated source of energy. A single gallon of petroleum provides the energy equivalent to 47 days of human labour. The major fossil fuel, and the first to be exploited at scale was coal. More recently, a growing share of fossil fuels have been derived from oil and natural gas.

Unfortunately, the production and use of fossil fuels are major sources of climate-changing greenhouse-gas emissions. The burning of fossil fuels to generate energy ejects carbon dioxide (CO_2) into the biosphere. Although carbon dioxide is not the only greenhouse gas leading to climate change, it is the dominant one, accounting for approximately 72 per cent of total greenhouse-gas emissions. The second-largest source of greenhouse gas is methane. which contributes 18 per cent of total emissions. Although coal mining and oil and gas extraction are not the only source of methane emissions (agriculture is a major contributor), they nevertheless are a major contributor to their emissions.

Calculating the net impact of different energy sources on the climate is a complex process. Within each energy family, there is a spectrum of technologies operating with varying degrees of efficiency. Moreover, it is necessary to consider the lifetime energy costs of each fuel source. This latter point is often overlooked when, for example, it is claimed that renewables such as wind-power have no harmful emissions. This may be true when the windmills are being turned by the wind. However, CO_2 is produced throughout the cycle of wind power production and use. It results from the manufacture of the windmills, their installation (cement production is a major contributor to global CO_2 emissions), their maintenance and repair, their dismantling at the end of their lives and in the distribution of the energy to users. The lifetime CO_2 emissions of nuclear power are similarly very large when compared to their recurrent operating emissions. Moreover, many sources of renewable energy, such as wind and solar power, are intermittent. Until new energy storage technologies are developed, renewable energy needs to be combined with 'base-power' generated by nuclear power and fossil fuels, if energy supplies are to be continuously and reliably available.

Notwithstanding these caveats on the complexity of carbon dioxide emissions, there is an unambiguous scaling difference in the emissions of the major sources of energy. Table 4.1 and Figure 4.4, viewed in tandem, provide an overview of the lifetime CO_2 emissions of various energy sources. The numbers are, of course, approximate, but they nevertheless paint an illuminating picture of the consequence of relying on fossil fuels as the primary source of energy. The table provides estimates of the lifetime CO_2 emissions of different energy sources, measured in grammes of CO_2 emissions per kWh of energy produced. It shows very substantial differences. The highest emitters are the fossil fuels – coal, oil and natural gas. For example, compared to hydro power, CO_2 emissions from coal are 100 times higher, oil 78 times higher, and between 45 and 60 times higher for natural gas. These adverse figures for oil and for gas (and particularly fracked natural gas) are exacerbated by their emissions of methane. This is emitted at various points along their value chains, and in some respects is more damaging to the climate than is CO_2.

Figure 4.4 shows the contribution of different sources of energy over a long time period (1800–2019), showing how the Mass Production paradigm has strongly favoured environment-damaging sources of energy. Renewables with a low CO_2 footprint – hydro, solar and wind – have only entered the energy frame relatively recently. Even today, they contribute only a small proportion of total supplies. By contrast, the three major fossil fuels – coal, crude oil and natural gas – have dominated supplies in the past and continue to do so in the present. In 2017 their contribution to total global energy combustion was 43, 36 and 20 per cent respectively, together accounting for 84 per cent of total global energy supplies.[3]

But energy is not the only resource which has been pillaged from the earth's surface. The United Nations Environment Programme (UNEP) has developed an indicator which provides a picture of the dramatic rise in overall global resource extraction.[4] How can a single metric capture the combined value of such a diverse range of

Table 4.1 Range of approximate CO_2 emissions per unit of electricity produced, different sources of energy (grammes/kWh)

	Range of CO_2 emissions
Coal	960–1050
Oil	780
Natural gas	450–600
Nuclear	66
Solar	50
Wind	34
Traditional biomass (wood, agricultural waste)	14–25
Hydro	10

Source: compiled from D. Nugent and B. K. Sovacool (2014), 'Assessing the Lifecycle Greenhouse Gas Emissions from Solar PV and Wind Energy', *Energy Policy*, 65: 229–44

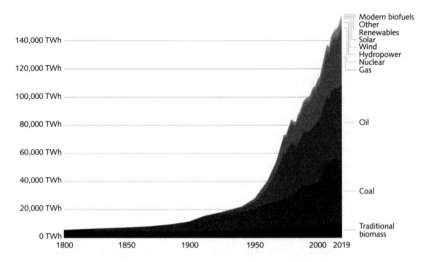

Figure 4.4 Energy equivalent global output of different energy forms, 1800–2019 (terawatt hours)

Source: data from Our World in Data (https://ourworldindata.org/energy)

raw materials? Can 'apples and bananas' be grouped together in a single measure, and, if so, should the indicator be their weight, their financial value, their calorific content or some other metric? The measure which was settled on – their combined tonnage – is therefore very imprecise. But it is nevertheless useful in providing an illustrative snapshot of overall trends. UNEP groups this pattern of resource use into four sets of natural resources. The first are non-metallic minerals, primarily construction materials and chemical and fertilizer minerals. The second are metal ores, primarily iron ore, copper and precious metals. The third is biomass, primarily grazed biomass, crops, wood and timber. And the final set of resources are fossil fuels – coal, oil, gas and biomass.

Unfortunately, data are not available to illustrate the sharp growth in consumption after the post-1950 Great Acceleration. But Figure 4.5 shows the growth in production of the combined tonnage of these four sets of material inputs for the more recent period between 1970 and 2010. Between 1970 and 2020, the quantity of resources used globally almost trebled. All four sets of resources experienced rapid growth. The rate was highest for non-metallic mineral products, primarily used in construction and agriculture.

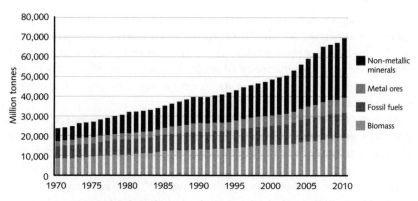

Figure 4.5 The growth in global total resource supply, 1970–2010 (million tonnes)

Source: United Nations Environment Programme (2016), *Global Material Flows and Resource Productivity*

So, what can we conclude from this overview of resource extraction? The volume of what humankind takes from the earth has grown dramatically, particularly after the post-1950 Great Acceleration. And, at least insofar as energy resources are concerned, the environmental eye seems to have been off the ball. Whatever the intentions of energy extractors, the overwhelming source of supply has been those materials which most damage the environment. Moreover, until very recent years, little thought has been given to the environmental consequences of the way in which these resources have been pillaged from the environment. For example, in many cases, waste gases emanating from oil-wells have been flared (set alight), despite their potential use in the chemicals sector. Flaring is cheaper than capturing gases, despite the fact that it pumps greenhouse gases, as methane, into the atmosphere. Similarly, the world's mining sector has shown little regard for the environment around mines, resulting in large 'tails' of noxious dumps which pollute water supplies and local inhabitants.

'Making' with what is 'Taken' – are we using the earth's resources more efficiently?

So much for what and how humankind takes from the environment. But how efficiently are these resources used? Have we learnt to do more with less? Improvements in the efficiency with which we use resources is known as 'relative dematerialization'. At first glance, there is good news on this front. In many countries, and particularly in the high-income countries, there has indeed been a significant improvement in the efficiency of resource use across all sectors of the economy. For example, if we focus on energy efficiency, Figure 4.6 shows the trend between 1990 and 2014.

However, 'relative dematerialization' may or may not translate into 'absolute dematerialization'. That is, improvements in resource efficiency may be overwhelmed if overall output increases at a faster rate. Consider the experience of the improvements in energy efficiency in the EU in the four sectors shown in Figure 4.6. In each case, despite progress in energy efficiency (relative dematerialization), absolute energy use increased. In the transport sector, for example, total CO_2 emissions grew between 1990 and 2002 (Figure 4.7) despite improvements in energy efficiency (Figure 4.6). This was a consequence of a reduction in public transport, increases in the volume of goods transported and the growth in private ownership of cars. In the household sector, significant improvements in efficiency were matched by an increase in the ownership of electrical appliances.

Thus, seen through an environmental sustainability lens, the increased materials intensity of production and household

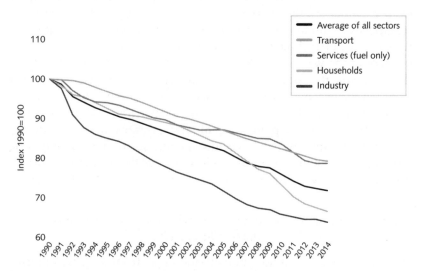

Figure 4.6 Index of energy efficiency in the EU, 1990–2014 (1990 = 100)
Source: Intelligent Energy Europe (https://ec.europa.eu)

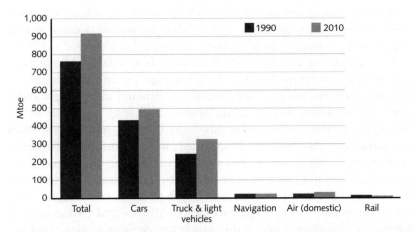

Figure 4.7 Variation of CO_2 emissions from transport in the EU, 1990 and 2010 (million tonnes energy equivalent)

Source: Intelligent Energy Europe (https://ec.europa.eu)

consumption in the European Union offers a depressing story. However, in reality these observed negative trends underestimate the severity of the increasing absolute use of resources in the *global* economy in three important respects. First, as will be shown in Chapter 5, the global economy experienced a significant structural shift after the mid-1980s. Increasingly, the large firms dominating the global economy began to 'slice up' their supply chains. They relocated many of their supply chains from their home environments to low-cost producers in the developing world, and particularly in China. Since manufacturing is a prime user of natural resources, this global outsourcing led to a fall in resource use in the high-income economies. But, by the same token, it increased resource use in the developing world. Hence, the appropriate indicator for resource efficiency is not the ratio between resource inputs and output in a given economy, but between resource inputs and final consumption. For example, whilst greenhouse-gas emissions in the UK fell by 18 per cent between 1990 and 2007, the greenhouse-gas intensity of aggregate consumption in the UK increased by 9 per cent.[5]

Second, resource use in low-income countries has grown not just due to the relocation of materials-intensive activities in global supply chains, but also because of rising incomes in emerging economies. As we saw in Chapter 3, rates of economic growth in heavily populated developing economies (particularly China and India which, together, make up more than one-third of the global population) do not mirror the declining trend in the industrially advanced countries.

And, third, the character of demand in low- and middle-income economies is different from that in the high-income economies. In the rich-country group, as incomes grow, demand increasingly shifts from the consumption of manufactures and food to the demand for services. Services are relatively light users of natural resources compared to other sectors. By contrast, in low- and middle-income economies, rising incomes feed into an increase in the demand for manufactures and agricultural products, both intensive users of natural resources. Moreover, and perhaps even more significant, economic expansion in lower-income countries – and particularly in China – involves very heavy investments in economic infrastructure. As we saw in Figure 4.5 above, construction materials were the dominant sub-sector of increasing resource use in the non-metallic minerals sector, and copper and iron ore are intensively used in buildings and infrastructure.

Overviewing these trends, the United Nations Environment Programme has calculated the materials footprint of global consumption. This includes all of the four major families that we have described above and aggregates them into a single composite measure. It estimated that global material use increased from 7 tonnes per capita in 1970 to 10 tonnes per capita in 2010. Coupled with an increase in global population, this means that the 'use' of the four categories of materials shown graphically in Figure 4.5 grew from 23 billion tonnes in 1970 to 70 billion tonnes in 2010. So much for 'relative dematerialization'!

Consumption: 'Using' what is 'Made'

The products which we are offered as consumers have a critical environmental impact. Both the 'taking' of resources from the biosphere and the subsequent 'making' into final products result in harmful emissions, not just of greenhouse gases but also of chemicals and other environmentally damaging pollutants. And then there is the problem of waste when products reach the end of their useful life and are discharged into the biosphere as waste. So what determines the character of final demand in our economic systems? Four sets of factors shape the extent and nature of consumption – the number of users, their incomes, the types of products available and the manner in which products are consumed.

The first two of these determinants are relatively uncomplicated – the more consumers and the higher their incomes, the greater their use of the earth's resources. Here there is a striking contrast in the share of the high-income countries in global population and in global economic consumption. The high-income countries make up only 7 per cent of the global population, but they are responsible for almost half of total global consumption. Thus, although the share of low- and middle-income countries is growing rapidly, if we are to explain the thirst for resources and the impact of 'making' on the environment, we must therefore begin with the nature and extent of use in the high-income world.

So what drives the character of final consumption in these leading high-income countries? To understand this, we need to turn to a long tradition of economic analysis, stretching back from Adam Smith in the eighteenth century, through Karl Marx in the nineteenth century, and to Joseph Schumpeter in the twentieth century. This highlighted the central role played by entrepreneurship in economic growth. Essentially, the argument is as follows. Competition erodes profits. The solution to escaping from competitive pressures is to be found in innovation. Innovation increases efficiency, results in the introduction of new, improved and differentiated products, and allows entrepreneurs to tap new markets. Innovation is thus central to capitalism and is often referred to as the 'Schumpeterian engine of growth'. But innovation is not Darwinian in the sense that there is only 'one best way'. New technologies are malleable. So it is not surprising to see a link between the character of a techno-economic paradigm and the direction of innovation. This draws our attention to the manner in which the Mass Production paradigm influenced the 'life' of the products and the individualization of consumption, two critical determinants of humankind's negative impact on environmental sustainability.

The 'obsolescence' of products determines how long they are used before they are discarded into the environment. Some innovations are intrinsically superior in a technical sense and contribute to an improved environment. For example, as the costs of renewable energy have fallen sharply and are now lower than coal-fired plants in many countries, it makes environmental sense to build new wind and solar farms and to scrap coal mines and coal-fired power stations. Other innovations which involve new products make an important contribution to welfare and efficiency in the economy as a whole. Their introduction can be relatively easily defended in environmental terms. The mobile phone is a case in point. How would we have been able to manage during the Covid-19 pandemic without the mobile phone? Mobile apps were central to Covid-19 test and track programmes. And even before Covid, the mobile phone allowed people to connect to others whilst on the move, kept families and friends in touch and greased the worlds of commerce and industry. Of course, there are also downsides to mobiles – for example, conversationless family meals, square-eyed grandchildren and the dissemination of fake news. But, as with all products, consumption comes at an environmental cost. Mobile phones may have been manufactured without adequate environmental care or may be difficult to recycle at the end of their lives.

At what stage does a mobile phone reach the end of its 'useful life'? I have just replaced a functioning iPhone 6 with a new, faster and more expensive iPhone X. True, it stores more photographs, is faster and impresses my friends, but it is not clear in what respects it makes possible what was previously impossible. How much of the earth's resources were pillaged to manufacture and deliver the iPhone X to me? And how do I discard my old, 'obsolete' mobile without damaging the environment? I have stored the 'obsolete' iPhone 6 in a junk-box awaiting responsible recycling. But the frightening element of this junk-box is the layer of old phones which my iPhone 6 rests on. And did we really have to replace our TV last year? Has our new TV been manufactured in an environmentally friendly manner, and was our 'obsolete' TV recycled in an environmentally responsible manner?

The example of the mobile phone represents a case of what economists refer to as trade-off – to what extent are new and additional 'real benefits' justifiable in environmental terms? However, there is a very different driver of environmentally damaging obsolescence which cannot be considered in these terms. This is when, in the search for profit, corporations deliberately design products to wear out or to be unrepairable. For example, many children's toys incorporate soft metal screws and materials which are unable to withstand hard or prolonged use. Another form of planned obsolescence involves designs which deliberately limit the useful working life of equipment. Computer printers are a case in point, where printer manufacturers inhibit the refilling of ink-jet printer cartridges. This has led to the dumping of more than 350 million cartridges per year (many of which are not even empty) into landfills, in the US alone.[6] (How many 'exhausted' cartridges have I jettisoned unnecessarily in the writing of this book, and with what negative impact on the environment?) In the US, Hewlett Packard was forced to compensate consumers and to change its designs which had automatically prevented printers using the ink remaining in cartridges after an undisclosed expiration date.[7] A further type of planned obsolescence is when products are designed to make repair difficult. For example, many washing machines incorporate wear-prone bearings into the drum so that they cannot be replaced without changing the drum as well. And back to my mobile, where Apple deliberately used pentalobe screws which cannot be removed with conventional tools in order to inhibit self-repair.

Systems obsolescence is a relatively new strategy that entrepreneurs use to induce customers to purchase new products. This is a growing phenomenon in the case of 'platform technologies'. These involve a range of complementary products that are interconnected by using a common software. I might prefer to use an Android mobile phone, but it does not synch seamlessly with my Apple computer. When the systems provider chooses to discontinue support for its software (as Microsoft has done in the past with its Windows operating systems), users are left with no other option but to jettison products which meet their needs perfectly well. Exploiting this systems dependency, in 2018 Apple and Samsung incorporated into their software updates a feature which slowed down older mobile phones (such as my iPhone 4). This induced users to replace their existing functioning phones with newer 'faster' models.[8]

One of the characteristics of these various forms of planned obsolescence is that many consumers are savvy to the waste involved in replacing products that either meet their needs satisfactorily or could continue to do so were they constructed for greater durability and repairability. So, if a competitor emerges that challenges these obsolescence-promoting product strategies, consumers will rapidly switch their purchasing preferences. Hence, there is a strong incentive for producers to conspire to limit competition. Perhaps the most famous case of this is the 'Phoebus Cartel' of the major firms producing incandescent light bulbs in the 1920s. The major producers in Germany (Osram), the UK (AEI) and the USA (General Electric) met and agreed to limit the life of bulbs. As a result, the life of the average light bulb fell from 1,500 hours to 1,000 hours. Indeed, Thomas Edison's first commercial bulb in 1881 lasted 50 per cent longer than the average light bulb in the mid twentieth century.[9]

All of the above examples show the harmful environmental impact when, in the search for profit, firms deliberately limit the functioning life of a product. However, these strategies designed to promote consumption by building obsolescence into their products pale into insignificance in the face of strategies promoting 'perceived obsolescence'. The vast advertising industry is bent on persuading consumers that what they have, or might have, is unacceptable. It is true that some advertising plays an important function in informing consumers of new products or of new characteristics in products. However, this represents a minority of the advertising spend. The bulk of advertising is designed to play on consumer preferences by persuading them to 'want' objects which they do not 'need' (and often in order to impress people they don't like!).

In 1960, Vance Packard vividly documented the cynicism of the US advertising industry. His book *The Hidden Persuaders* provided numerous examples drawn from advertising industry journals, businesspeople and politicians.[10] His parody of his findings is depressingly prescient (many of his fanciful examples, designed to be humorous, are in fact with us today) and worth quoting at some length:

> Spokesmen for industry like to speculate about tomorrow even more than the rest of us. They invite us to peer out onto the horizon and see the wondrous products their marketing experts are conceiving for us. We are encouraged to share their dreams and to tingle at the possibility of using voice writers, wall-sized television screens, and motorcars that glide along highways under remote control. Most of these marketing experts, despite their air of chronic excited optimism, are grappling with a problem that would frighten the wits out of less resolute people. That problem is the specter of glut for the products they are already endeavouring to sell. If we could probe the real dreams of these marketing people as they slumber restlessly at night, we would find ... that they are in their private world of the future, where selling has again become easy because the haunting problem of saturation has been vanquished. This Utopia might be called Cornucopia City. ... The motorcars of Cornucopia will be made of a lightweight plastic that develops fatigue and begins to melt if driven more than four thousand miles. Owners who turn in their old motorcars at the regular turn-in dates – New

Year's, Easter, Independence Day, and Labor Day – will be rewarded with a one-hundred-dollar United States Prosperity-Through-Growth Bond for each motorcar turned in. ... One fourth of the factories of Cornucopia City will be located on the edge of a cliff, and the ends of their assembly lines can be swung to the front or rear doors depending upon the public demand for the product being produced. When demand is slack, the end of the assembly line will be swung to the rear door and the output of refrigerators or other products will drop out of sight and go directly to their graveyard without first overwhelming the consumer market. Every Monday, the people of Cornucopia City will stage a gala launching of a rocket into outer space at the local Air Force base. ... One officially stated objective of the space probing will be to report to the earth people what the back side of Neptune's moon looks like. Wednesday will be Navy Day. The Navy will send a surplus warship to the city dock. It will be filled with surplus play-suits, cake mix, vacuum cleaners, and trampolines that have been stockpiled at the local United States Department of Commerce complex of warehouses for surplus products. The ship will go thirty miles out to sea, where the crew will sink it from a safe distance. As we peek in on this Cornucopia City of the future, we learn that the big, heartening news of the week is that the Guild of Appliance Repair Artists has passed a resolution declaring it unpatriotic for any member even to look inside an ailing appliance that is more than two years old. The heart of Cornucopia City will be occupied by a titanic pushbutton super mart built to simulate a fairyland. This is where all the people spend many happy hours a week strolling and buying to their heart's content. In this paradise of high-velocity selling, there are no jangling cash registers to disrupt the holiday mood. Instead, the shopping couples – with their five children trailing behind, each pushing his own shopping cart – gaily wave their lifetime electronic credit cards in front of a recording eye. Each child has his own card, which was issued to him at birth. Cornucopia City's marvellous mart is open around the clock, Sundays included. For the Sunday shoppers who had developed a churchgoing habit in earlier years, there is a little chapel available for meditation in one of the side alcoves.

Parody aside, as Figure 4.8 shows, the spend in the US advertising industry grew rapidly during the twentieth century, and particularly after 1950. As we saw in the earlier discussion, 1950 witnessed the onset of the Great Acceleration, which is widely thought to represent the turning-point in the transition from the Holocene to the Anthropocene Era.

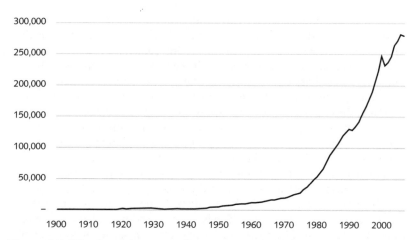

Figure 4.8 US advertising expenditure, 1900–2007 ($m)
Source: data with permission from Douglas Galbi (www.galbithink.org)

But, even when innovation leads to the introduction of products that are intrinsically new or superior, are more reliable and are easier to repair than the products they replace, an issue with important environmental consequences is their mode of consumption. Can they be used by more than one person? For shared use may reduce the overall quantity of demand and the overall environmental impact of final consumption.

Transport is an example of an innovation trajectory central to Mass Production. In Chapter 5, I will show that economic growth since the Industrial Revolution has depended on the growing physical separation of people from their workplaces and the transport of inputs and outputs to increasingly distant final markets. The environmental issue is not just whether this process of distancing has occurred, but how the communication arteries are constructed.

Since the automobile was invented in the late nineteenth century, privately owned and privately used cars have increasingly substituted for public transport. Key to this development was the deliberate subversion of public transport in the US. In the late 1930s, a group of automobile manufacturing, tyre manufacturing and gasoline firms formed a company called National City Lines. This bought up electric streetcar systems in twenty-five cities and replaced low-cost and relatively non-polluting electric vehicles with gasoline-powered buses. After the war, reflecting the pressure exerted by these firms to support individualized transport, the US Federal and state governments invested heavily in highways rather than subways and other forms of mass transit. The automobile then came to dominate transport, not just in the US, but globally. In 2017, there were more than 1.2 billion private cars on the road, with annual sales of 79 million. By contrast, annual sales of all buses in the same year were just over 200,000.

This privatization of mobility has major implications for environmental sustainability. Cars require three times more energy per passenger mile than do buses and rail. In EU countries with relatively poorly developed public transport systems (Germany and Austria), the average car travelled 14,000 km per year. In countries with relatively well-developed public transport (Eastern and Central Europe), the average distance per car per year was only 8,000 km. But it is in this latter group of public-transport-intensive economies that the decline in the share of public transport has been most rapid. Whilst the energy efficiency of cars in the EU increased by more than 16 per cent between 1990 and 2010, more than one-third of this efficiency gain was offset by a switch from public to private transport.[11]

'Waste', in and after 'Use'

There is thus a direct link between artificially stimulated overconsumption and environmental sustainability. But it is not just overconsumption that threatens sustainability. Virtually all production and consumption leads to the ejection of residues into the biosphere. These emissions into the biosphere arise as a direct consequence of activity in the 'taking' of the earth's resources, the 'making' of products and in 'consumption'.

We have already considered one set of emissions, with particularly harmful environmental consequences – that is, greenhouse gases such as carbon dioxide and methane. But these are by no means the only discharges that damage our ecosystem. Residues from chemicals used in agriculture are another particularly damaging source of waste. Around 3 million tons of pesticide are applied globally every year, at a cost exceeding $40 billion and, as I will show in Chapter 7, this is a direct consequence of the character of Mass Production agriculture. The long-term use of pesticides and herbicides in agriculture has left a large legacy of chemical residues in the earth's terrestrial and aquatic systems. A recent study of residues in eleven EU countries found that over 80 per cent of tested soils contained pesticide residues. Chemical contaminants are not confined to the specific localities of agricultural production, but are dispersed widely through wind- and water-driven erosion. The most common chemical residues in these eleven EU countries were glyphosate (suspected of being carcinogenic to humans) and DDT (which, because of its toxicity, is banned from application).[12] These waste materials are found in rich countries with extensive regulatory systems which seek to limit chemical use. In other countries with lower environmental standards, and in particular microenvironments, pesticide residues are even higher. As we will see below, not only are many of these chemical residues toxic to humans and other vertebrates, but they are especially damaging to insect life, with potentially devastating harmful impacts on medium- and long-term food production.

Another large and environmentally significant set of 'waste' ejected into the biosphere is plastics. Plastics are produced in enormous volumes – more than 400 million tons a year. The global sales of the largest fifty plastics companies exceed $1 trillion. Of this, just over one-third is destined for single-use packaging; 15 per cent is used in buildings and construction; 14 per cent is incorporated in textiles; 10 per cent in consumer products; and 7 per cent in transport. Because of its versatility as a material, because of its ease of manufacture and because of its relatively low cost, the plastics-intensity of global economic output has grown astonishingly since plastics were first introduced in the late 1930s. In terms of weight (kilogrammes per $ of GDP), by 2000 the use of plastics was more than double that of the next most utilized material input (aluminium).[13]

Plastic is insoluble in water and biochemically inert. However, the consequence of the widespread use of plastics is that there is a growing global mountain of plastic waste, since, unless purposively designed to degrade naturally, most plastics degrade very slowly – 50 years for a plastic cup, 400 years for a plastic bottle, 450 years for a disposable nappy and 600 years for a fishing line.[14] And despite increasing attempts to recycle plastics, progress has been slow. Leaving aside the accumulated mountain of plastics, less than 10 per cent of ongoing annual plastics production is recycled globally. In excess of 6.3 billion tons of plastic waste litters the earth's surface and its oceans.

It is only in recent years that we have come to recognize the particularly harmful impact of plastic pollution in the sea. Each year more than 36 million tons of plastic waste are deposited into the world's ocean sediments. Marine plastics litter harms over 600 species, and 15 per cent of marine species are endangered by ingestion and entanglement with plastics. At current rates, by 2050, 99 per cent of seabirds will have ingested plastics. Even the eggs of northern fulmar birds in the Arctic contain hormone-disrupting phthalates, a residue of chemicals which increase the flexibility of plastic products.[15] Microplastics are a particularly damaging source of marine pollution. These comprise very small fragments of plastics (5 millimetres or smaller) which have fallen off the large variety of plastics products, such as packaging, bottles, bags, textiles, fishing nets and cosmetics. It has recently been discovered that a major source of microplastic discharge is from motorcar tyres. It was estimated that in 2014 there were between 15 and 25 trillion pieces of microplastics in the world's oceans alone.[16]

As I will show in later chapters, this ejection of waste into the biosphere is a central characteristic of the 'linear' Mass Production paradigm, and is in sharp contrast to the 'circularity' of production and consumption which is made possible by Information and Communications Technologies.

4.3 It All Adds Up to a Crisis in Environmental Sustainability

Humankind's misuse and overuse of the earth's natural resources and the wilful and careless ejection of waste into the biosphere has driven the transition from the Holocene to the Anthropocene Era. What will be the medium- and long-term impact of this transition in the earth's environment? Focusing on long-term trends, an international team of earth systems scientists who evidenced the character of the Great Acceleration (shown in Figure 4.2 above), identified nine 'Planetary Boundaries'.[17] Together, these determine the character of the biosphere and provide the Holocene-like conditions which have allowed life as we know it to flourish on earth. These critical boundaries are:

1 A loss in biodiversity which can lead to abrupt and irreversible changes to ecosystems and severely reduce agricultural productivity.
2 Climate change which, amongst other impacts, has the capacity to disrupt agricultural production and lead to a melting of the

ice-caps. This will both result in a rise in sea levels and, through feedback effects such as changes in sea temperature, reinforce the disruption of the global climate.

3 Levels of chemical pollutants and novel entities such as radio-active materials, nanomaterials and microplastics which threaten many life forms with irreversible change.
4 The thinning of the stratospheric ozone layer which filters out ultraviolet rays, affecting the health of humans and other life forms and atmospheric processes which lead to climate change.
5 An increase in atmospheric aerosol loading which affects cloud formations, atmospheric circulation and rainfall patterns.
6 The acidification of oceans which undermines marine life and changes the sea temperature, thereby affecting weather patterns.
7 Altered flows of nitrogen and phosphorous and chemical residues resulting from widespread use of fertilizers, pesticides and herbi-cides which run into the water system, affecting marine biodiversity and ocean temperatures.
8 The degradation of freshwater systems which sustain life and agriculture, and which affect weather patterns.
9 Changes in land use which affect biodiversity and carbon emissions and hence have an impact on climate change.

In each of these Planetary Boundaries, limits were identified, beyond which the conditions for life on earth would be threatened. For example, to limit climate change, the concentration of CO_2 should be lower than 350 parts per million; 75 per cent of once-forested land should remain forested; and the annual use of fertilizers should be limited to 62 million tonnes of nitrogen and 6 million tonnes of phosphorus. By 2015, each of these four Planetary Boundaries had been transgressed. The concentration of carbon dioxide in the atmos-phere is over 400ppm and rising. Fertilizer use is currently more than twice the recommended limits, and only 62 per cent of land that could be forested still stands as forest, reducing their capacity to act as a carbon sink.

Although 'only four' of these Planetary Boundaries have been transgressed so far, the consequences for climate change are already evident. These dangers are now widely recognized and, with a few exceptions such as the Trump-era US and the Bolsonaro-era Brazil, almost all of the world's governments have agreed to support and implement the 2015 Paris Accord. This seeks to limit the increase in global temperatures to 1.5 degrees above pre-industrial levels. This is a daunting objective. In order to limit global temperature rises to 1.5 degrees, annual emissions need to fall to 25 giga-tonnes or less. However, in 2016 global CO_2 emissions were 52 giga-tonnes and, on historic trends, they will rise to 58 giga-tonnes by 2030. Instead of limiting warming to 1.5 degrees, this trajectory means that it is estimated that the global temperature will rise by 2 degrees or more by the turn of the century.

Table 4.2 shows the International Panel on Climate Change's estimates of the severe consequences of this impending warming of the global climate. Even at the conservative 1.5-degree level, there will be major impacts with respect to periods of extreme heat, the loss in ice, the rise in global sea levels, the loss of vertebrate / plant and insect species, disruptions to local ecosystems, Arctic ice-thaw, crop yields, coral reefs and fish. At a 2-degree temperature rise, each of these impacts is magnified considerably. Perhaps even more problematic is that these changes become cumulative and self-reinforcing. Thus, even if corrective actions are taken at some point in the future, changes in the global climate and the biosphere will have become irreversible and self-perpetuating.

How do we make sense of these frightening macro trends? How might they affect our lives in the near future? To what extent will they

Table 4.2 Projected impacts of global warming at increase of 1.5 °C and 2 °C

Impact	1.5 °C	2 °C
Extreme heat – global population exposed at least once every 5 years	14%	37%
Arctic ice – number of ice-free years	1 every 100	1 every 10
Sea-level rise by 2100	0.4 metres	0.46 metres
Vertebrate species loss	4%	8%
Plant species loss	8%	16%
Area of global land with shift in local ecosystems	7%	13%
Amount of arctic permafrost thaw	4.8m sq kms	6.6m sq kms
Reductions in crop yields in tropics – e.g. maize	3%	7%
Decline in coral reefs	70–90%	99%
Decline in marine fisheries	1.5m tonnes	3m tonnes

Source: compiled from K. Levin (2018), '8 Things You Need to Know about the IPCC 1.5 °C Report', World Resources Institute blog (www.wri.org)

impinge on my own generation and the lives of our children and their generation? What prospects are there for the sustainable livelihoods of our grandchildren and their descendants?

Three examples show the scale of risks. The first, and most topical, concerns the rise of zoonotic diseases such as Covid-19. The destruction of the world's forests has led to the increasing impingement of human settlements by animals which have previously not coexisted closely with people. The result has been the spread of novel zoonotic diseases such as SARs, MERS and, most recently, Covid-19. The Covid-19 pathogen appears to have evolved from bats and passed through pangolins to humans. Previously, both bats and pangolins have lived in lesser proximity to human habitats. Assuming that Covid-19 is brought under control, this does not remove the possibility of the emergence of other deadly zoonotic viruses. In fact, left unchecked, the increasing destruction of natural habitats makes it even more likely that other, and perhaps even more dangerous, zoonotic viruses will develop.

The second example of the harmful impact of environmental change is the catastrophic impact of pollution and climate change on insect and plant diversity. The diversity of the ecosystem is crucial to the sustainability of the future of our food supplies. A review of seventy-three studies on trends in insect life revealed an astonishingly rapid rate of population decline.[18] In terrestrial ecosystems, Lepidoptera, Hymenoptera and dung beetles have been most affected, and four major groupings of aquatic life (Odonata, Plecoptera, Trichoptera and Ephemeroptera) have lost a considerable proportion of species. In Germany, a population-monitoring study over twenty-seven years revealed a 76 per cent decline in flying insect biomass. In the US, the number of honey-bee colonies plummeted from 6 million to 2.5 million between 1947 and 2010. By point of comparison, the development of our complex insect ecosystem has taken 400 million years since the end of the Devonian period.[19] Amongst other things, the diversity of plant pollinators such as insects and birds is critical to the maintenance of our agricultural systems. Without them, we will not be able to grow nutritious crops such as fruit, nuts and many vegetables, and will increasingly have to rely on less nutritious crops such as corn, potatoes and rice.

The spread of large-scale (mass production) agriculture has resulted in a major narrowing of diversity, both within and between crops and livestock. In 2019, the United Nations Food and Agriculture

Organization (FAO) reported that two-thirds of global food output was accounted for by only nine crops, and forty types of livestock provided the bulk of meat, milk and eggs.[20] Disease in any one of these large-volume crops poses a major threat to sustainable food production. The crisis facing the global banana industry is a case in point.[21] (Since I eat a banana with my breakfast every morning, this is a particularly worrying development, for me at least!) Virtually all currently traded bananas in the world are derived from a plant stock developed in the 1930s by a gardener in Cavendish House in Derbyshire, England. The Cavendish banana not only accounts for the bulk of global trade but also serves one-quarter of the Indian, and virtually all of the Chinese, domestic markets. Before the 1950s, the global banana industry was dominated by the Gros Michel variety, but this was wiped out by the 'Panama Disease' in the space of a few years. The problem now is that, in recent years, the Panama Virus has successfully adapted to attack the Cavendish variety. It is spreading rapidly through this global monoculture, with potentially devastating impacts on the lives of millions of banana farmers. The loss of species diversity within the global banana industry has severely undermined the capacity to develop new fungus-resistant varieties of bananas.

The third example of large negative impacts which have already appeared as a consequence of humankind's destruction of the earth's environment is the increasing frequency of natural disasters. Munich Re, one of the world's largest insurance companies, has a direct interest in assessing these risks. It is extremely concerned – perhaps frightened would be a better word – at the trend over the past three decades. The company classifies four categories of significant natural disasters which are large enough to affect the claims made against it and other global insurance companies. As Figure 4.9 indicates, between 1990 and 2016 the incidence – by number of events – grew more than threefold. If this were not bad enough, the severity of these individual natural disasters grew as well.

All of these disasters have major economic costs, not just to the insurance industry but to economic output as a whole. And, as world population increases, these costs will be magnified. Scientists estimate that at least $67 billion of the $90 billion cost of Hurricane Harvey in the Caribbean in 2017 was attributable to climate change.[22] But it is not just the economic costs which are a source of concern. Climatic events lead to the disruption of ecosystems and to considerable human suffering. Amongst the consequences of this are not just famines and disease, but also a rise in forced migration as affected populations seek to escape hazardous living conditions.

The way in which societies are organized and governed determines the extent and nature of humankind's environmental footprint. As Dorothy Sayer observed, 'A society in which consumption has to be artificially stimulated in order to keep production going is a society founded on trash and waste, and such a society is a house built upon sand.' So what is the economic motor which has driven our world into an environmental crisis? What forms of social and political organization have allowed this environmental crisis to unfold? What, if any, are the threads which draw these sustainability crises together? This is the subject matter of the chapter which follows.

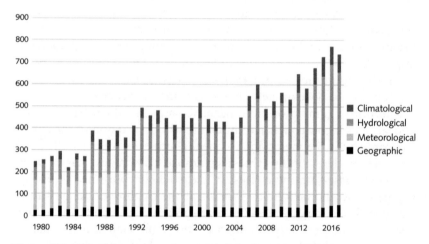

Figure 4.9 Rising frequency of natural disasters, 1980–2017

Source: data from Munich RE, NatCatSERVICE – The natural catastrophe loss database

5

Mass Production Runs Out
of Steam

It is now time to assemble the findings of the three previous chapters into an integrated story explaining the evolution of systemic crises in the post-World War 2 global economy.

We saw in Chapter 2 that the post-World War 2 decades witnessed a Golden Age, followed by a protracted slowdown in productivity growth, investment and economic growth. It culminated in the Great Recession after 2008, the sharpest economic downturn since the Great Depression in the 1930s. It also left a global economy in a parlous state of systemic vulnerability – speculation, debt, volatility and a disruption to the global trading architecture. In Chapter 3, we observed coterminous developments in society and politics. The post-war Golden Age decades were accompanied by a relatively cohesive social environment. As a generalization, liberal democratic political systems were largely supported by the populace. Then, after the 1980s, growing inequality and social exclusion led to the unravelling of this social compact. Fuelled by xenophobia, and manipulated by a rapacious neo-liberal-promoting plutocracy, a number of high-income economies (and notably the largest, the US) descended into variants of populism. Accompanying these developments in the economy and society, but without an equivalent to the positive economic and social developments of the post-war Golden Age, the environment was increasingly degraded as a result not just of the character of the Mass Production paradigm, but also of the overweening footprint of the human species.

Are these coterminous developments in the economy, society and the environment linked in any causal way? Or are they merely coincidental? In this chapter, I will draw on what has come to be termed the *techno-economic paradigm* framework to show that the economic, the social and the political developments co-evolved and were part and parcel of the same system. I will show that many of the unfolding developments in the environment were also intrinsically linked to the character of the Mass Production paradigm. In subsequent chapters, I will argue that there is a real opportunity of reversing this descent into multiple crises through the shaping of the new post-Mass Production paradigm, driven by Information and Communications Technology.

5.1 Learning from History – Successive Techno-Economic Paradigms since the Industrial Revolution

Growth surges and techno-economic paradigms

The growth slowdown in the advanced economies over the past two decades is not a unique historical event.[1] In the three centuries since the Industrial Revolution, there have been similar episodes in which growth has surged over a number of decades, to be followed by a period of stagnation before a new growth surge has emerged. In each of these phases, the transition to the new order has been punctuated by some form of crisis, generally involving a period of a burst 'financial bubble' and often accompanied by major social disorder. A distinctive feature of these surges is that they are of such significance that they affect not only all sectors of the economy but also a large number of countries.

The most compelling explanation for their existence – one which informs the analysis in this book – is that the growth surges are driven by the introduction and diffusion of major disruptive 'heartland technologies'. These technological revolutions are complemented by political and institutional structures, norms, patterns of behaviour and the unwritten rules within which economic production occurs.

Our brief journey into the theory of techno-economic paradigms begins with the ideas of the Austrian economist Joseph Schumpeter. In his early work in 1911, Schumpeter identified the crucial role played by entrepreneurship in driving forward economic growth.[2] As we saw in the previous chapter, he argued that the distinctive role of entrepreneurs was to turn inventions into profitable use – that is, to innovate. Innovations might involve new products, new production processes and new forms of organization. They provide entrepreneurs with the capacity to escape from the competitive pressures that erode their profitability. Schumpeter argued that standing above the everyday process of entrepreneurial innovation were periods of major economic and social disruption caused by the diffusion of a series of major disruptive technologies. The generalized diffusion of these technologies – which I will refer to as 'heartland technologies' – ushered in a period of 'creative destruction'. That is, they rendered a great number of existing technologies obsolete and destroyed the economic viability of much of the old order. On the positive side, however, Schumpeter argued that these disruptive innovations provided enormous potential for a new growth surge. This in turn would be sustained for some decades before itself being eroded by a new wave of innovation-led creative destruction.

Freeman and Perez built on these pioneering ideas to distinguish four categories of technological innovation.[3] The first are *Incremental Changes*, which occur on a routine and regular basis as production proceeds, involving minor modification to processes, and changes to product and organization. The second are *Radical Innovations*, which comprise discontinuous changes, generally arising out of research and development. For example, nuclear power stations could not emerge from incremental changes in coal-fired power stations. Nor could synthetic textiles emerge from improvements in cotton textile production. Changes in a *Technological System* are the third category of innovations. They comprise limited systemic changes involving a number of related sectors, often resulting from a combination of incremental and radical innovations. For example, synthetic chemicals are extensively used in the health, plastics and agricultural sectors. The final set of innovations are *techno-economic paradigms*. These involve the diffusion of heartland technologies, a cluster of innovation systems which are so significant that they affect all sectors of the economy. Crucially, these paradigms are not limited to production technologies. They involve complementary societal-level changes in institutions, in structures of governance, in residential patterns and lifestyles, and in values and behavioural norms.[4]

What, asked Freeman and Perez, are the characteristics of the heartland technologies which lie at the core of techno-economic paradigms? The first condition is that they have widespread applications across a number of sectors. The second is that they offer decisive and demonstrable cost reductions, improvements in existing products and the introduction of new products and services. Third, the cost of the new technology is falling rapidly, with the expectation that its price will continue to fall further for the foreseeable future. And, fourth, there must be no practical limits to its supply.

Drawing on Schumpeter's framework of disruptive heartland technologies, Freeman and Perez (and latterly, after Freeman's death, Perez[5]) identify a series of successive techno-economic paradigms that have dominated the trajectory of the high-income economies since the Industrial Revolution in the early eighteenth century. Each of these paradigms proceeds through a series of stages which are shown graphically in Figure 5.1. The first stage sees the invention of the core technology, the *Big Bang*. This is followed by a period in which the core technology is *developing*. It begins to be applied in a number of related innovations, clearly evidencing its revolutionary potential to transform production and introduce new products. In this stage of paradigm development, the financial sector plays an important

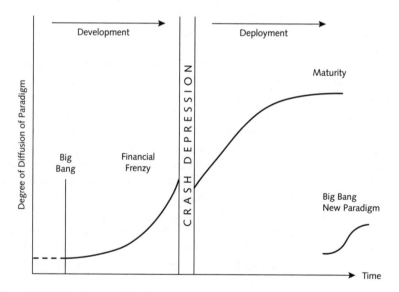

Figure 5.1 Six phases of techno-economic paradigms

Source: author's elaboration of Perez, *Technological Revolutions and Financial Capital*

constructive role. It provides the financial resources to allow new entrepreneurs to experiment with and develop the new technologies.

A few hugely profitable successes at the beginning of the development of these new radical technologies reveal their transformative and profit-generating potential. The financial sector is so excited by the potential of the new heartland technology that it pours finance into too many new ventures. These *frenzied* financial inflows are far in excess of what the productive sector can absorb. This results in a rapid increase in share prices in firms working with the new technology. And then ... the bubble bursts. It becomes apparent that much of the anticipated financial gains are built on unrealistic expectations of the profitability of these new enterprises and of an infinitely sustained increase in their share prices. The whole economy is then disrupted by a financial crisis. Most of the speculative financial assets which have flowed into new technologies become nearly worthless.

This party-spoiling financial crash is followed by a deep economic recession and unfolding social and political turmoil. Anger at the rise in inequality, the growing number of workers with redundant skills and the rise in unemployment fuels a surge of populism. This disruption endures until new patterns of political leadership emerge which allow for the new heartland technology to be rapidly *deployed* across the economy and society. The success of these policies ushers in a third phase of the wave, a 'golden age' in which the revolutionary heartland technology achieves its potential. It sweeps through and transforms the whole economy. In this stage of rapid technological diffusion, instead of the financial sector being decoupled from production as it was during the phase of financial speculation, it becomes a handmaiden to economic growth. But, eventually, the gains from the new techno-economic paradigm diminish, productivity growth and investment slow and the wave *matures*.

Crucially, as the paradigm begins to atrophy, a new heartland technology emerges, laying the grounds for a new techno-economic paradigm. Its character is not pre-ordained and deployment of the new system can take a number of directions. And, critically, its development and deployment are not automatic. It requires decisive action by governments and key stakeholders to resist the reactionary social forces which seek to hang on to the old and outdated. These reactionary forces are powerful, having benefitted greatly from the old order. They are the fetters holding back the transition to the new paradigm. But since each paradigm involves a mating of values and norms with patterns of technological innovation, it is not just the fetters exerted by powerful vested interest which hold back the advance of the new paradigm. Transition is also held back by the blinkers of embedded social behaviour and attitudes which had developed to support the old order.

Learning from history

This analytical framework is derived from empirically grounded enquiry into the development of the advanced economies. Perez identifies five techno-economic paradigms since the early eighteenth century.[6] The first two waves originated in England. The third and fourth waves originated in Germany and the USA. And the most recent wave originated in the USA and is diffusing rapidly in Asia and smaller and more flexible high-income European countries. These paradigms are:

1 The introduction of water power in the late eighteenth century. This new form of inanimate energy was initially used to transform the textile industry, and then diffused to other sectors. The development of canals allowed innovating firms to reduce their costs, extend their market reach and deepen the division of labour. For example, canal boats could carry more than ten times the weight of a horse-drawn cart and, within a year of opening, the new Bridgewater canal reduced the cost of coal in Manchester by two-thirds.[7] This paradigm lasted until approximately 1830.

2 The introduction of coal-fired steam power after the 1830s facilitated a greater division of labour and more efficient mechanization across a range of economic sectors. The development of railways and the introduction of telegraphy aided its extension to new and more distant markets. For the first time, inputs into production and perishable foods could be brought from afar to local markets, and national brand names began to develop. This paradigm exhausted its growth potential by the 1870s.

3 The development of the steel and the electricity industries after the 1870s deepened and widened the capacity to mechanize production and introduce new products across a range of industries. Steel was also central to the development of long-range cross-border transport. Together with the development of telegraphy, this widened the span of markets across continents.

For example, steamships enabled Britain to become 'the factory of the world'. Within fifty years of their introduction for commercial transport, the cost of carrying goods by sea fell by more than 70 per cent and the geography of markets was no longer determined by the direction of wind currents.[8] It also opened the door to mass migration from Europe to North America and was instrumental in the development of an industrializing US. This paradigm lasted until World War 1.

4 The Mass Production paradigm originated in the early years of the twentieth century. Cheap oil and new forms of factory organization allowed for the development of the automobile and other forms of mass and long-distance transport. Cheap oil was also the feedstock for the plastics, the chemicals and the pharmaceutical industries which rapidly grew in importance during the twentieth century. As I will show below, the Mass Production paradigm exhausted its potential by the 1970s but was granted a 'stay of execution' through its global extension after the mid-1970s.

5 The most recent period has seen the emergence of the Information and Communications Technology paradigm. The core technologies were developed in the 1970s. They vastly improve the productive potential of existing industries. They also led to the development of wholly new products and services. But, critically, they also provided the means to control the complex interflows of information, people, components and products which allowed for the deepening of globalization.

Each of the first four paradigms was characterized by a burst financial bubble – the canal mania bubble between 1793 and 1797; the railway mania bubble between 1836 and 1847; the Baring bubble between 1890 and 1893; and the stock market bubble of the 1920s. (The Baring bubble, named after a major trading company which had to be rescued by the Bank of England, involved a frenzy of speculative investment into raw material-producing economies such as Argentina). Each of these bubbles and subsequent financial crises marked a turning point in the evolution of the paradigm and heralded the transition to a 'golden age' when the heartland technology was deployed and when it realized its full potential. But these turning points were characterized by massive social and economic upheavals. Chillingly, not all transition phases were peaceful. For example, it took the Great Depression of the 1930s and World War 2 (resulting in the loss of approximately 80 million lives, 3 per cent of the global population) to usher in the transition between the development and deployment stages in the Mass Production paradigm.

Naturally, this analytical framework is not free from controversy. At almost every point in the story, it is possible to query a specific element – for example, in the timing of starting- and end-points and the links between the core heartland technology sectors and other sectors exploiting these heartland technologies. The historical sweep is so large, the range of technologies so diverse and the geographical canvas (the global economy) so broad, that in disputing detail it is easy to be sceptical of the whole analytical construction. But this would be to miss the wood for the trees. The 'trees' are the details of specific events, specific technologies and specific locations. The 'wood' is the repeated historical surge in growth trajectories, the significance of the core heartland technologies in these surges, the increasing extension of markets and, crucially, the development of institutions, and the forms of productive and social organization which support the widespread diffusion of a whole range of related economic and social technologies.

5.2 The Development, Deployment and Atrophy of the Mass Production Paradigm

There are two analytical building blocks which I need to put in place before I apply this techno-economic paradigm framework developed by Freeman and Perez to a description of the techno-economic paradigm which dominated the global economy in the twentieth century. The first is to clear up an important issue of nomenclature. I will use the term 'mass production' in two different ways. In its capitalized form – Mass Production – I refer to the combination of economic and social factors which accompanied and facilitated the growth surge after World War 2. This was the era of the Mass Production paradigm. In its lower-case form, 'mass production' refers to the specificities of production organization in individual firms and workplaces. The significance of this distinction will become apparent in the recounting of the rise and fall of the techno-economic paradigm which dominated the twentieth century.

The second building block draws on the analysis by Adam Smith of the growth of industrial production in the eighteenth century.

Smith observed that the surge in growth in the first techno-economic paradigm resulted in large part from growing productivity. In turn, the growth in productivity was driven by an increasing division of labour. Using the example of the manufacture of pins, he showed that breaking the production process down into discrete stages, each of which was performed by dedicated labour, was the key to productivity growth. This was because labour productivity was increased since workers did not have to waste time changing tools. They could thus specialize in the precise skills required for their stage of operation. In the same way, dedicated machinery could be developed to mechanize these specialized tasks. Smith added a further and very important dimension to his analysis of the division of labour. This was that the extent of the division of labour was determined by the size of the market – the larger the market, the greater the scope for specialization.

The 'Big Bang' in Mass Production was followed by speculative frenzy, a financial crisis and the Great Depression

The Big Bang of the Mass Production paradigm was the development of mass production in the automobile sector. This was pioneered by Henry Ford's Model T car, which was introduced in 1908 and then manufactured on a mass scale from 1913. Ford's mass production factories involved the application of five complementary innovations. First, work patterns were reorganized and routinized. This involved the careful measurement of all tasks in production, the training of workers to perform the specific tasks which they were allocated and the use of task-measurement of performance to increase both the intensity and productivity of workers. Ford famously observed that he employed his workers to follow instructions, not to think. Second, the changes in work-organization were complemented by the introduction of special-purpose machinery which could operate at great speed and without interruption. Third, since the special-purpose machinery was inflexible, the final product was standardized, even with respect to its colour. Ford proudly marketed the Model T as being 'available in any colour as long as it is black'. As in the case of the specialization of tasks, this meant that dedicated machinery could be developed which could work without the interruption required to change product specifications. Further, a stable product meant that components could also be standardized, allowing for specialization and productivity growth along the supply chain.

Fourth, Ford internalized virtually all of the manufacturing cycle into a single plant in River Rouge, Michigan.[9] This comprised 1.5 km² of factory floor space. It had its own docks to unload ore, coal and other raw materials, as well as 100 miles of internal railtracks. And, finally, contrary to established practice in US manufacturing, which sought to minimize wages, Ford doubled the wages of his workers to $5 per day and reduced the working day from nine to eight hours. The reorganization of his plants had increased the pace and intensity of work. This raised the danger that workers trained in specialized skills would move on to firms with less onerous working conditions. Moreover, Ford realized that production could only be expanded if people – even factory workers – had the incomes to buy cars. He believed, correctly, that raising wages in his plants would spur higher wages in other factories and hence expand the demand for his products.

Ford's introduction and refinement of this mass production organizational system improved the performance and quality of the car and allowed for easier repair. But it also resulted in a significant reduction in its price. Between 1909 and 1916, the price of the Model T fell from $825 to $345 (from $24,270 to $7,933 in current 2020 prices) and further to $260 ($3,918 in current prices) in 1925. Between 1912 and 1927, Ford produced and sold more than 15 million Model T cars.[10] So significant were these reductions in price and improvements in product that the principles of mass production diffused rapidly to other auto manufacturers and then began to spread to other sectors.

The critical element of Ford's related innovations is that they fused new technologies (specialized machinery) and a new design philosophy (standardized products) with changes in work practices, factory organization and Ford's relationship with suppliers. The social and the technical were thus intertwined within his production system. This fusion of the social and the technical was reflected in the wider roll-out of mass production in other firms and sectors.

The American and European economies expanded steadily during the 1920s. The diffusion of Ford's pioneering mass production system outside of the automobile sector was complemented by the growth of mass consumption, in part fuelled by a boom in housing construction. In the US, growing prosperity led to an era of heady optimism. Cheap and easy credit also led to a frenzy of highly speculative investments in the stock market. Citizens across the income scale borrowed money from banks and mortgaged their properties to take advantage of what seemed to be an unstoppable boom in share prices. Between 1921 and 1929 – a period of stable retail prices and moderate economic growth – average share prices grew by more than four times.

The party came to an abrupt end in October 1929.[11] In the space of two months, the index of share prices crashed by 48 per cent. Some specific examples of America's leading firms illustrate the resulting carnage.[12] The share price of the largest industrial company, General Electric, fell by 46 per cent. Du Pont Chemical and US Steel witnessed share price falls of two-thirds, and the share prices of the Radio Corporation of America fell by 94 per cent. Consumer demand collapsed, partly because so many ordinary US citizens had lost money in the stock market crash, and partly because there was a generalized loss of confidence in the system.

One of the consequences of this collapse in equity prices and confidence was that the US public began to lose faith in banks. There was a rush to claim money invested in bank deposits. At the same time, agricultural commodity prices fell by 60 per cent and the farming sector was unable to repay the heavy borrowings which it had used to expand. This resulted in a wave of bank failures, with one-fifth of banks collapsing between 1930 and 1933. The crisis, which began in the US financial system, spread rapidly across the US economy and then to the global economy. Banks in Germany, Austria and Hungary were rapidly and particularly badly affected. In a short time, the banking crisis spread across Europe and to many developing economies. Global trade halved as countries introduced tariffs to protect domestic industries, and global commodity prices collapsed. Unemployment rose to 25 per cent in the US, and to more than 33 per cent across Europe. Between 1929 and 1932, the size of the global economy fell by 15 per cent.

The deployment of Mass Production and the post-war Golden Age

So, in the context of this major financial crash and economic depression, how did changes in the organization of production introduced in a single factory complex on the River Rouge in Michigan, USA, between 1908 and 1913, develop into a techno-economic paradigm which dominated the global economy, transformed social relations and shaped the environment in the second half of the twentieth century?

Henry Ford's innovation at the productive level clearly satisfied the conditions of being a heartland technology. That is, it provided massive cost savings, led to the development of new and better-quality products, was widely applicable across virtually all sectors (including services and agriculture), was characterized by falling costs and was in unlimited supply. Although the productivity gains provided by mass production had become increasingly apparent during the 1920s and 1930s, the scale of the potential gains became graphically evident in the factories churning out weapons during World War 2. For example, applying the principles of mass production to aircraft manufacture, the number of combat planes produced in the US increased from 1,771 in 1939 to 37,861 in the first eight months of 1945 – that is from less than 5 per day to more than 150 per day.[13]

As in each of the previous techno-economic paradigms, the transition from the development to the widescale deployment phase of the Mass Production paradigm required decisive political leadership and involved new patterns of consumption and lifestyles. During the depth of the Great Depression in the 1930s, Roosevelt's New Deal Program created employment and incomes and built skills in the labour force. After World War 2, in both the US and Europe, governments made massive investments in the infrastructure required to support the rapid growth in car ownership and the associated changes in residential and consumption patterns. The growth in suburbanization after the war was accompanied by the expansion of household consumption of durable consumer goods, such as TVs, refrigerators and other household appliances. The private sector rapidly responded to these new conditions and, as we saw in Chapter 4, advertising expenditure grew sharply to promote and reinforce consumption.

The result was a 25-year Golden Age of rapid growth and relative social harmony between 1950 and the mid-1970s. This was similar in many ways to the *Belle Époque* ('Beautiful Era') in the last quarter of the nineteenth century, during the heyday of the previous techno-economic paradigm, of steel and electricity. This had seen decades of economic prosperity, widespread social optimism, cultural and scientific innovation, peace in Europe and the US, and the extension of European power to colonies in Africa, Asia and Latin America.

Maturity deferred: the globalization of Mass Production

As we saw in Chapter 2, by the mid-1970s economic growth rates began to decline. The gains accruing from the rapid diffusion of mass production organization had been reaped and the boost offered to productivity growth had begun to run out of steam. There were two structural reasons for this declining performance. First, as was evident in Henry Ford's pioneering introduction of mass production between 1907 and 1929, the initial gains from the new form of production organization were substantial. But once the structural transformation had been made, the incremental productivity gains were at a lower rate. Economists refer to this as 'diminishing marginal productivity'. Second, mass production required the standardization of product, and achieved this by building increasingly large plants using specialized equipment. That worked well in the post-World War 2 decades when consumers were hungry for virtually anything that producers offered them. But, as incomes rose and basic needs were satisfied, consumers wanted new products, increased variety and higher-quality products. The inflexible large-scale mass production manufacturing plants found it very difficult to satisfy this increasingly demanding market.[14]

There was an additional impediment to growth which also arose from the central character of the Mass Production paradigm. Its reliance on the internal combustion engine and automobilization provided oil producers with monopoly power. By limiting the production of oil, the Organization of the Petroleum Exporting Countries (OPEC) was able to push up oil prices considerably in 1973 and 1979. Coupled with the exhaustion of the gains arising from mass production, this led to a prolonged period of 'stagflation'. This saw a combination of rising prices and stagnant output. This combination of factors, all intrinsic to the character of the Mass Production paradigm, had an impact on corporate profitability. In the US, the rising-trend share of corporate profits in domestic income between 1951 and 1966 – the heyday of the Golden Age – was followed by a downturn between 1966 and 1990 (Figure 5.2).

So, how did the Mass Production paradigm stave off this crisis of maturity? It achieved this by going global – that is, by increasingly extending markets from the national to the transnational economy. This required the development of major institutions of global governance such as the International Monetary Fund (IMF) and the World Bank, with the remit to promote global economic stability and

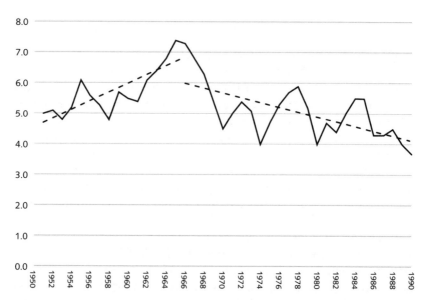

Figure 5.2 US corporate profitability as share of domestic income, 1951–1966 and 1966–1990 (post-tax profits as a share of domestic income, %)

Source: data from Federal Reserve Bank of St. Louis

growth, and to assist with the expansion of global trade. In 1951, the European Coal and Steel Community was formed in order to promote cross-border trade. It rapidly increased its scope and membership, evolving into the European Economic Community (EEC) in 1957, and then the European Community (EC) in 1993. Both the EEC and the EC increasingly performed functions to manage demand and to facilitate trade. But the crucial policy innovation promoting the growth of globalization was the reduction in the obstacles to international trade. The General Agreement on Tariffs and Trade (GATT) was established in 1947 and was superseded in 1993 by the World Trade Organization (WTO). Between 1947 and 1999, the average import tariffs of GATT/WTO member countries had fallen from 27 to 5 per cent, and many of the non-tariff barriers (such as quotas) which had been widely used and which had restricted global trade were abolished.[15]

These various global institutions provided the enabling environment for the globalization of mass production. The primary actor that could take advantage of these developments, and that promoted their development, was the corporate sector. Access to external markets enabled firms to deepen the division of labour in their operations, which, as we saw earlier, was key to productivity growth. The key development here was the introduction at the corporate level of new policies towards the use of external suppliers. This led global firms to unwind the internalization strategies which Henry Ford had developed in the vertically integrated River Rouge plant manufacturing the Model T which I described earlier.

There was a threefold logic that had underwritten the internalization strategies which Ford had introduced in his factories and which had spread widely throughout the advanced economies. First, communication with suppliers was a difficult and costly process – it was better to do the work in-house and save the hassle and cost of dealing with unreliable and distant suppliers. Second, suppliers could not be trusted since there was a danger that they might steal the knowhow of the outsourcing firms and pass this on to their rivals. And, third, suppliers were reluctant to make the necessary investments in specialized equipment and technology to serve their customers' needs. This was because they were concerned that their customers might switch their sourcing at short notice. This would leave suppliers with costly specialized and redundant equipment. Thus, whilst the lead firms with their massive internalized operations might have preferred a different arrangement – one in which they could concentrate on those parts of the manufacturing cycle and product development in which they had unique capabilities – it was not worth the cost or risk of dealing with unreliable and untrustworthy suppliers.

Three developments reduced the need for this corporate strategy of internalization. The first was a change in the organizational relationship between lead firms and their suppliers. The origins of this development were to be found in what came to be called the 'Toyota Manufacturing System'. Toyota invested in the development of long-term relationships with a small number of suppliers whom it judged it could trust. Along the chain, inventories would be reduced and production would occur on a just-in-time basis. This system involved trust not only in the business relationship between Toyota and its suppliers, but also in the capacity of the suppliers to improve their products and to reduce their prices. When suppliers ran into problems, instead of Toyota switching to alternative suppliers, it invested resources in assisting them to overcome their difficulties.

Over time, as this supplier–customer relationship improved, Toyota tasked its suppliers with assisting their own suppliers in a like way, and this ricocheted down the supply chain.

The Toyota Manufacturing System was developed in the 1960s and 1970s. It diffused rapidly across the Japanese auto industry. The competitive advantages of this strategy were enormous.[16] It allowed Toyota, Nissan and their followers to concentrate on their special capabilities (design, drive train manufacture and assembly) and to outsource the production of much of the lower value-added and highly specialized components to others. Thus, whereas in the 1970s the American auto firms were producing almost 70 per cent of the value of their cars in their own plants, their Japanese rivals were adding less than 50 per cent of total product value. In the mid-1980s, the Toyota Manufacturing System was adopted by the US and European automobile industries and then by vast swathes of industry in the global economy, and not just in manufacturing.

A second factor which allowed the lead firms to reduce their commitment to internalization was the development of new Information and Communication Technologies. This significantly reduced the costs of communicating with suppliers. Although it was only during the late 1990s that email and the internet provided massive gains in the cost and efficiency of knowledge transfer, it was already the case from the late 1980s that improvements in telephony and the digitization of knowledge were reducing – and would continue to reduce – the costs of information transfer. For example, computer-aided design was developed in the early 1980s. It allowed for the precise specification of components to be easily transmitted directly to suppliers' computer-controlled equipment.

A third facilitator of globalized mass production was the development of containerization in the shipping industry. The introduction of modular containers in the 1950s revolutionized seaborne freight and transhipment. Containers reduced the need for warehousing. They allowed for the mechanization of the labour-intensive loading and unloading of freight, and increased the speed of turnaround in ports. The growth of containers for sea transport was rapid and sustained, and currently more than 90 per cent of global non-bulk trade is transported in more than 700 million containers.[17]

But containerization required a range of complementary developments – in ship-design, in infrastructure (purpose-built docks and quays), in metrification (executed through the International

Organization for Standards, ISO), in road transport and in customs procedures. It also led to the massive displacement of labour and the destruction of what had previously been very powerful trades unions in ports. Further, it both required and precipitated changes in design philosophy. The introduction and diffusion of containers is thus an example of how major technological developments require complementary changes across industries, in global governance, in social organization and in power relations.

From the perspective of the corporate sector, the globalization of Mass Production did the trick. In the US, after twenty-five years of a trend fall in corporate profitability between 1966 and 1990 (Figure 5.2), the share of profits in domestic income began to rise (Figure 5.3). Of course, this rising profitability was not only a result of the internal crisis of mass production organization, since the data in Figure 5.3 reflect the share of *post-tax* profits in domestic income. However, as we saw in Figure 2.5 corporate tax rates in the US were uniquely stable (being unchanged between 1988 and 2017) amongst the major high-income economies.

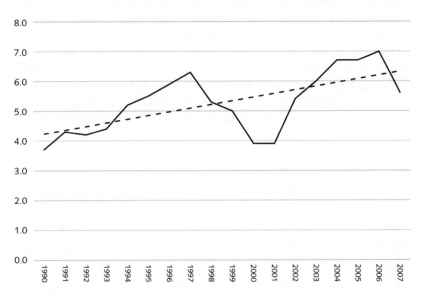

Figure 5.3 US corporate profitability as share of domestic income, 1990–2007 (post-tax profits as a share of domestic income, %)

Source: data from Federal Reserve Bank of St. Louis

Complementary policy changes in low- and middle-income countries

The reduction in trade barriers and the development of communications technology and containerized transport occurred at the same time that many emerging economies were making the transition from an inward-facing to an outward-facing development strategy. This change in development strategy in low-income economies after the mid-1970s was not a coincidence. It was driven by advanced economies' aid programmes, supported by the imposition of neo-liberal economic orthodoxy in the developing world by the IMF and the World Bank. The combination of developments matched perfectly the need of lead corporations in the advanced economies for low-cost suppliers as they made the transition from internalization to core competence strategies and outsourcing. Increasingly, much of the factory production which had historically taken place in the advanced economies was outsourced to low-wage economies. The entry of China, the former Soviet Union, India and other emerging economies into the global economy provided an almost inexhaustible reservoir of cheap and skilled labour. As Table 5.1 shows, wages in emerging economies were much lower than in the advanced economies, and not just for unskilled labour.

Economists refer to core-competence outsourcing strategies as 'the slicing of the value chain' in a process of 'vertical specialisation'.[18] Extended beyond national boundaries, this led to the rapid development of Global Value Chains.[19] Particularly in those parts of manufacturing which involved the assembly of many components, but also in services and agriculture, the production of final products was

Table 5.1 Post-tax wages in global economies, March 2009 ($)

	Building labourer	Skilled industrial worker	Engineer
New York	16.6	29.0	26.5
London	9.7	19.0	22.1
Beijing	0.8	2.3	5.8
Delhi	0.5	2.1	2.9
Nairobi	0.6	2.0	4.0
Ratio of rich–poor	20.4	10.9	5.8

Source: compiled from B. Milanovic (2012), 'Evolution of Global Inequality: From Class to Location, from Proletarians to Migrants', *Global Policy*, 3, 2: 125–34

segmented into increasingly finely specialized sub-processes. These global supply chains became increasingly complex, and economies became ever more interconnected. For example, the Apple iPhone 3 was sold in the US for $399, and was exported from China at a price of $175. However, the value which was actually added in China, where the phones were assembled from imported components using imported equipment, was only $6.50.[20] The consequence of this division of labour is that global trade is no longer dominated by the exchange of domestically produced final products (for example, cars for wheat). Instead, global trade is increasingly made up of intermediate products (such as parts of parts, stages in software production, and call centres in retail and customer support). Economists estimate that trade in Global Value Chains now accounts for more than 70 per cent of total trade.[21]

As I type this page, my attention turns to the myriad of gadgets on my desk, and to the toys which have just been delivered for my grandchildren. Written on the base and packaging of almost all of these artefacts are the words 'Made in China', signifying that they have been shipped across the globe to meet my needs. But I know these words are seldom accurate. 'Made in China' may also mean 'Assembled in China using Components Shipped Across the World'. This highly complex global production system which rescued the Mass Production paradigm from its growth atrophy depends critically on the stability and security of the global communication network. Any disruption of this infrastructure threatens growth, jobs and incomes in both the consuming high-income countries and the low- and middle-income countries supplying their needs.

Enter the Covid-19 pandemic … This has exposed the deep penetration of global supply chains in the latter stages of Mass Production, no more so than in the health sector. Vital Personal Protection Equipment was in short supply and global production was concentrated in a few countries, and particularly in China. For some weeks after the onset of the pandemic, it proved difficult to obtain paracetamol – the key ingredient was manufactured in China and the pills were produced in India. Production in the auto sector ground to a halt; the Jaguar – Land Rover plant in the UK could not obtain a small electronic component which was required to produce key fobs. Large volumes of milk and beef were wasted since they could not be delivered to distant markets. Many of these problems were a direct result of the extended globalized production systems which had rescued the Mass Production paradigm from its atrophy after the mid-1970s.

5.3 Economic and Social Sustainability during the Mass Production Paradigm

The systemic interactions between the economy and society in the Mass Production paradigm can be separated into two periods. The first was a phase of positive win–win synergy. Economic growth fostered the development of social behaviour and political institutions which directly supported sustained economic growth. However, after the end of the Golden Age in the mid-1970s, this positive synergy began to collapse. Developments in the economy resulted in patterns of social development which not only were unsustainable, but also eroded the fundamentals of sustainable economic growth. Thus, whilst the primary driver of change in social and political relations emanated from the economy, the two systems – the economic and the social/political – interacted and co-evolved.

The synergistic close fit between economic and social sustainability in the Golden Age

We can observe this synergistic fit between economic and social sustainability by drawing on the analysis provided in Chapters 2 and 3. The development and deployment phases of the Mass Production paradigm (between 1912 and World War 2, and 1950 and the mid-1970s, respectively) were redolent of links between technology, the economy and society. I have already shown how Henry Ford's mass production line required a combination of changes in physical technology (the introduction of special-purpose machinery), factory layout, work organization, payment systems and inter-firm relations. So much for the factory and firm level. But what about the technical, the economic and the social interconnections at the macro and paradigm level? Here, too, the links were wide and deep. A few examples, some of which were described in earlier chapters, illustrate these interactions.

Government played a key role in sustaining demand and in matching mass production with mass consumption. Welfare payments provided incomes to consumers. Massive public investment programmes in infrastructure and housing provided the arteries for automobilization, suburbanization and mass consumption. Developments in the US (the economy leading the deployment of the Mass Production paradigm) illustrate the interconnections between government policies, lifestyles and mass consumption. In 1965, state expenditure on highways totalled $26 billion, the largest ever public works programme in US history.[22] Between 1946 and 1955, the production of automobiles quadrupled. Together with large-scale house-building, automobilization promoted suburbanization. The number of out-of-town shopping malls increased from 8 in 1945 to 3,840 in 1960.[23] And the number of televisions – the window through which the advertising industry promoted mass consumption – grew dramatically. In 1946, 7,000 US homes possessed a TV. A mere three years later, the number had grown to 172,000 households. The share of households possessing TVs expanded rapidly from 20 per cent in 1950 to 90 per cent in 1960.[24]

The diffusion of mass production at the plant and inter-firm level was similarly reflected in the societal-wide structure of industrial relations. The prevalence of large factories in Mass Production was closely associated with the development of industrial unions and employer–employee bargaining councils. In countries with centralized state provision of social services, large unions also dominated the service sector. Through much of the high-income world, this structure of industrial relations was backed by supportive legislation. Job security and 9-to-5 working hours became the norm in this mass production work compact. A 'fair' distribution of the returns from production was generally accepted, with labour's share of total national income largely stable.

At the political level, there was a generalized acceptance of the legitimacy and effectiveness of the liberal democratic political structures which delivered this supportive policy regime. These involved frequent elections resulting in centrist governments which favoured the moderated growth of capitalism and the deepening of globalization. During the heyday of the Mass Production paradigm, liberal democracy and its associated institutions were increasingly accepted as the legitimate political order across the world. Thus, as we saw in Chapter 3, when the Soviet Union collapsed in the late 1980s, the influential political scientist Fukuyama triumphantly proclaimed that he was witnessing 'the end of history'.

Beyond politics and the productive sector, changes in lifestyles and gender relations complemented the requirements of the 'economic engine' of Mass Production. Social attitudes were actively shaped to reinforce consumerist lifestyles, including with respect to gender. In the early years of the Mass Production paradigm, the role of women was moulded and then remoulded to fit the changing needs of the economy. During the war, a shortage of male labour in the US required women to work in factories producing armaments. However, when their husbands returned to civilian life and wanted their jobs back, these women were sent back home. Suddenly, the ideal and 'normal' image for women was no longer a worker dressed in overalls, but a mother and homemaker, using 'machines' (that is, appliances) in the home. This transition was supported by the rapidly growing advertising industry. Fashion magazines were filled with images of elegant and glamorous women. They were uniformly white, with blond tresses and wearing flowing dresses, often with a cigarette elegantly balanced in their long-fingered slim hands.

The erosion of synergy between economic and social sustainability after the Golden Age

The interconnections between the economic and the social in the pre-maturity phase of the Mass Production paradigm were reinforcing of each other. It was predominantly a time of belonging, of optimism and of 'progress'. But from the late 1970s, an era of economic and social crisis (which I described in Chapters 2 and 3) set in. Sustainable economic growth became increasingly problematic, and social cohesion fractured. Here, too, as in the case of the Golden Age of Mass Production, the social and the economic were closely intertwined. The rising inequality consequent on the growth of the Mass Production economy resulted in growing social exclusion, absolute poverty and insecurity. This in turn bolstered the power of the plutocracy, which resulted in the 'triumph' of neo-liberalism. This policy agenda ate away at the fundamental underpinnings of economic growth. In recent years, building on dissatisfaction in rust-belt sectors that were hurting badly from global competition, there has been a rising tide of protectionism – for example, in a tit-for-tat imposition of tariffs between the world's two largest economies, the US and China. This political development, set in train by Mass Production's growth trajectory, has eroded the sustainability of globalization which, as we saw above, rescued mass production from its productivity crisis.

The link between the Mass Production economy and the social was not confined to policy agendas. It was also reflected in lifestyles, values and norms. As I showed in Chapter 4, mass consumption was an essential complement to mass production. The productive system spewed out more and more products. Consumers willingly gobbled up this output, conspiring to throw away products which were not past effective use, and allowing themselves to be duped into wanting things they did not need. But during the Vietnam War, which occurred at the beginning of the turning-point in the paradigm, the values and lifestyles backing mass production began to erode. What started as civic political opposition to the war rapidly morphed into a counter-culture, initially in the US and then globally. Many of the values of the fringe hippy movement in the late 1960s then went mainstream. This resulted in innovations in lifestyles such as those promoting non-industrialized farming, organic foods and social consumption. It also resulted in the growth of politicized civil society institutions 'speaking truth to power'. Growing awareness of the working conditions in global value chains led to consumer campaigns opposing the use of cheap child labour and unsafe working conditions in low-wage economies.

These developments – in income distribution, in economic policy, in global governance and in values and lifestyles – undermined the foundations of Mass Production's growth machine. The paradigm required stability, a rule-based trading system and a population willing to participate in mass consumption. But, at the same time, each of these and associated developments were challenged as a direct outcome of the character of Mass Production. The paradigm was increasingly at war with itself, floundering as a consequence of its own internal contradictions.

5.4 The Crisis in Environmental Sustainability during the Mass Production Paradigm

As we saw in Chapter 4, although the unfolding environmental crisis since the Great Acceleration after 1950 reflected the character of the Mass Production paradigm, the roots to the environmental crisis go much deeper. They reflect not only the character of previous techno-economic paradigms since the onset of the Industrial Revolution (for example, coal-powered steam energy), but also the development of settled agriculture more than 13 millennia ago.

Mass Production deepened the degradation of the environment. The mass consumption which was a direct complement to mass production intensified the taking and wasting of resources. As I will show in Chapter 8, the neo-liberal macro policy regime (which argued that the market would ensure a stable and prosperous world) introduced a range of incentives that exacerbated the negative impact of growth on the environment. Polluters were not charged for their discharges, materials were used wastefully and the primary source of a transport-intensive paradigm – hydrocarbons – wreaked havoc on the climate. Deepening globalization during the mature phase of the Mass Production paradigm resulted in an explosive growth in climate-damaging sea and air transport as products criss-crossing the globe became a major contributor to climate change.

But, as in the case of the economy and society, there was a two-way interaction between the environment and society. Environmental decay helped to fuel the demise of liberal democracy and to undermine the potential for sustained economic growth. Livelihoods have become increasingly precarious for many, and growing environmental disasters contributed to an increase in the mass migration which populist leaders and the plutocracy exploited to seize the reins of social and economic power. The populist politics which were introduced were fused with climate denial, none more obvious and damaging than Donald Trump's decision to withdraw from the Paris Agreement on Climate Change (COP) adopted by 196 countries in 2015.

5.5 Mass Production: The Balance Sheet

The causal links between the evolving crises in the economy, in society and in the environment and the diffusion of Mass Production should not blind us to the overwhelming contribution which this techno-economic paradigm has made to human welfare. On the positive side, it provided the means for societies to improve living standards dramatically, to develop cures for diseases which had ravaged humanity for centuries and to fund flourishing expressions of culture. It provided new products and experiences to expand the horizons of humankind. And it even provided the resources for humankind to visit the moon. Perhaps most significantly, these benefits were not limited to the high-income countries. Following the global spread of Mass Production after the 1980s, an increasing number of the global population shared in these positive developments.

On the 'dark side' of the equation, as in previous techno-economic paradigms, this progress was punctuated adversely at three points of its evolution. The first was the Great Crash and the Depression of the late 1920s and 1930s, and the devastation of World War 2. This threw a great many people into destitution and despair and cost many millions of lives. The second dark period is that which emerged after the mid-1980s. The high-income countries experienced growing inequality and absolute poverty, falling rates of economic growth and a severe weakening of the social fabric. And the third was the Global Financial Crisis in 2007–8. Millions of people around the world, and particularly in the high-income countries, witnessed a sudden fall in incomes and job security. The decades-long increase in life-expectancy was abruptly reversed, an increasing number of homeless populated the streets, and opiod and other drug use mushroomed.

And then, and most recently, there is the sudden and catastrophic Covid-19 pandemic. To what extent has this resulted from the character of the Mass Production paradigm? There is a danger of trying to explain too many things through the lens of techno-economic paradigms. Many elements of the Covid-19 pandemic were unrelated to the character of Mass Production. For example, the wet–dry food markets in parts of Asia have existed in one form or another for decades. Any increase in their scale, whether a result of Mass Production or any other techno-economic paradigm, would increase the likelihood of the emergence of a zoonotic pandemic such as Covid-19. On the other hand, the pandemic is not unrelated to Mass Production. The despoliation of the environment in Mass Production, the destruction of the world's forests and species and the advance of monocultural agriculture undoubtedly contributed to the growth of this zoonotic disease. Further, the globalization of supply chains was a major factor in the extraordinarily rapid transmission of a local zoonotic outbreak in Wuhan, China, to the four corners of the world in a matter of a mere three months.

What of the future? Have we reached the 'end of history'? Are these crises of sustainability in the economy, in society and in the environment insoluble and with us forever? Are there alternatives which can allow us to construct a more sustainable world? Learning from history – that is, from the successive historical evolution of techno-economic paradigms since the early eighteenth century – it is possible to envisage an achievable form of social and economic organization that may lead to the development of a more sustainable world. It is to this agenda that our attention now turns.

6

Information and Communication Technologies: The Motor of the New Techno-Economic Paradigm

So far, we have focused on the past. What have been the major developments in the economy, society and the environment since World War 2, and how have they been interconnected? But it is now time to think forward. The techno-economic framework which provided us with the opportunity to understand historic developments can also be used to provide us with the capacity to transition to a more sustainable future. This is the subject matter of the remaining chapters in this book.

I begin in this chapter by explaining the character of Information and Communications Technologies (ICTs) and show how they reflect the transformative character of the heartland technologies described by Schumpeter, Freeman and Perez. Then, in Chapter 7, I will describe in some depth three sets of ICT innovations which illustrate not just their potential to drive future economic growth, but also the manner in which they simultaneously can bolster social and environmental sustainability. Each of these case-studies in their own way is an exemplar of the systemic changes involved in the transition of techno-economic paradigms. In the final two chapters, our attention will turn to the policy agenda – how can we shape the direction of the evolving ICT techno-economic paradigm to maximize its beneficial transformative impact? Imparting directionality to the evolution of ICTs is imperative, since, as we will observe in Chapter 8, the positive transformative potential of ICTs can easily be overwhelmed by their capacity to undermine social, political and environmental sustainability.

The technical material in this chapter will be familiar to some of my audience and I apologize to you for what might seem to be a statement of the obvious. But not all readers will be familiar with the character of ICTs and why they are indeed the heartland technology which will power the economy, society and the environment in decades to come.[1]

6.1 The Emergence of the New Heartland Technology

Like almost everyone, I have become increasingly reliant on various electronic technologies. My first academic paper in a peer-reviewed journal was published in 1975. I had written it by hand, and then laboriously typed and retyped it on a portable Olivetti typewriter which I had lugged out from the UK to Kenya. This draft had then been retyped – with copious use of Snopake – by the secretary at the Institute for Development Studies at the University of Nairobi. Before posting it off for publication, I proudly took it home to show my wife, and left it on the dining-room table overnight. At that stage, we had a pet goat who slept on a mat near the table. As it happened, it appears that he didn't always sleep on the mat since that night he jumped on the table and defecated all over the paper. At least it was a novel way to miss a publishing deadline! To this day, my wife extolls the sagacity of this goat.

This book, by contrast, has been written using two interconnected laptop computers. Heaven knows how many drafts and redrafts I have gone through, and even now I am tempted to change a few words in the preceding paragraph. With previous books I have written, I have employed a research assistant (or two or three). This time I did all the primary research myself, relying heavily on the internet. I also prepared almost all of the graphs and tables, although in some cases I was expertly assisted by Annie James in New Delhi, and Courtney Barnes and Chris Grant in South Africa. Various drafts were read and reread by friends and colleagues around the world. Interviews were conducted via Skype, and copious notes were exchanged by email. I even managed to glance furtively at the sports results periodically as I was 'working'. All of this was only made possible by my reliance on a plethora of electronically controlled equipment.

Of course, the impact of computing and other electronic technologies is much more significant than my stumbling attempts to type with more than two fingers and to keep up with software updates.

ICTs have application across the full range of economic and social activities; they offer very significant rewards for their use; their price has fallen dramatically and will continue to do so for some time to come; and there are few practical limits to their supply. They are, in other words, a new disruptive and transformative heartland technology, equivalent in historical significance to the heartland technologies which have driven previous techno-economic paradigms. However, there is a key difference between ICTs and previous heartland technologies. Water power (the first wave), steam power (the second wave), electricity and heavy engineering (the third wave) and mass production, automobilization and hydrocarbons (the fourth wave) all transformed productivity by substituting increasingly efficient inanimate energy for human energy. By contrast, ICTs transform productivity by drawing on what might be called 'intellectual energy' to drive the development of the emerging smart knowledge-intensive economy.

In order to appreciate the character and significance of ICTs, we need to return to Figure 5.1 (which is reproduced below as Figure 6.1). In each techno-economic paradigm, the Golden Age of

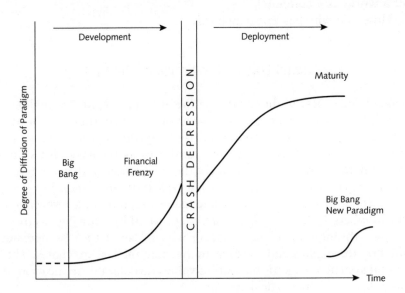

Figure 6.1 Six phases of techno-economic paradigms

Source: author's elaboration of Perez, *Technological Revolutions and Financial Capital*

deployment decays into a mature phase in which the expansionary surge slows and then atrophies. It is during this maturity phase that the new heartland technology is invented – Perez refers to this as the 'Big Bang'. So, just as the paradigm that dominated the second half of the nineteenth century began to mature, Henry Ford 'invented' and refined mass production to manufacture the Model T between 1908 and 1927. Similarly, the key inventions powering ICTs – the transistor, the integrated circuit and the microprocessor – occurred during the deployment period of the Mass Production paradigm.

Although ICTs played an important role in the global extension of Mass Production after the mid-1980s, they did not begin to diffuse more widely across the spectrum of economic and social activities until the turn of the millennium. As we will see, ICTs are now 'everywhere'. For better or worse, directly and indirectly, they suffuse almost every set of human activity. In the words of the CEO of IBM, Satya Nadella: 'Digital technology, pervasively, is getting embedded in every place: every thing, every person, every walk of life is being fundamentally shaped by digital technology – it is happening in our homes, our work, our places of entertainment. It's amazing to think of a world as a computer.'

How and why has this happened?

6.2 Digital Logic – the Brains of the System

Digital logic lies at the centre of the ICT paradigm. In analogue systems, measurement proceeds without interruption, as in the values 0, 1, 2, 3, 4, extending all the way through to infinity. By contrast, digital measures (often referred to as binary systems) are of a different order. Instead of a continuous indicator, they are based on the capacity to measure through a system of on/off indicators. So, if we think of a series of electronic 'gates', representing respectively the numbers 1, 2, 3 and 4, we can count to 10 by allowing electrons to pass through all of these 'gates'; we can count to 6 by opening the first three gates and to seven by opening the last two gates. This digital system allows for measuring values through the application of an *either–or* binary logical system.

In the same way that counting can be reduced to a series of either-or switches, so logical systems can be represented through a series of *yes–no* decisions. For example, I want to invite you to the cinema tonight. Step 1 – 'Are you free tonight?' If the answer is no, I close the conversation. If the answer is yes, 'Would you like to see Film A or Film B?' If the answer is Film A, 'Would you like to go to the show at 17:30, or 20:00?' And so on, and, depending on your proclivity, this may even extend to an agreement for an add-on dinner, with or without romantic candles and soft music, and who knows what lies beyond ... . So, even romantic and carnal bliss can be reduced to binary logic.

The heartland technology which dominates and drives the emerging post-Mass Production paradigm involves the application of this digital yes–no system to both measurement and decision-making. This system of counting and logic can be applied to virtually all representations of knowledge, including visual displays, music and other seemingly unrelated phenomena.

6.3 The Evolution of ICTs

The capacity of ICTs to transform economic and social relations follows from its phenomenal power to record information, to store information, to process information and to transmit and receive information.

The story begins with a series of inventions which occurred during the deployment period of the Mass Production paradigm. During the 1940s, binary logic had been used to calculate the trajectory of shells fired from artillery guns. These early computers were driven by thermionic valves. But valves were cumbersome, unreliable and consumed much energy. In 1947, Bell Laboratories in the US invented the transistor. This provided the ability to process a digital step electronically by allowing for or interrupting the flow of electrons. Unlike thermionic valves, these 'solid state' transistors supported binary logic systems without any moving parts. Subsequently, the integrated circuit (many transistor gates on a single device) was invented in 1958, and this was followed by the invention of program-mable circuitry (the microprocessor) in 1971. The primary raw material used to manufacture these devices – 'chips' – is silicon, derived from sand and in virtually unlimited supply. Building on these three key inventions, phenomenal progress was made in the capacity of electronic chips to record and store data, to communicate this data and to analyse its content.

How have these key inventions matured into a transformative heartland technology?

Data storage and communication

The ability to capture, record, communicate and use information is intrinsic to the survival and progress of virtually all species. For example, trees absorb changes in the natural environment, analyse these changes and then communicate the results to other trees through their root systems.[2] Other trees receiving this information then adjust their absorption of nutrients from the soil as a consequence of this information transfer. Notwithstanding this communication capability in trees and other species, the densest and most elaborate forms of data collection, communication and use are those between humans.

The first task in the effective use of information is to capture data. For many hundreds and thousands of years, humans absorbed data about their environment through their five senses. The primary instruments used to communicate this information were signs, sound and language. The development of writing around 3500 BC vastly improved the capacity of humans to record and communicate information. But this form of data-recording involved a laborious process and access was limited to a selective few. The invention of the printing press by Gutenberg in 1439 removed this constraint. The capacity of humans to record, store, and then to transmit information was transformed by this pathbreaking technology. His printing press made possible the repetitive production of written texts and allowed for a widening of access to information. The growth of literacy and numeracy in Western Europe allowed this flow of information to diffuse widely and was a necessary accompaniment to the Enlightenment, and then to the Industrial Revolution which began in the early eighteenth century.

Much of the data relevant to human activity involves the recording of change. For example, changes in heat, light, sound, pressure, magnetism, chemistry and motion are central to production processes. Change is also central to the functioning of the body, to the environment and to human emotions. The capacity to record these changes requires the development of sensors. Heat gauges measure the temperature of machines, water gauges the flow of water, and thermometers the temperature of the human body. Since the 1970s, miniaturized electronic components have transformed our capacity to monitor changes rapidly, accurately and cheaply. These sensors are able to withstand hostile environments. They are reliable and have the capacity to transform analogue readings (that is, values ranging from nought to infinity) to the binary signals that are the currency of digital logic systems.

A second recent and important development in data capture has seen the widespread use of bar codes. These provide for the identification and tagging of individual objects, for example individual components and finished products in manufacturing processes, individual items on supermarket shelves, dosages of medicine, airport boarding passes and domestic appliances. These bar code readings too are easily transformed into digital logic systems.

Following data capture, to be useful, recorded data has to be transmitted to other receptors so that effective responses can be identified and implemented. A key element in the advance of the Industrial Revolution was the invention of telegraphy in 1809. This provided a qualitative leap forward in the capacity to transmit information rapidly, cheaply and across large distances. More recently, an innovation of perhaps even greater significance was the invention in the early 1970s of the capacity to transmit data electronically. Electronic data interchange (EDI) rests on the ability to reduce logical and counting systems to binary logic and then to transmit this binary data rapidly and cheaply through the electricity network. Initially, this electrical transmission network depended on cabling, but increasingly digital information is being transferred very rapidly and cheaply through wireless networks. Developments in computing and the internet have led to sustained and significant reductions in the cost of data transfer, and increases in the speed of transmission and in the reliability of data interchange. It is this combination of electronic data-processing capability and the capacity to transmit these data electronically which defines the heartland technology known as Information *and* Communications Technology. This capacity to transfer data electronically is arguably as momentous and transformative as was the invention of the printing press by Gutenberg in 1439.

Having recorded and transmitted data, the challenge is then to store the data before it can be analysed and utilized effectively. Here, as in the case of sensing technologies, electronics provides the capacity for massive advances in the storage of data in digital form. As storage capabilities and user needs have altered, the locus of data storage has also experienced major changes. Until the end of the twentieth century, data storage was predominantly decentralized in individual computers and local computer networks. But over the past two decades, cloud computing has grown in importance. Here, data are transferred via the internet to and from the point of data capture and data use to centralized data storage facilities with massive storage capacity. Many of these data warehouses are targeted at the corporate sector. But cloud storage is not just a service provided to corporate customers. ICloud, Dropbox and Google Drive are widely used by individual consumers. The reason for this rapid growth of cloud computing is that it reduces the cost of storing and maintaining data. It also provides for a backup of data in case individual computer systems fail and, with suitable safeguards, enhances data privacy. Firms such as IBM and Amazon derive an increasing share of their revenues from cloud storage, and more than half of their revenues are currently generated from their cloud computing and related software services.

Computer-integrated and flexible production systems

The growing capacity to record data in detail, and to transmit these data seamlessly between different objects in different locations, depends on the adoption of the common currency of digital logic in both the objects sending and those receiving these data. Once this synergistic capability exists, there are enormous advantages to be reaped. Think for the moment of a factory consisting of a range of unconnected machinery lacking digital control systems. All of the instructions required to transfer the work-in-progress between workstations have to be recorded on paper or transmitted through verbal instructions. This requires a costly set of transcribing activities and meetings. But it is also prone to error in transcription or in the process of 'Chinese whispers' as instructions are relayed verbally between a range of workers. And then the individual machines have to be programmed or to be manually guided as they perform their tasks. If there is any alteration in the product, this requires the machines to be stopped as the controls are reset. And because these alterations are almost always a function of human input, they will inevitably often be imprecise. Contrast this with a system in which machines are linked together electronically, and where the instructions guiding the machinery are controlled using the same common currency of digital logic. Fewer workers are required, there is less scope for human error, machinery does not need to be stopped to change specifications, and much higher levels of precision are possible.

Thus the advantages of computer-integrated production systems are clearly very substantial in controlling production *within* individual factories. However, when the same principles are applied in the management of production *between* different factories, the advantages are multiplied. For, without the benefit of face-to-face communication within individual buildings and factories, the prospect of errors and delays in verbal and written communications between geographically separated facilities are increased. Moreover, with digital data and electronic controls, it makes virtually no difference whether the machines are next door or thousands of miles away in different countries. For example, in many global supply chains, design occurs in the head office and the specifications are fed seamlessly and directly to factories producing the product in emerging economies. As in the case of the advantages accruing within individual factories, digital logic and electronic controls not only enhance communication between machinery, but also significantly improve the flow of knowledge required to coordinate and control production and supply chains within and between factories and countries. Thus, it is not just in manufacturing that these integrated and connected databases provide massive benefits. Think of the manner in which our health data are stored and communicated. When we visit our doctor, she will have access not only to all of our past visits to her practice but to the data generated in our interactions with many other institutions in our health system – our visits to specialists, our immunization records, our blood-test and scan results and (increasingly) data fed to her by the electronic devices we wear recording our ongoing health status.

Over the past decade, a new and related technological development has emerged in manufacturing, which, as we will see below, has particularly important implications for the character of the post-Mass Production paradigm. This is known as 3D printing. Here, a design is transformed into a product by adding successive layers of an extruded raw material such as high-quality plastic resin or specialized metal to form single complex shapes. There is a key difference between this technology and traditional machinery. Over the centuries since the onset of the Industrial Revolution, machining involved a reduction in the size of raw materials. Metals and wood were cut into shape and drilled and then joined together. This involved a process of *subtractive* manufacturing. By contrast, 3D manufacturing builds up a product by adding successive layers to raw materials. For this reason, it is sometimes referred to as *additive* manufacturing.

This new technology has three particularly important advantages over traditional machining techniques. First, it saves on the use of inputs since there is no shedding of material. Second, it allows for the building of complex shapes. A product or a part which previously would have required the assembly of a number of different components can now be produced as a single integrated unit. For example – and with alarming consequences – handguns can now be produced in a single manufacturing operation from a design template fed by a computer (and now available as free software on the web). And, third, 3D printing provides for highly flexible production. Instead of producing an article in large numbers (in order to save the costs of changing machinery specifications), additive manufacturing allows for one-off production. The 3D printer can produce one or as many items as are required with little cost penalty.

The Internet of Things

The capacity of digital-logic electronic systems to facilitate the interconnection of machinery in factories applies equally to the interconnection of a whole range of everyday objects. This is referred to as the Internet of Things (IoT) and it is this development that provides what might be referred to as 'the lungs' of the emerging ICT techno-economic paradigm.

Electronic controls and sensors are embedded in products which capture and record data. This data is linked via the internet to other electronically controlled products and services and to large databases. An important frontier for the application of the IoT is what has come to be called 'the smart home'. For example, lighting fixtures, refrigerators, washing machines, heating systems, thermostats and home security systems can relay their performance and can be controlled at a distance. This allows homeowners to change their heating settings in their home, to observe who is in their houses, to switch appliances on and off and to record the food in their fridges from a distance. A major emerging arena for the diffusion of the IoT is in monitoring the human body. Electronic sensors monitor physical, and perhaps also emotional, states, and can feed this information into automated systems and to medical specialists. This data can assist with the monitoring of patient health and with treatment in emergencies. But, of course, the most widely used IoT device is the mobile phone. Mobile phones are connected digital-logic electronic systems and, by their nature, enable communication with other electronic devices and with databases. In 2020, there were more than 10 billion mobile connections globally and, if portable tablet computers are included, there were 14.2 billion connected mobile devices.[3] This compares with a global population of 7.6 billion.

Big Data and Artificial Intelligence

The spread of the IoT, and the capacity of the range of connected devices to sense, record, monitor and communicate data through the use of digital logic and electronic technologies at very detailed levels, have resulted in an avalanche of information. The detailed numbers of data generation, transmission and storage are mind-boggling and, of course, subject to considerable estimation errors. In 2017, IBM estimated that 90 per cent of all data recorded globally had been recorded in the previous two years. In the same year, it projected that, by 2020, the quantity of electronic data collected daily would be equivalent to more than 147,000 gigabytes for every person on the earth.[4] It is difficult to comprehend this number. But as a point of comparison, 1 gigabyte of memory will store more than 1,000 family pictures.

There have been increasing attempts to make productive use of this vast and rapidly increasing avalanche of data, which has come to be referred to as 'Big Data'. Big Data comprises datasets which are so large that their analysis cannot be undertaken by conventional software tools. The size of the challenge is enormous since the data needs to be tagged so that links between apparently unrelated databases can be identified to provide insights into non-obvious developments, to identify hidden trends and to search very large datasets to explore hypotheses.

Much of the data captured in very large databases is 'senseless' – that is, it is generated, stored, often transmitted and then is left fallow. The critical factor enabling the use of Big Data is the development of Artificial Intelligence (AI). AI involves machine-learning. That is, having analysed a given set of data, the 'machine' (generally an electronic device which submits instructions to people or other machines) makes decisions involving actions or inactions. And then, depending on the outcomes of these actions or on new data fed into the system, the machine automatically adjusts the decisions it makes in future actions. AI and machine-learning are often characterized as being unrelated to human intervention and therefore posing dangers to society and the environment. Whilst these dangers are evident, it is important to recognize that every AI application is inspired by a human-defined algorithm. This comprises a set of instructions given to the system which explains how data is to be analysed and what sets of actions are required.

Big Data and AI reflect both the frontier of ICTs development and a summation of the rewards accruing from their diffusion. Three brief examples of their use and impact illustrate the technology's disruptive potential. First, economists have traditionally measured the size of the economy through periodic surveys. But the data so collected is dated and uncertain, and estimations of economic performance are subject to frequent revision. Since a range of investment decisions and government expenditure are predicated on these estimates, these numbers are of considerable economic and policy performance. Big Data provides the capacity for real-time and accurate estimates of economic activity. It turns out that indicators such as the footfall in shopping centres and the number of large delivery trucks on particular highways are very accurate measures of activity in the whole economy.

Second, for the corporate sector, getting the right products to the customer when she needs them, without holding unnecessary and potentially unfashionable stocks, is the key to profitability. When suppliers are located across the globe and when products may take weeks to emerge from factories assembling components drawn from suppliers across the world, this is no simple task. An increasing number of large firms – and Amazon is currently the best example – have developed the capacity to analyse in detail minute changes in consumer behaviour in one product area and to link this with considerable accuracy to their propensity to consume in other areas. Walmart processes more than 20 million transactions a day from its point-of-sale terminals in the US, and uses this to control its stocking policies and to estimate forward orders.[5] And, finally, self-driving cars depend on the capacity to use massive datasets to pilot vehicles, and then to change the path and speed of the car depending on new data which is fed to each individual car. This enables the car to avoid unexpected dangers and to self-pilot around traffic jams.

6.4 Beyond Mass Production

So, the development of ICT technologies unquestionably satisfies the criteria for being a heartland technology. First, digital logic can be applied to a very wide range of social and economic activities. ICTs thus have pervasive uses. Second, there is abundant evidence in our daily lives and across the spectrum of recorded activities that ICTs not only reduce the costs of production but vastly improve the range of products which we can consume. Third, ICTs have benefitted from extraordinary cost reduction. As the demand for integrated circuits has grown, developments in their manufacture have resulted in very significant and sustained reductions in their costs (per binary decision-making capacity). With unrelenting progress, they have become also smaller, much faster with enhanced processing power and flexibility, and with improved reliability and a sharp reduction in energy consumption. An indication of these major, related technological advances is what has come to be called 'Moore's Law'. That is, that the capacity of microchips doubles every two years, with equivalent reductions in costs.

As an indication of the reduction in the price of electronic circuitry, the price of 1 gigabyte of memory fell from \$2m in 1956 to less than 2 cents in 2019.[6] Whereas the first chip in 1947 consisted of a single transistor, in 2017 a commercially available chip contained more than 50 billion transistors.[7] In 2020, a top-range smart phone incorporated more than 9.5 billion transistors.[8] Finally, since the basic building block of most of these electronic components is silicon (which makes up around a quarter of the earth's surface by weight), the raw material is in abundant supply. A major potential impediment to their production and use is that they depend on electricity but, as we shall see in later chapters, the rapid advance of renewable energy technology provides the capacity not just to increase the supply of energy but to do so without contributing to climate change, and in many cases at a lower cost than hydrocarbon-based and nuclear energy.

Given these heartland characteristics of ICTs, a few brief examples illustrate their transformative potential and their capacity to respond to the economic, social and environmental challenges which I documented in earlier chapters. I shall draw on these developments in Chapter 8 when I outline an agenda for building more sustainable futures.

.

ICTs provide the capacity to revive productivity growth

As we saw in Chapter 2, the rate of productivity growth – one of the major drivers of economic growth – fell in all of the high-income economies after the early 1970s. This resulted in large part (as we saw in Chapter 5) from the exhaustion of the benefits of mass production in the productive sector. This decay was caused by a number of factors. Initial productivity gains were delivered by the standardization of products. But, as time wore on, consumers wanted more variety. In the sphere of production, there were one-off and large initial benefits arising from the introduction of special-purpose large-volume machinery. But, after these early gains, the subsequent incremental changes in machinery generated smaller productivity benefits. Mass production required large-scale factories, and this in turn led to the increasing geographical separation of production and consumption. But, although taking advantage of cheaper labour in emerging countries enabled firms to reduce their costs and to improve or maintain their profitability, this did not improve underlying productivity. Moreover, global supply chains became increasingly unattractive because of the logistical costs of shipping components and products across geographically dispersed production facilities, the costs of the transport infrastructure and the riskiness of long-distance supply chains, particularly in an era of a global pandemic.

ICT-enabled flexible and integrated production systems offer the prospect of overcoming many of these constraints. New products and services provide the potential for sustained consumption (albeit of a different and more environmentally beneficial character). In the sphere of production, electronically controlled equipment such as robots and 3D machinery provide abundant opportunities for labour- and materials-saving technological change and for reducing material inputs. Similarly, so does the introduction of new forms of organization within and between firms. For instance, producers who had previously guessed what customers might want and produced-to-forecast are able to save inventories and reduce waste by making-to-order. ICTs offer scope to reduce scale in production, and thereby to reduce the transport and logistical costs of transferring products from the site of production to the final consumer. Many of these ICT-enabled technologies are at an early stage of their development and offer considerable improvements before their productivity enhancements will inevitably tail off, as has been the case in the transition into maturity in previous techno-economic paradigms.

ICTs provide the capacity for decentralized production, and thus for bringing residence, production and consumption closer together

Henry Ford's pioneering Model T production line in the early twentieth century required large production volumes to defray the high costs of the specialized equipment used to produce standardized products. Following the same logic, as globalization deepened from the early 1980s, very large factories – and whole towns and cities – were dedicated to the production of components and products for export to global markets. For example, 5,000 footwear firms in JinJiang in China employ more than 500,000 workers, and produce 20 per cent of global production of sports shoes and sneakers.[9] Much of the inputs, and almost all of the output, of these factories have to be transported large distances, often across national borders. The increasing separation of work and consumption was thus a central feature of the Mass Production paradigm.

The aggregation of large numbers of workers in a single location was not only driven by the adoption of costly specialized equipment. It also resulted from the need for extensive communication in the workplace. In manufacturing, the different divisions of a firm – strategy, design, production and marketing – need to exchange information frequently, and on an ongoing basis. Similarly, interpersonal communication is central to the functioning of government and the service sector (for example, healthcare and hospitality). In mass production, these information flows required face-to-face contact and this resulted in large factories and offices. The consequence of this pursuit of scale was that very large numbers of people commuted from home to their places of employment. Hence, it was not just that production and consumption became increasingly separated in the Mass Production paradigm, but so too did work and residence.

In an ICT-enabled post-Mass Production world, there is enhanced scope for decentralized production and smaller establishments. In the manufacturing sector, integrated and flexible machinery reduces the need for gigantic factories churning out standardized products which then need to be shipped to customers, often across vast distances. At its extreme, additive manufacturing allows for one-off production. Similarly, the combination of a network of smaller units and remote working can also substitute for large offices in the service sectors. These developments are made possible by the internet, which allows for the required information exchange without face-to-face contact.

The contribution which ICTs can make to more localized patterns of living and work were brought into sharp focus during the Covid-19 lockdowns. The pandemic resulted in a massive boost to remote working. This allowed firms, healthcare and other public services to continue to operate in an era of social distancing (although perhaps physical distancing is a more accurate phrase). While there were clearly costs to the erosion of face-to-face information exchange, it became clear that in many cases there was no deep need for people to work in physical proximity. It demonstrated the costs of path-dependency, of continuing to rely on organizational and work practices which had been developed to support the (now decaying) Mass Production techno-economic paradigm.

Bringing work, residence and consumption closer together contributes to better health and the strengthening of social and environmental sustainability. Studies have shown that the more time people spend commuting, the greater their propensity to catch influenza and other bugs, and the greater the levels of personal anxiety. Closer proximity between residence and work, and remote working, enable workers to spend more time with their families and in their communities. Moreover, during the pandemic lockdown, many people and firms discovered that remote working resulted not only in a happier workforce but, unexpectedly, also in new sources of worker creativity. And, perhaps most importantly in the current context, the greater proximity of residence, production and consumption provides considerable environmental benefits. The reshoring of production from distant economies will reduce the need for the air travel and shipping which are required to grease global supply chains. This extensive transport infrastructure is one of the major causes of climate change. Decentralized production and remote working will also slow, and perhaps even reverse, what has seemed an unstoppable trend towards increased urbanization, with its associated environmental and health costs.

*ICTs can provide the capacity to customize products to meet
individual needs*

The flexibility of ICTs provides the capacity for the mass customization of products and services. This offers major welfare benefits. One of the most graphic cases is personalized healthcare. This is of interest not just because of its obvious social impact, but also because it is largely outside the manufacturing sector where many of the ICT-related innovations are seen to be concentrated.

Traditionally, the delivery of healthcare was organized around the principles of mass production. Consumers were largely undifferentiated, pharmaceuticals were standardized and produced in bulk, and care was delivered in large hospitals. Personalized healthcare provides the capacity to transform this pattern of health provision. It is now recognized that different individuals respond in different ways to the same drug. Drug formulations therefore are most effective when they are tailored to the physiology of each individual and to the aetiology of each pathogen. These developments depend upon a detailed analysis of DNA in both individual patients and individual pathogens. Devices worn by the patient and connected to databases allow for the state of an individual's health to be monitored in real time. This enables diagnosis and the delivery of specific medical interventions on an up-to-the-minute basis. At the same time that large hospitals are specialized in particular health problems, decentralized polyclinics improve healthcare at the local level. In addition, there is considerable scope for the optimization of hospital organization and treatment regimes through data-based analysis of staff deployment, medicines and patients.

These developments transforming healthcare are all driven by ICTs. The equipment used in DNA analysis and the development of personalized pharmaceuticals are all heavily dependent on electronic sensors, large computerized databases and AI. The real-time monitoring of individual health states depends on Big Data, computer-integrated health records and electronically controlled IoT devices such as 'intelligent' wrist-watches. And not only do polyclinics depend on integrated databases, but the cost of specialized equipment is falling as electronic controls become cheaper and more sophisticated. So it is not surprising that pharmaceutical firms are increasingly collaborating with major software companies to exploit the power of Big Data and AI in drug development and personalized medicines. In the first half of 2019, Sanofi and Google partnered to develop a 'virtual innovation lab' to aid new drug development; Eli Lilley invested $550 million in a joint venture with AI firm AtomWise to speed up drug discovery; and Verily, the health unit in Google's parent company Alphabet, joined with Novartis, Otsuka, Pfizer and Sanofi to accelerate clinical testing using digital technology.[10]

What more graphic example of the central role played by ICTs in the health sector can there be than the world's frantic attempt to cope with and overcome the Covid-19 pandemic? The detection of the virus, the rapid sequencing of its genome in Wuhan, the transmission of this data and the equipment required to test whether patients currently have, or have had, Covid-19 all depended centrally on ICTs. So too does the ability to contain the spread of the virus – for example, through test, track and trace, and through mobile phone apps. And each of the more than 150 attempts to develop a Covid-19 vaccination requires ICTs to analyse natural organisms, to synthesize elements and, perhaps most importantly, to allow the scientific and corporate community to collaborate across disciplines and geographical space.

ICTs can provide the capacity for shared, rather than individualized, consumption, and for repairable rather than throwaway products

The growth of mass consumption after 1950, aided by an explosion of spending on advertising, resulted in a frenzy of individualized consumption. Products were designed to have short lives, to rapidly become unfashionable and to be discarded after use. In this environment – at least in the high-income economies – the repairability and reuse of products was generally unthinkable. As I showed in Chapter 4, this has had disastrous impacts on the environment.

One of the most glaring examples of these trends was in personalized transport, specifically in the form of the automobile. As we saw in earlier chapters, the automobile was central to the development and diffusion of the Mass Production paradigm. During the Golden Age of the paradigm's evolution in the 1950s and 1960s, cars were deliberately designed to have a limited life, and components were designed to be thrown away rather than to be repaired. Internal combustion engines spewed out a combination of climate-damaging emissions which were harmful to human health. Many of the improvements made in the efficiency of internal combustion engines were eroded by building costly new features into ever larger cars. And taking advantage of technological advances (for example, in the improved energy efficiency of the internal combustion engine) required the discarding of a well-functioning and usable car and its replacement with a new vehicle. Perhaps most damaging, most of this materials-intensive stock of automobiles was unused. In 2018, the average car in the USA was parked for 95 per cent of the time.

The incorporation of ICTs in the manufacture and in the controls of cars has the capacity to mitigate these negative environmental characteristics. Greener production systems reduce emissions during manufacture. The development of automated self-driving (or driver-assisted) cars reduces the attraction of personal ownership of individual vehicles, and Uber, Lyft and other car-sharing schemes allow for a much greater utilization of cars. Car ownership thus becomes socialized rather than individualized. Electric-powered cars have a much less harmful environmental impact than autos powered by internal combustion engines. Moreover, electric cars can be remotely reprogrammed to take advantage of technological innovations. There will consequently be a much reduced need to scrap cars as new technologies are developed. This reprogrammable capacity of electric cars will be an important future development and is not pure fantasy. The strategy was pioneered by Tesla which makes frequent use of software updates, and has been adopted by the world's largest car producer, Volkswagen. The principle of upgrading product performance through software updates is not limited to cars and mobile phones. It applies equally to other electronically controlled equipment such as household appliances and machine controls.

ICTs can enhance the capacity for greener production systems, and for the development of renewable energy

In Chapter 8, we will see how 'smart' (that is ICT-enabled) green growth provides the capacity for the renewal of sustainable economic growth. On the production side of the equation, the more efficient transformation of inputs into outputs depends on the ability to monitor processes accurately in real time, reliably and at low cost. In addition, incremental improvements in process require the continual adjustment of equipment. These improvements in what we called 'relative dematerialization' in Chapter 4 are made easier if the machines are electronically controlled. The optimization of workflow and the reduction in the carbon footprint within – and especially between – factories depends on the internet, computer algorithms and the diffusion of integrated production systems. The design of new 'green products' and shared-use and reusable products depends not only on the use of ICTs in the design and controls of these products, but also on IoT and extensive peer-to-peer communication.

A particularly important contribution to environmental sustainability is the substitution of renewable energy for fossil fuels. ICTs play a central role in the development of these green energy systems. To be safe, solar panels require AC and DC isolators; inverters adjust to variable energy generation; the junction box which allows for the integration of multiple panels is an assembly of electronic components. In wind power, ICTs are critical to the sensors which monitor the yaw of the blades, imbalances in rotors and rotor damage. They are also at the heart of the inverters and transformers which feed current into the grid. At a systemic level, the integration of multiple energy sources in the national grid, and the control and distribution of electricity, depend heavily on electronic control systems. So too do the smart meters in the home and AI-enabled thermostats which contribute to energy efficiency.

ICTs provide for peer-to-peer communication that enhances civil society

As we have seen, the most widely diffused IoT object is the mobile phone. Unlike previous generations of telephony which allowed for one-to-one verbal communication, the mobile phone enables the connection of very large numbers of people. It also allows for simultaneous interchanges through voice, text and pictures. And it does this at a low and descending cost, with distance often being irrelevant to the form and nature of the communication.

Much of the attention given to the social and political consequences of interconnectivity has focused on its capacity to degrade social cohesion and to strengthen the power of the powerful. The use of Facebook and other social media for the distortion of electoral processes in the US and Europe was chronicled in Chapter 3. But, despite these nefarious abuses of mobile connectivity, peer-to-peer communication has multiple benefits that promote social solidarity and social sustainability. These features enable parents to keep track of the welfare of their children and to alert friends and relatives to emerging problems. Social media also provide warning of advancing environmental hazards, such as tsunamis and storms. In May 2019, smartphones and social media were used to alert residents to advancing tornadoes in Dayton, USA, limiting personal injuries and deaths. Smartphones have been widely used in social protest movements, such as the Arab Spring in 2010 and in Hong Kong in 2019. The rapid viral spread of the #MeToo movement against sexual harassment is a further testament to the power of social media to mobilize civil society movements. 'Speaking truth to power', the clarion call of protest movements over the world, depends literally on the capacity provided by ICTs to 'speak' and to be 'heard'. As one of the leaders of the democracy protestors in Hong Kong observed in a letter to the *Financial Times* in 2019:

> pro-democratic lawmakers stayed on the frontline to monitor any unlawful use of power by the policemen, while at the back netizens live-streamed and texted to ensure the supply of water, umbrellas and medicine. There was also a digital frontline. Forum members voiced their thoughts on strategy, others voted up or down and followed up with actionable next steps. Members also created infographics to help rebut any unfounded accusations in a timely manner. Within a few hours, over HK$5m was raised in a member-initiated campaign for front-page international newspaper ads ahead of the G20 meeting.[11]

6.5 Not Just Roses, Also Weeds in the Garden

The transformative potential of a heartland technology has both a positive and a negative side. Indeed, this was a key insight in Schumpeter's metaphor of 'gales of creative destruction' which sweep away what have been viable enterprises and jobs and replace them with new firms, new technologies, new products, new skills and new jobs. So far in this chapter, I have focused on the bright side of the diffusion of ICTs. But there is of course also a dark side, as some examples show.

The first example is cybercrime. This operates over the internet and depends on the interconnectivity of devices (computers and mobile phones) – that is, the IoT. This interconnectivity is supported by a host of ICT-enabled systems, including cryptocurrencies such as Bitcoins (which make it impossible to verify the recipients of stolen funds) and the dark web (which enables malign actors to communicate in absolute privacy). The scale of cybercrime is astonishing.[12] A report by McAfee (a firm specializing in the control of cybercrime) estimated that its economic costs rose from \$400 billion in 2013 (0.62 per cent of global GDP) to \$600 billion in 2016 (0.8 per cent of global GDP). However, cybercrime is in its infancy. It still predominantly consists of interventions guided by human beings. But what will happen when 'advances' in Artificial Intelligence and machine-learning are applied to the cybercrime industry? Not only will this lead to the development of novel forms of crime, but when these systems are freed from human control, they may become unstoppable and increasingly damaging to the economic and social fabric, and to the environment.

A second alarming application of ICTs is the development of automated weaponry. Weapons based on Artificial Intelligence and machine-learning are increasingly being provided with the capacity to 'learn' from experience, to adjust their responses to perceived threats automatically, and then, crucially, to take action independent from human control. For example, in both China and the US, military strategists are calling for swarms of armed drones to patrol the skies, with the capacity to launch attacks without human guidance.

Third, as we saw in Chapter 3, the invasion of privacy through the harvesting of personal data has provided fodder for businesses to shape our consumption patterns and to enhance the capacity of the plutocracy to steer the policy agenda and to undermine democratic processes. The analysis of very large datasets and the application of AI algorithms enabled Cambridge Analytica to play what seems to have been a transformative role in the election of Donald Trump in 2016, in the UK Brexit Referendum and in elections in an alarmingly large number of countries.

And, finally, there is the impact of ICTs on employment. The potential of robots to substitute for human labour is clear. Think, for example, of the pictures of serried ranks of uniformed assembly workers inserting silicon chips onto printed circuit boards in the factories of Foxconn, which employs more than 1 million workers in China. Faced with the capacity of robots to do the same work cheaply and efficiently, Foxconn committed to introducing 1 million robots in its Chinese plants. A widely cited study in 2017 by two researchers from Oxford University predicted that, in a worst-case scenario, 47 per cent of jobs in the US were at risk as a consequence of the diffusion of robotized automation and Artificial Intelligence.[13] For example, 9 million people in the US are employed in the transport sector, and the roll-out of automated vehicles threatens a great many of these jobs. It is not just the number of jobs that will be radically affected, but also the skill profile of employment. An OECD study estimated that the major area of job displacement will be in low-skilled work and the work performed by younger workers. Around 20 per cent of workers below 20 in the OECD economies work in these threatened jobs.[14] AI is now also challenging the work of a variety of skill-intensive tasks. Many professional jobs are subject to automation, including in the legal profession and in medical diagnosis.

I am acutely aware of the potential for a 'dark side' to triumph in the development and diffusion of ICTs, as is evidenced in these examples. I will argue in the final two chapters that we are at a crossroads, and 'directionality' is critical. Which fork in the road will we hurtle along? One direction will take us to a more sustainable world; the other is the road to environmental disaster and prolonged economic and social unsustainability. Thus, we need to steer the ICT techno-economic paradigm in a direction which builds sustainable futures. This requires a focus on both maximizing the potential for generating beneficial outcomes and minimizing the malevolent use of ICTs to promote war, to deepen inequality and to extend environmentally damaging overconsumption.

In this book, I have chosen to argue the case for the positive, and to explore what is required to deliver more sustainable outcomes. In the final chapter, I discuss what political and economic coalitions this may require. Focusing on the potential for building sustainability may be a panglossian idyll. But at least it provides us with a sense of optimism, and a roadmap for action. It may be a hard struggle, but the underlying character of the ICT heartland technology provides abundant scope for more beneficial outcomes. So let's go forward in a positive direction. In the following chapter, I offer three case-studies which illustrate the transformative potential of ICTs for building a more economically, socially and environmentally sustainable future. Each of these case-studies exemplifies the systemic interactions which are characteristic of techno-economic paradigm shifts.

7
Transformative Change in Practice

In the two previous chapters, I described the historical significance of Information and Communication Technologies and argued that their widespread deployment offers us the opportunity to build a more sustainable world.

In Chapter 5, I recounted how a limited number of heartland technologies have had a major disruptive impact on the course of economic and social sustainability since the Industrial Revolution. Heartland technologies offer dramatic improvements in cost and performance; their price is on a falling trajectory and consumers have the expectation that this will continue in the future; they have application across the full range of economic and social relations; and there are no limitations to their supply. So significant are these attributes that they have a transformative impact on the economy, on society and on the environment. Technology, economy and society co-evolve in waves (sometimes referred to as surges) of approximately five to six decades.

In Chapter 6, I described how ICTs, the most recent heartland technology, were invented during the heyday of the Mass Production paradigm, and how they helped to stave off the atrophy of Mass Production by extending the paradigm to the global level. I also offered some insights into why ICTs are economically, socially and environmentally transformative. They have the capacity to revive economic growth. By enabling decentralized production, they can be applied to serve to bring production, consumption and residence closer together. They allow for the customization of products to meet the needs of different types of consumers. They facilitate shared use, and thus reduce the environmental impact of mass consumption. They provide scope for the greening of production. And they provide the potential to strengthen civic participation.

In this chapter, I present three case-studies to illustrate the transformative potential of the new ICT techno-economic paradigm. The first of these cases is already 'mature' – mobile telephony has had a demonstrable transformative societal impact in Kenya and other low- and middle-income economies. The second example – small-scale distributed renewable power generation – will illustrate how different the world might look now if ICT-enabled technologies had been available at a time when large-scale 'mass production' hydroelectric dams were constructed. The third case-study – precision farming – describes the transformative potential of new technologies which are beginning to have an impact in the agricultural sector. As we will see, to a greater or lesser extent all of these characteristics of a heartland technology are evidenced in each of the three case-studies.

7.1 Mobile Telephones Transform the Financial Sector and Facilitate Economic and Social Inclusion

One of the most important arenas of innovation in ICTs has been the development of mobile telephony. This not only provides low-cost access to verbal communications and to the transfer of data, but does so in a manner which transforms the communications infrastructure. The fixed-line telephones which revolutionized communications after the late nineteenth century operated through a centralized and hard-wired grid. This required the construction of costly transmission lines, and this often excluded poor, isolated and distant consumers from access to communication channels. By contrast, mobile telephony provides access on a much more distributed scale, without the need for costly hard-wired interconnections.

Mobile telephony has spread with extraordinary speed. As we saw in the previous chapter, there are now currently more than 4.3 billion mobile phones in use. And, since many phones serve a number of users, there are an even larger number of individual connections. As Figure 7.1 shows, in the high-income countries, the number of connections now exceeds one per inhabitant. (Many users have more than one account.) In developing countries, in 2018, there were more than 60 accounts per 100 inhabitants, fewer than in developed

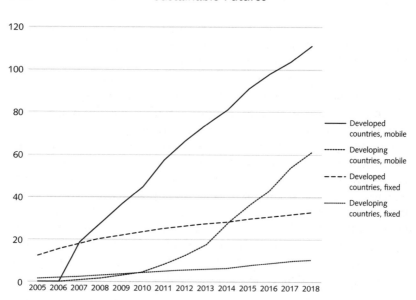

Figure 7.1 Broadband connections per 100 inhabitants, 2005–2018
Source: data from International Telecommunications Union

economies, but nevertheless evidencing a substantial pattern of connectivity. By contrast, the equivalent figures for fixed-line phones were 61 and 10, respectively.

Mobile phones have promoted financial inclusion and renewable energy in Kenya

Mobile phones were introduced in Kenya after the mid-1990s. The number of subscriptions grew rapidly, comprising over half of the adult population by 2003. A number of foreign firms, including Vodaphone from the UK (operating through a Kenyan subsidiary, Safaricom), invested early in this rapidly expanding market. Responding to the desire to promote the Millennium Development Goals (MDGs), the UK's aid agency made a grant to Safaricom to develop a mobile phone app to promote access to financial transfers for low-income citizens. M-Pesa was launched in 2007, under the banner 'Send Money Home'. ('Pesa' means 'money' in Swahili.) It was designed to facilitate money transfers from the largely urban-based formal sector to family members in rural areas. Subscriptions grew rapidly. By 2013, the number of Safaricom M-Pesa customers had grown fifteen-fold, from 1.7 million to 17 million users. By 2017, Safaricom was no longer the only company providing mobile banking services. With the entrance of other providers, the number of users of mobile banking had grown to 26.2 million. Transferring money in small transactions is a labour-intensive operation. By 2017, 17,000 money agents were involved, significantly exceeding the combined numbers of all other forms of financial service providers (Postbanks, post offices, bank branches and ATMs).

Critically, the development of M-Pesa was made possible through changes in the regulatory environment. The initial response of the formal banking system to the disruption posed by mobile finance was hostile. The four largest banks lobbied the Minister of Finance to stop its diffusion, accusing M-Pesa, *inter alia*, of being a Ponzi scheme and facilitating fraudulent transfers. The Kenya Bankers Association called for an audit of mobile banking, and for it to be incorporated within the existing banking legislation. Fortuitously, albeit in difficult circumstances, politics intervened – every cloud has a silver lining. In 2007, there was a wave of post-election violence which crippled much of the economy and led to the shut-down of the formal banking sector. This was a boon to M-Pesa since mobile money transfer was unaffected by the closure of physical establishments. The Kenyan Central Bank quickly recognized this and other advantages of mobile banking. It thus resisted the pressures exerted by the formal banks to limit M-Pesa, although a number of new regulatory measures were introduced to protect the mobile banking sector from money-laundering and related potential problems.

M-Pesa has contributed to economic growth and sustainability in Kenya.[1] It has deepened the monetary economy and facilitated the transfer of money from savers to investors. But it has also made a major contribution to social sustainability by promoting the inclusion of rural inhabitants, women and the poor. Some examples make these impacts clear. Within two years of M-Pesa's launch, 50 per cent of M-Pesa users were previously unbanked households. The rate of uptake of mobile banking has been highest in low-income households, and the proportion of households completely excluded from financial intermediation fell from 41 per cent in 2006 to 17 per cent in 2016. An important transformative characteristic has been that a high proportion of users are women, live in rural areas and are relatively less well educated. Reflecting the character of this customer base, mobile banking is predominantly used for small payments. Although in 2014 it accounted for only 7 per cent of total national payments value, this comprised two-thirds of total financial transactions. Additional non-monetary benefits were that access to M-Pesa credit allowed poor households to withstand variable financial flows, and that a reduction in holdings of physical cash reduced the incidence of mugging and robbery.

Mobile money has grown rapidly in economies which are poorly served by the traditional banking sector and which have large numbers of rural residents who have traditionally been excluded from the financial system. In Kenya, where mobile money was pioneered, by 2019, 58 per cent of adults had mobile finance accounts. In Uganda, Tanzania and Somalia, the equivalent figure was 35 per cent, and it was 20 per cent in Sub-Saharan Africa as a whole. This contrasts with a global average of a mere 1 per cent. M-Pesa has now diffused to a number of other economies, including Egypt, Lesotho, Mozambique and South Africa in Africa, Afghanistan and India in Asia, and Romania and Albania in Eastern Europe.

Social inclusion through access to renewable energy

The success of M-Pesa as a cheap and accessible form of money transfer has begun to have an impact on other sectors, illustrating the systemic character of ICTs. As in the case of finance, access to cheap energy also plays a transformative role in the lives of the poor. The capacity to recharge mobile phones provides households, even in remote regions, with access to the external world, and availability of cheap electricity improves the storage of food and enables children to do their homework. A South African study some years ago estimated that reading by electric lights is more than 180 times cheaper than using candles.

In 2011, one of the developers of M-Pesa combined with two colleagues to establish M-Kopa. M-Kopa uses the ubiquity and cheapness of M-Pesa to market renewable solar energy technology. It targets poor and rural households who do not have access to the main electricity grid, and provides far cheaper energy to small-scale users than does the large grid. Users are offered a set of packages which they can either purchase in a one-off transaction or pay off over a year or more via their mobile phones. In mid-2019, M-Kopa customers could purchase a 1.8W solar panel plus four LED bulbs, a rechargeable LED torch, a rechargeable radio and a phone charger cable for a lump-sum payment of $186. Alternatively, the same package was available with a downpayment of $30 and a further payment – paid through M-Pesa – of $0.50 per day for 14 months. A 30W system (powerful enough to drive a refrigerator as well) came with a 24-inch colour TV, and cost $540, or a deposit of $60 plus a daily payment of $1 for 20 months.

Take-up was rapid, and by 2018 there were more than 400,000 household customers in Kenya, Tanzania and Uganda, and a further 500,000 M-Kopa sets on order. By then, 100,000 of the larger solar panels, which provide access to solar TV, had been assembled in Kenya. M-Kopa is installing the capacity also to assemble the smaller panels domestically. Although the value added in its manufacturing activities was limited, employment was created domestically, including for engineers and technicians. There is also scope for deepening local content as volumes grow.

Mobile telephony and techno-economic paradigms

So how does this story of mobile telephony in Kenya (and then subsequently in other low- and middle-income countries) illustrate the transformative and systemic character of ICTs? First, beginning with the requirements of a heartland technology – mobiles offer a combination of new and cheaper forms of communication; their price has fallen (although many consumers prefer to pay more and to 'upgrade' to more powerful devices); they have ubiquitous uses (not just for social interaction, but also for transferring and storing money, for marketing agricultural produce, for obtaining agricultural extension services and for promoting the diffusion of small-scale renewable energy); and there are few limits to their supply.

Second, they have played an important role in fostering economic, social and environmental sustainability. Mobiles play an invaluable role in economic and productivity growth in agricultural production and in small-scale manufacturing and trading. They provide access to inputs, knowledge and customers. In the social sphere, mobiles have strengthened social inclusion, facilitated the transfer of money from high-income urban areas to low-income rural outposts, allowed families to keep in touch with distant friends and relatives, and supported threatened individuals and communities in times of conflict. In contrast to large-scale fixed-line telephony, mobiles support economic activity and social life in distant areas formerly cut off from effective communication with the outside world, and help to diminish the geographically centralizing trajectory of economic growth. Their contribution to environmental sustainability is evidenced by the role which they play in the dissemination of renewable energy. In each of these cases, there is an interconnection between the contributions of mobile telephony to economic, social and environmental sustainability – sustainability is simultaneously strengthened in each of these spheres of activity.

Finally, the disruptive character of this revolutionary technology is evidenced in the attempts made by the formal banking sector to limit its diffusion. It required decisive and visionary policies by government to overcome the fetters to change emanating from large-scale financial firms that had previously dominated financial intermediation in Kenya.

7.2 Renewable Energy, Large Dams and Hydroelectric Power

As we saw in Chapter 5, the techno-economic paradigm preceding Mass Production was driven in large part by the diffusion of electricity. Electric power was much cheaper than water- and steam-powered energy. Moreover, because of the numerous and diverse sources of its inputs (coal, and then oil and gas), it was in effectively unlimited supply. It thus met all the conditions of being a heartland technology. Although more than 150 years have passed since the introduction of electricity, cheap electric power remains a core technology in the twenty-first century. The organization of society today – both production and consumption – is unthinkable without the pervasive availability of electricity. The rapidly deploying ICT techno-economic paradigm is a copious user of electricity too, so the centrality of electricity to economic and social activity will endure for many decades to come.

Historically, fossil fuels have been the primary energy-generating source of electricity. But, although they continue to play a dominant role, they are not the only source. Amongst the alternatives are nuclear power, hydroelectric power and a cluster of smaller-scale renewables such as wind, solar power and biomass. Although the share of hydroelectricity in global power generation declined after 1970, it remains a significant contributor. It accounted for more than

15 per cent of global commercial energy production in 2014 (Figure 7.2), and is a disproportionately important source of power in many low- and middle-income economies.

Hydroelectric power can be generated at both a small-scale 'micro-hydro' level and at a large scale. Although, in some cases, large-scale hydroelectricity is produced by tapping the rapid flow of large rivers, invariably it relies on very large dams as a source of water-driven energy. The investments required for these large hydro projects are very significant. For example, the Grand Ethiopian Renaissance Dam commissioned in 2020 cost more than $4.8 billion (excluding the cost of transmission lines), equivalent to 5 per cent of Ethiopia's total GDP. Because of the size and complexity of these very large hydroelectric projects, cost and construction-time over-runs are the norm, and typically are even greater than in the case of nuclear power stations, and are many times greater than those in renewable power schemes (Figure 7.3).

Hydroelectric schemes offer many benefits to society. They provide long-life and low-priced electricity. They often also harness river flows for agricultural irrigation. Thus, large-scale hydro dams can

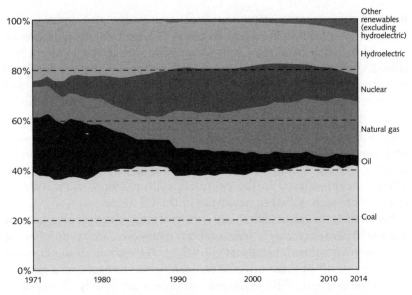

Figure 7.2 The global share of different energy sources, 1971–2014
Source: Our World in Data (https://ourworldindata.org/energy)

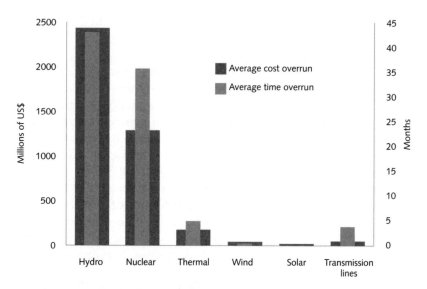

Figure 7.3 Frequency and cost escalation of electricity infrastructure projects (based on analysis of 411 projects)
Source: data courtesy of Benjamin Sovacool

have a transformative impact on local economies, and, indeed, they were a key element in President Roosevelt's New Deal Program which rescued America from the Great Depression during the 1930s. Their construction provides employment and presents a market for local industry. They provide electricity to cities, industries and mines, and support economic growth. The electricity they generate literally lights up the lives of many citizens, including some of the poor. Alternative carbon-based electricity has disastrous environmental costs and also undermines social and environmental sustainability. For example, beyond driving climate change, coal-mining is polluting and has adverse health effects. In the twentieth century, more than 100,000 coal miners were killed in accidents in the US alone.[2]

Nevertheless, large dams are not without their problems. Set against hydroelectricity's low carbon emissions are a number of adverse environmental impacts (Box 7.1). Whilst not all dams suffer from any or all of these adverse environmental impacts, as a general rule some or most of these adverse outcomes are widely observed.

The net contribution of large-scale hydroelectricity to economic sustainability is open to question. The construction of these dams

Box 7.1 Negative Impact of Large Dams

- Around 400,000 km^2 of land worldwide has been submerged due to the construction of dams.
- In flat basins, large dams can cause flooding of large tracts of land, destroying wildlife and fauna and altering local habitats.
- Large amounts of plant life are submerged and decay anaerobically (in the absence of oxygen), generating greenhouse gases such as methane.
- The migratory patterns of river animals like salmon and trout are affected.
- Dams can restrict sediments that are responsible for the fertile lands downstream. Farmers respond by using chemical fertilizers and pesticides to compensate for the loss in productivity.
- Large dams are frequently breeding grounds for mosquitoes, and cause the spread of malaria and other diseases such as bilharzia.
- Farmers downstream who used to wait for the flooding of the fields to plant their seeds are affected. Although dams can mitigate the harmful consequences of periodic flooding, when they exceed peak capacity or fail, there can be devastating consequences for downstream residents.
- Dams serve as a heat sink. The water is hotter than the normal river water. When released into the river downstream, warm water can affect animal life.
- Although hydroelectric power is 'green' in that it substitutes for fossil fuels such as coal and oil, dam construction involves a great deal of heavy fossil-fuelled transport. Dam construction also uses very large quantities of cement, which is a major source of greenhouse gases. Cement production is responsible for approximately 10 per cent of total global carbon dioxide emissions.
- Although built for long lives, large hydro schemes require costly maintenance. In 2019, more than half of existing dams had either required or were due for significant repair and upgrading.

Source: www.internationalrivers.org/environmental-impacts-of-dams

takes many years and involves tying up large quantities of valuable finance for a long period before the economic returns can be reaped. Many dams become heavily silted with soil runoffs from agriculture and operate well below their notional levels of capacity. In some cases, drought reduces the capacity of these dams to operate efficiently and, given that these large fixed dam structures are by their nature immovable, climate change threatens to reduce further their economic viability. In addition, the economic efficiency of large hydro energy generation is reduced because between 7 and 14 per cent of generated power is lost in the distribution of power in large centralized grid systems.[3] The longer the transmission lines, the greater the loss of power. Moreover, as can be seen from Box 7.1, many of the negative environmental costs of large dams are not included in the price charged to consumers. So the relatively low price of hydroelectricity to the consumer seldom equates to its low cost.

Large hydroelectricity dams also challenge social and political sustainability and reflect the social and political character of the Mass Production techno-economic paradigm. This centralizes, at scale, the production of energy and then distributes it over long distances via the grid. Because of the high cost of building the transmission grid, it ideally supports the geographical concentration of users, and large rather than small users. The land required for the dams is extensive, and local populations have invariably to be relocated. In many low- and middle-income countries, these relocated populations are poor and politically powerless, and their needs are inadequately met. Large-scale hydro requires massive investments and provides fertile opportunities for corrupt purchasing, reinforcing the inequality of power and income. The massification of economic power is not just a phenomenon at the purchasing side of the equation, since large-scale hydro also involves very large construction firms supported by their governments and aid agencies. In recent years, Chinese state-owned construction firms have been particularly active in building large hydro dams in Asia, Africa and Latin America. For example, the large Grand Ethiopian Renaissance Dam was funded in large part by Chinese loans. In 2016, China promoted the establishment of the Asian Infrastructure Investment Bank to support its global Belt and Road programme.

As a result of the large environmental footprint of large dams, their construction is often accompanied by widespread opposition from adversely affected groups, and sometimes the degree of popular opinion is sufficient to abort these mega projects. For example, the proposed $3.6 billion Myitsone Dam in Myanmar would have been the fifteenth-largest hydro power station in the world, generating 6,000 MW of electricity. It was to be a joint venture between the China Power Investment Company (one of the five largest Chinese state-owned electricity companies) and the Myanmar government. Most of the power would be exported to China. However, the dam would have flooded 447 square kilometres and 47 villages, and would have submerged historical temples, churches and heritage sites. It would also have had a devastating cultural impact on the Kachin communities who would have been most affected. Further, it was only 60 miles from the Sagaing earthquake fault line. Despite the power of an authoritarian military government, the opposition to the dam was so vocal that the project was suspended.[4] Similarly, following vocal opposition, in March 2020 the Cambodian government announced that it would cease the construction of new hydro dams on the Mekong Delta for at least the coming decade.

The adverse socio-political consequences of large-scale hydro are not confined to individual countries, but are also a source of geo-political tensions. Large dams concentrate water for use in the country which builds the dam, at the cost of downstream users in other countries. For example, the Grand Ethiopian Renaissance Dam will affect the flow of the Nile River as it passes through Sudan and Egypt. This has already become a source of tension and raises risks of future conflict between these countries.

The impact of large hydro in the Zambesi River basin

By its nature, large-scale hydroelectricity has a massive societal impact and illustrates the systemic interaction between economic, social and environmental sustainability. This is illustrated in the case of large-scale hydro in the Zambezi Valley in southern and central Africa. The Zambezi River makes its way from the western region of southern Africa to the Indian Ocean on the east coast. It is Africa's fourth-largest river and flows for 1,600 miles through six countries – Zambia, Angola, Namibia, Botswana, Zimbabwe and Mozambique (Figure 7.4). The river has been used to power the very large Kariba and Cahora Bassa hydroelectricity dams, as well as two smaller dams.

The Kariba Dam divided two former British colonies (then Southern and Northern Rhodesia, now Zimbabwe and Zambia).

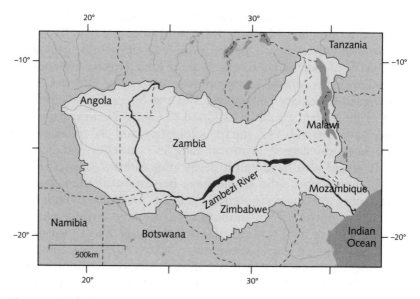

Figure 7.4 The Zambezi river basin

It was constructed during the 1950s and 1960s to meet the needs of urban and industrial sectors in both countries, and the mining sector in what was then Northern Rhodesia. The first stage, with a capacity of 705 MW, was built during the 1950s. The second stage was completed in the 1970s. This provided an additional 610-MW capacity. Although 'small' in comparison to megaprojects such as the suspended Myitsone Dam in Myanmar (6,000 MW) and the recently completed Grand Ethiopian Renaissance Dam (6,000 MW), Kariba was very large in the African context at the time of construction. It not only provided abundant energy, but also reduced the price of power significantly. Between 1961 and 1977, the general price index in Northern and Southern Rhodesia rose by more than 75 per cent, but the price of electricity fell by 30 per cent.

This impressive provision of low-cost energy predominantly benefitted high-income and large-scale users. But the costs were borne by the local population and the environment, as some examples illustrate.[5] The expanded water base extended the spread of predator tiger fish and crocodiles, which had previously been confined to the Zambezi's primary channel. The potential for expanding the commercial fishing industry had been recognized early in the dam's development. But, despite the intention to develop small-scale and artisanal fishing, in both economies the governments favoured large-scale expatriate firms. The development of the tourism industry reflected a similar trajectory of verbal commitments to inclusion, but with the resources and opportunities allocated to large-scale and foreign firms. On the Zimbabwe side, the river frontage was extended to 5 km, making way for national parks and hunting concessions. This required the resettlement of 23,000 people some distance from their previous livelihoods. In Zambia, the prime land was allocated to an expatriate who used paramilitary forces to drive out the indigenous population. He subsequently stocked the land with elephants, which frequently foraged on local crops.

An additional unanticipated consequence of the construction of the Kariba Dam, and the downstream Cahora Bassa dam, was that the enhanced water control offered by the dams led local inhabitants to move closer to the river. Ironically, this made them more vulnerable to flooding, due to water releases at times of high rainfall. In 2000, this flooding affected 635,000 people in Mozambique, 180,000 of whom were forced into emergency shelters. Finally, a striking feature of this investment in large-scale hydroelectricity is that it still did not provide energy for the mass of the population. In 2016, only 28 per cent of the Zambian population had access to electricity, and those excluded were predominantly out of the reach of the centralized electricity grid.[6]

In technical terms, many of these adverse impacts arising from the Kariba Dam could have been mitigated. However, in reality, large dams are coterminous with the concentration of power which serves the interests of the political and economic elite, as seen in the case of the fishing and tourism sectors. Thus, in principle, the resettled populations could have been relocated in ways which were developmentally beneficial. But in reality, their interests were over-ridden. Here the World Bank was complicit. The Report which it used to justify its loans for the Kariba Dam referred to the need to resettle 29,000 people. The real number was 57,000.

Large dams also support irrigation

Large dams do not just provide power. They are also often linked to large-scale irrigation systems. Irrigation is an important driver of agricultural production and rural incomes, and can make an important positive contribution to economic growth. Notwithstanding their contribution to economic sustainability, large dam-fed irrigation schemes have characteristically undermined social sustainability. In 1996, the World Bank reviewed its experience with the funding of fifty large dams, with an installed generation capacity of 39,000 MW and providing irrigation to 1.8 million hectares of agricultural land. These were deemed to be carbon saving since they replaced 51 million tonnes of fuel (although this environmental judgement excluded the carbon dioxide emitted in the manufacture of the cement required to build the dam, and in the heavy earth-moving required to construct these dams).

Despite the promise offered by these large dams, they had significant negative developmental consequences. In 2003, drawing on the internal World Bank review of its support for fifty large dams, an evaluation concluded that:

> The 50 dam projects displaced about 830,000 people, and only half showed a satisfactory resettlement outcome. Hirakud dam, India, built over 1948–57, displaced 100,000 persons and submerged 167,376 acres of land ... Sardar Sarovar, India is expected to displace about 100,000 people (30,000 from Gujarat and Maharashtra and 70,000 from Madhya Pradesh).... In some cases landholders have not been compensated, for example farmers were stripped of their land during the Semry I project in Cameroon.[7]

Is there an alternative to large-dam hydroelectricity?

In summary, large-dam hydroelectricity is an exemplar of the Mass Production paradigm. When large dams produce electricity at or near full capacity, they provide large volumes of low-priced (and often also low-cost) electricity which underwrite the economy and society and provide water for agricultural irrigation. But, as with mass production in general, these advantages of scale are challenged by multiple disadvantages. The real cost of supply is generally much higher than the costs to the economy as a whole. Their social impact reinforces concentrations of users in industry, cities and towns, at the expense of users who live in relatively unpopulated areas and who cannot afford to cover the costs of connecting to the distribution infrastructure. Moreover, the scale of these dams is such that they require, and reinforce, the concentration of finance, corporate power and political power. In many countries with weak governance, large dams have helped to fuel corruption and inequality. Finally, although hydroelectricity reduces the carbon footprint of energy supply, large dams have a very significant negative environmental impact.

But, in the face of these complex trade-offs, is there an alternative, short of building hydrocarbon-based power plants? Are there other viable forms of energy supply? Might these alternatives not only deliver energy more cheaply and have more benign environmental impacts, but do so in a way which allows for different and more sustainable patterns of social organization?

The development of ICT-enabled renewable energy transforms the opportunities for a more sustainable form of energy provision. Over the past decade, renewable energy technologies have matured. Their major drawback is the intermittent nature of many forms of renewable energy. For example, wind-powered systems, and to some extent solar-power generation, are weather dependent. But even with existing technologies, there are ways of working around this intermittent power supply. For example, surplus renewably generated energy can be used to pump water up a hill or mountain, and when weather interrupts supplies, this water can be used to generate hydro power. For the future, a range of technologies is being developed which will vastly improve the economics and feasibility of energy storage. These include batteries, such as those being produced in Tesla's solar-powered battery storage plants in Australia and the USA. Moreover, the supposed benefit of reliable supply from large hydro is increasingly questionable as climate change leads to altered and intermittent rainfall. In 2019, the world's largest waterfall, the Victoria Falls on the Zambezi River, which feeds into the downstream Kariba Dam, slowed to a trickle.

Wind, solar and thermal renewable energy is increasingly cost-competitive with fossil fuel, nuclear and large hydroelectric energy. In Texas, the heart of the US oil and gas industry, electricity generated by wind and solar power projects is now cheaper than that produced by coal-fired power stations.[8] These competitive advantages follow from sustained technological progress. The cost of solar power fell by 80 per cent between 2009 and 2016; in the same period, the costs of onshore wind power fell by 30–40 per cent. As the number of installations increases, costs fall further.[9] It is estimated that a doubling of onshore wind capacity results in a 9 per cent reduction in investment costs and a 15 per cent fall in electricity prices. Given the growing cost-competitiveness of renewables, and aided by

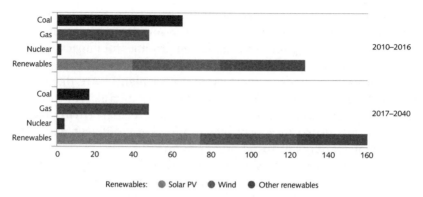

Figure 7.5 Global average annual net capacity additions by energy source
Source: data provided by the International Energy Authority

government schemes incentivizing the adoption of renewable power, global investment in renewable energy doubled from $168 billion in 2009 to $326 billion in 2017. Renewables increasingly dominate capacity growth at a global level, and this is projected to grow even faster in the future (Figure 7.5).

Large hydro, renewables and techno-economic paradigms

The striking contrasts between the sustainability impacts of large-dam hydroelectricity and distributed renewables such as solar and wind power is not a story of renewables versus non-renewables. Instead, it exemplifies the contrasts between two paradigms, both producing renewable energy. On the one hand is the scale-intensive, environmentally damaging and centralizing inflexibility of Mass Production renewable energy generated by large dams. On the other hand stands the environmentally benign, small-scale, distributed, flexible and low-cost ICT-enabled renewable energy. If, instead of focusing on large-scale hydro, we had considered large coal-based power plants or nuclear energy, the same inter-paradigm contrasts would have been evident. Similarly, had we compared small-scale distributed hydro to large-scale hydro, we would also have been able to draw a similar inter-paradigm comparison.

But, critically, this is not a rehearsal of the story about small versus large which was central to the Appropriate Technology movement during the 1970s and 1980s.[10] The character of small distributed production has changed over the past five decades. In the earlier period, during the heyday of Mass Production, the adoption of small-scale technologies had to swim against the tide of technological inferiority and the higher cost of small-scale production. But now, with the deployment of the ICT heartland technology, small-scale and distributed technologies draw production and consumption closer together and provide for more equitable and sustainable social outcomes. Crucially, too, in the case of electricity generation, it also has a considerably better impact on the environment.

7.3 Precision Farming and Robots in Agriculture

This blog by a British farmer in Shropshire (Sam Watson-Jones) tells an interesting story:[11]

> On the wall of my office on our farm in Shropshire, there is an old tithe map from the 1840s. ... The tithe map shows our farm as it was 180 years ago and when I first looked at it, I found it difficult to translate the map I was looking at to the farm I know today. I could see the farm house on the same site that it is today, but I couldn't make sense of the fields.
>
> Eventually, the picture became clear to me and I realised that what used to be around sixty small fields, each individually lined with a hedge, is today two 30 hectare blocks right next to the farm house.
>
> As I studied the map more closely I realised that the way the fields had been divided up made sense – there is a clay seam that runs through both fields and these parcels had been divided up. Further up the bank the soil type changes, going more loamy before becoming very sandy at the top, and again the hedgerows reflected the changing soil conditions.
>
> As I pondered on this, it occurred to me that each patch would have been managed individually, possibly by different people. We know that some parts were run by the villagers at the time, and names like 'Common Leasowe' indicated which fields these might have been.
>
> Whoever was in charge of each patch would have had a defined area of soil which they knew intimately – they would have understood the characteristics of the soil, how and when to work it, which crops grew best in which conditions and so on. As the crops grew, they would have checked them every day, learning all the time about what worked and what didn't. The minute attention to detail must have been incredible. Importantly, the management and cropping of the sandier patches at the top of the field would have been entirely different to the management of the heavier patches at the bottom.

Then I thought about how we manage it today. ...

All of the hedges have gone, I am sorry to say – ripped out by my great-grandfather and grandfather in an effort to increase productivity using machines at a time when the country was desperate for more food post World War Two.

What was sixty fields is now just two.

Now we think of those two fields as two uniform production facilities. We still have an understanding of the variation in soil type but, if we are honest, it isn't fully reflected in our management of the field. There is some variation in seed rate, chemical and fertiliser application but probably in a counter-productive way – where there are patches which are not as good as others, we typically increase our application of inputs to compensate.

Today's farming system is designed around making the machinery as efficient as possible; it is not designed to make the soil as healthy or as productive as possible. We have decided to have two big, square, 30 hectare fields because it means a quicker job for the sprayer, a quicker job for the combine harvester.

The extension of mass production in mechanized farming

Had the words 'farm', 'tractor' and 'agriculture' been substituted with the words 'factory', 'machinery' and 'manufacturing', this story could easily have fitted into the discussion of economic decline in Chapter 2 and the degradation of Mass Production in Chapter 5.

In Chapter 2, I evidenced the emerging crisis of economic sustainability in the Mass Production paradigm, with falling productivity growth and growing levels of debt. The experience of the UK economy as a whole is mirrored in the performance of the agricultural sector. Figure 7.6 shows the pattern of crop yields in two major cereal crops, wheat and barley, between 1948 and 2017. Naturally, the yields bounce up and down on a yearly basis as weather patterns vary. But the dominant trends are clear. Yields grew steadily between 1948 and 1984. Thereafter the pace of yield-growth slowed, petering out after 1993. Land productivity has stagnated. Thus, without putting more land into agricultural production, output cannot grow. This is equivalent to investment in new machinery in factories, except that, unlike the supply of machinery, there is a limit to the amount of land available for farming.

But what has caused stalled productivity in UK crop production? Figure 7.7 breaks down the productivity contribution of different

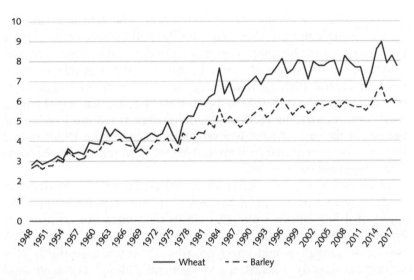

Figure 7.6 Wheat and barley crop yields in UK agriculture, 1948–2017 (tonnes/hectare)

Source: data from Department for Environment, Food and Rural Affairs, *Agriculture in the United Kingdom 2017*

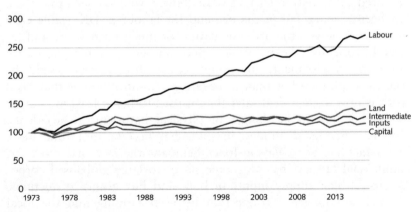

Figure 7.7 Sources of productivity growth in UK agriculture, 1973–2019 (1973 = 100)

Source: data from Department for Environment, Food and Rural Affairs, *Agriculture in the United Kingdom 2017*

inputs used in the production of these crops. The data in Figure 7.7 covers all agriculture rather than just the main cereal crops (Figure 7.6). The picture emerging from this more detailed productivity data provides a more nuanced story. It shows that the productivity of land, of capital (that is, machinery) and of inputs into agriculture rose little after the mid-1980s. By contrast the productivity of labour rose continuously, more than doubling over this four-decade-long period. In the case of Sam Watson-Jones' farm, by the 1920s only 2 labourers were required to farm 460 hectares. In the 1840s, the same farm employed 48 workers.

Tractors are a prime driver of increased labour productivity. A modern tractor is designed for 'efficient' and rapid farming. The speed of a horse-drawn plough used in the nineteenth century was limited by the pace of the horses and by the heaviness of the soil. A two-horse plough would cover an area of around two-thirds of a hectare per day. By contrast, tractors generally plough at 8 km/h (and sometimes faster) and will turn over heavy soils to a greater depth.[12] A 300-horsepower tractor used on many medium-sized UK farms will plough a UK cereals plot of 20–22 hectares in one day. But it is not just ploughing that is mechanized on today's farms. So too are the full range of agricultural practices, including fertilizer and pesticide application, harvesting and off-field transport.

Is this emerging crisis in economic sustainability in UK agriculture mirrored by a crisis in social sustainability? We have seen that there has been a sharp fall in the demand for labour in UK arable crop production. Given the arduous nature of much farm work and (at least historically) the manifold opportunities open for alternative non-farm employment, this employment displacement could be seen as a 'plus' rather than a 'negative'. Another plus is that farm work is now a great deal safer than it used to be, at least in relation to a reduction in the danger of physical harm due to accidents. On the other hand, modern farming has become more and more like a factory. Sam Watson-Jones bemoans the fact that most UK commercial farmers have 'become slaves to large globalised corporations', which supply inputs in bulk and buy grains at auctions. There is no longer a connection between farming and the local economy for inputs, and no longer a connection between farming and consumers. Watson-Jones comments that 'farm management' is increasingly indistinguishable from 'factory management', and much of the intimacy and 'charm' in traditional farming has been lost. And there is less and less scope for small farms, particularly in the arable crops sector. A large tractor will set the farmer back by between £170,000 and £200,000, with the drill costing a further £70,000 to £100,000. Amortizing these costs requires intensive use, and this in turn requires large tracts of land. Moreover, although farm safety has improved due to a reduction in injuries, farm workers continue to be exposed to hazardous chemicals.

The environmental consequences of mechanized farming tell a sobering story. A tractor is a heavy beast. A 300-horsepower tractor used on a large UK farm weighs between 12 and 15 tons. The drill used for planting weighs a further 5–6 tons. Their use results in the compaction of soils, which leads to a series of environmentally harmful impacts. These include decreased seed germination, decreased root and plant growth, poor water drainage which leads to flooding and washed-out crops, reduced soil aeration and the erosion of top-soil. The combination of mechanized tilling and harvesting vastly exacerbates these problems caused by soil compaction in ploughing. The large footprint of tractor tyres and the weight of tractors also has an adverse impact on earthworms, which play a vital role in the aeration of soil. But perhaps the greatest adverse environmental impact of mechanized farming lies the results of its intensive reliance on chemical pesticides and fertilizers.

With current methods of bulk spraying, 40 per cent of fertilizer never gets absorbed by plants. The resultant run-off of fertilizers and pesticides has had major impacts on the character and extent of river- and sea-life. For example, in July 2019, the Yucatán peninsula in Mexico was overwhelmed by a sea of sargassum algae seaweed, more than 550 km long and larger than the total land-mass of Jamaica.[13] One hydrobiologist described it as 'the biggest environmental disaster for Mexico – these are some of the most biodiverse areas in the world'. Another scientist at the UNAM University in Mexico City concluded that 'the damage will become irreversible ... in years, not decades'. Although Sargassum algae is not new to this region, the overwhelming scale of this recent Mexican event is unique. It results in large part from the run-off of nitrogenous fertilizers from advancing large-scale mechanized farming in the Amazon Basin. Moreover, even when fertilizer is not washed into the water system, nitrogen is absorbed in the soil and is subsequently released. This has become a significant source of climate-changing gas emissions.

These harmful consequences of intensive chemical use in mechanized farming are only examples of a much wider problem. They exclude a range of other adverse social and environmental impacts, such as the impact of chemicals on the health of agricultural workers, the chemicals we absorb in the food we eat, the growing resistance to antibiotics, and the impact of pesticides on insect life and species diversity that I chronicled in Chapter 4.

The striking element of this unfolding horror story is that much of this adverse impact of mechanized farming results from the extension to farming of the principles of mass production first developed in Henry Ford's Model T factories in the early twentieth century. Ford's productivity growth was based on specialization of machinery and economies of scale. It involved the use of specialized machinery and the standardization of the final product. The same principles are redolent in the story of Sam Watson-Jones' farm. Land was treated as a standardized resource. The hedgerows separating distinct land plots were ripped out in order to allow increasingly large tractors to operate to maximum efficiency. The inability to take advantage of different soil characteristics reduced the capacity to produce crops with a variety of specific tastes and qualities. And the problems created in the process of production (for example, soil degradation) had to be rectified by the intensive use of environmentally damaging chemicals.

ICTs, robotics and machine-learning can transform mechanized farming

Is there an alternative to mechanized mass production farming? Yes, and one example is to be found in the development of precision farming. This allows for the specific characteristics of land to be taken into account at a very detailed level of planting. Seeds – and, in the future, seeds of different varieties – can be planted precisely where they are most likely to provide a high yield. Subsequently, each individual plant can be provided with just the right amount of fertilizer required to promote its growth. Those plants which are affected by disease are then dosed with the precise amount of pesticide required to meet the challenge to plant health, or will be zapped with a (renewably generated) electric current. Field trials at Reading University in the UK predict that this precise and targeted approach to crop production will reduce pesticide use by 90 per cent and fertilizer use by 95 per cent. It is estimated that one-third of all climate-damaging emissions in UK agriculture come from nitrous oxide deposits in the soil, which are residues of fertilizer use. Moreover, minimal-tilling practices in precision farming contribute to the burying of organic matter in the soil, which absorbs carbon.

Our British farmer, Sam Watson-Jones, speaks eloquently of these possibilities:

> Robotic monitoring systems, gathering data on every single plant and every square metre of soil, will create a truly digital understanding of our field. Artificial Intelligence analysing this digital view will allow us to see, and crucially to understand, the huge variation in soil types which is inherent in all of our fields.
>
> Highly accurate in-field action robots will be able to use this AI technology to vary the way that the soil is managed – planting seeds at different rates, or not planting at all, based on a prediction of profitability rather than on hope; treating only the plants that need to be treated and only with the amounts that they need. Ultimately, digital technology will enable us to move away from monocultures in fields to the point at which we are harvesting on a plant by plant basis.[14]

All of these innovations depend on the intensive use of ICTs. High levels of visual recognition are essential. Since the planting and plant husbandry are conducted at speed, this requires very rapid information processing. The system has to learn about changing environmental and growing characteristics, so machine-learning is critical. In turn, this requires the use of Big Data, and AI to interpret this data. Agricultural production thus transitions from the use of blunt, clumsy and low-technology machines that treat the world as a standardized environment, to a world of smart, flexible and learning machines.

There is growing commercial recognition of this coming disruption in agricultural farming practices. Not surprisingly, leading agricultural mechanization firms see the threat this poses to their traditional competences. At the same time, they see the opportunities open for expanded sales of new high-tech machinery. Because of its size and strategy, John Deere is a stellar example of this technological transition. Deere is the world's largest farm-machinery supplier, producing and servicing tractors, ploughs, drills and other equipment. In 2018, it employed 67,000 people in its global operations, and had sales of $37.4 billion and net income of $3.4 billion. In 2017, Deere acquired Blue River Technology, a firm then employing 60 people, for more than $300 million. Blue River was judged by a prominent industry journal to be one of America's 25 most technologically disruptive companies, and one of the 100 most promising AI companies in the world. The American Society of Agricultural and Biological Engineers placed Blue River as one of the 50 most innovative agricultural companies.

In its 2018 Annual Report, Deere explained the logic for this acquisition:

> Blue River puts Deere in a prime position to develop strong expertise in machine learning and artificial intelligence … Along with vehicle automation and electrification, artificial intelligence has the potential to reshape our industry. No one should doubt our resolve to secure and maintain a position of leadership in these areas.… Further, using the John Deere Operations Center, agricultural customers have stored data representing more than 125 million acres across the globe. Customers also embraced a service, Connected Support, that allows their dealers to remotely monitor the conditions of their equipment and send alerts when problems arise or are anticipated.

Deere imposes licence restrictions which forbid users to modify or repair their equipment. It claims that this provision is protected through the Digital Millennium Copyright Act enacted in 1998 to protect copyrighted software.

However, Deere's forays into AI and machine-learning are not guaranteed to succeed. Although its equipment facilitates the advance of precision agriculture, Deere is caught in the path dependency of its mass production heritage. Deere's precision agricultural machinery is driven by very large tractors. (I had wanted to include a picture of Deere's tractor in order to contrast it with the new small-scale precision machinery in Figure 7.8 below. However, perhaps because of its fear of new disruptive entrants to the sector, Deere refused permission to reproduce this picture. Readers who would like to compare the two approaches to precision farming graphically are referred to Deere's 2018 Annual Report.) It may save on the use of chemicals and raise crop yields, but tractors will continue to compact the soil and crush earthworms. Run-off into the water system, with all of its attendant harmful environmental impacts, will remain a problem. Moreover, the large tyre footprint of its tractors and associated equipment will continue to damage crops as large machinery traverses planted fields. Deere's path dependency complements the organization of agriculture in Mass Production, since its costly equipment reflects and reinforces the dominance of agriculture by large farms and firms in most of the high-income economies.

This path dependency is not unique to John Deere. One of the best-known business strategy texts published in recent decades was *The Innovator's Dilemma*, authored by Clayton Christensen in 1997.[15] Christensen chronicled how the dominance of very large companies was disrupted by flexible, new and innovative entrants. For example, in the 1980s, IBM, then the world's largest computer company, spurned the opportunity to enter the personal computer market. IBM was used to customers who processed large amounts of data on mainframe computers using hard discs. Who, they thought, would ever be interested in a machine whose storage capacity was a flexible floppy plastic disc holding a mere 512 kilobytes of data?

A similar story may be emerging in the case of precision farming. For example, the Small Robot Company is an innovative new market entrant in the UK – Sam Watson-Jones is a co-founder. It is developing its precision technology using an open-innovation strategy, drawing on researchers and graduate students in a number of universities. Equally important, it is developing its technology by working with farmers, who are experimenting with the technology. Some of these farmers have become shareholders. Unlike Deere, the Small Robot Company is developing self-propelled and battery-powered robots to perform the same functions which Deere is targeting through the use of petroleum-driven tractors. But it also takes a different approach with regard to the size of the technology and the manner in which farmers get access to it. A field will be serviced annually for £400 per hectare. The farmer does not have to purchase and maintain expensive tractors and ancillary farm machinery. For this annual fee, the farmer will be provided with the services of four robots, each weighing approximately 100 kgs (rather than 15 tons) and with a small footprint. The first robot, 'Tom', will gather precise data, producing an accurate soil and weed map (Figure 7.8). The second robot, 'Dick', will apply fertilizers and pesticide accurately. Where possible, it will zap weeds with electric charges and lasers, rather than using chemicals. 'Harry', whose development is a little further down the road, will plant scientifically. These three self-propelled robots will feed data continuously to their controlling robot, 'Wilma'. She acts as the Big-Data-AI brain of the system, gathering data and feeding instructions to Tom, Dick and Harry in real time.

Figure 7.8 'Tom' gathering data on soil and weeds
Source: Small Robot Company

The Small Robot Company is not the only new innovative entrant to the precision farming industry. Some examples show the breadth of effort. The Australian Centre for Field Robotics has been working for some years to develop a robot for weeding and spraying in horticulture. Saga Robotics is a Norwegian university spin-out which is focusing on precision farming in greenhouses and fruit. Fendt is a German company manufacturing tractors, which was established in the 1930s. Its MARS precision farming venture was partly funded by an EU innovation grant and involves the use of a swarm of small robots in the corn sector. DOTI, a Canadian firm, is following a similar path to Deere, seeking to automate existing processes. Their robotic tractors have a larger footprint than those of the Small Robot Company, although they are much smaller than the large tractors being developed by Deere.

The challenges confronting fully automated precision farming are daunting. Each of the firms described above is in the developmental stages. Most progress has been made in the development of detailed soil maps, and an increasing number of existing tractors already use GPS to refine their planting regimes. Currently, a great deal of research is being invested in the micro-dosing of individual plants with chemicals. The automated precision harvesting of crops is a little further down the innovation road. Not all – and perhaps none – of the firms described above may be commercially successful. But, even if they do not thrive, there is little doubt that ICT-enabled precision farming will be a disruptive factor which will transform the agricultural sector. In so doing, it will contribute to enhanced economic sustainability by increasing crop yields and saving inputs. Its environmental footprint may be even more beneficial to sustainability. And it is possible that, by facilitating the competitiveness of small farmers, it will also contribute positively to social cohesion.

And precision farming is not the only example of the transformative potential of ICTs in agriculture. Vertical farming is diffusing even more rapidly than the minimal-tillage experiments described above. Vertical farms involve the construction of multi-purpose buildings (and, in some cases, the cannibalization of unused buildings such as car parks). These buildings grow vegetables hydroponically in carefully regulated and electronically controlled environments. They can be built anywhere, and increasingly are being innovated by large supermarket chains on the outskirts of cities and large final markets.

Precision farming and techno-economic paradigms

The most significant impact of precision farming on sustainability is with respect to the environment. Agriculture's impact on the degradation of the environment has been huge. It has been, and continues to be, a major source of pollution due to its intensive use of chemical pesticides and fertilizer. Soil run-offs into rivers have led to erosion, a loss in biodiversity and marine pollution. The chemical intensity of agriculture and the increasing specialization on monocropping have been major contributors to species decline and to the growing vulnerability of an undiversified agricultural system to the danger of harmful pests, as we saw in the case of bananas in Chapter 4.

All of these characteristics are a direct result of the application of the principles of mass production to agriculture. The pursuit of scale economies with inflexible mechanization mirrors patterns in the manufacturing sector. The concentration on a limited variety of specific crops in the pursuit of scale economies in production mirrors

Henry Ford's dedication to a car 'available in any colour as long as it's black'. Treating all land as a homogeneous input reflects mass production's dedication to standardization.

And it is not as if this approach to agricultural production has been economically successful. As we have seen, increases in the UK in the productivity of the key resources – land and capital – have been stagnant. Increases in production have largely arisen from bringing more land into production, and falling profitability has been arrested through government subsidies.

The application of ICTs to agriculture – not just in precision farming, but also in vertical farming – promises to transform this sad story. ICTs provide the capacity to nuance agricultural production to specific land quality, and at the same time to diversify final products. Critically, the harmful environmental footprint of agriculture can be reversed through very significant reductions in the chemical intensity of production, at the same time providing for healthier foods. Attuning production to the differential fertility of land will not only reduce the application of chemicals but also increase the productivity of land. These developments represent a win-win outcome for environmental and economic sustainability. But not all stakeholders gain, and the historic giants of agricultural mechanization who continue to pursue a mass production approach to agriculture will stand to lose. How they will react to these circumstances is uncertain. Perhaps they will take steps to limit the diffusion of the new techno-economic paradigm, like the formal banking system in Kenya which tried to limit the spread of mobile banking, and the large dam-building consortia that have greased the palms of corrupt politicians and squeezed subsidies from their government's aid programmes. But, ultimately, they are walking against the winds of change.

7.4 Three Case-Studies – The Balance Sheet

In this chapter I have described three examples which show the transformative potential of ICT-based innovations. In each case, two alternatives are contrasted. The first describes the manner in which a set of products and services were provided in the Mass Production paradigm – fixed-line telephones, large-scale hydroelectricity and large tractors.

Each of these mass production technologies resulted in unsustainable outcomes. With respect to economic sustainability, they were increasingly characterized by static or falling productivity. Their profitability was only assured because the price at which they sold their products did not reflect the adverse social and environmental impacts of their operations. Their contribution to social sustainability was often negative since they reinforced unequal power structures. Moreover, their reliance on scale also contributed to the undermining of local communities and social cohesion. Large dams and mechanized tractor-based farming had very severe environmentally harmful impacts.

The new technologies, based on the use of the ICT heartland technology, stand in sharp contrast in each of these cases. They offer the potential for reviving stalled productivity growth and providing profitable opportunities for investors. They contribute to social sustainability by providing the capacity for small-scale production and consumption, and geographically distributed use. Their small scale of operations and their relatively low acquisition costs make them accessible to the relatively poor and disadvantaged, particularly in low-income economies. And, in each case, their environmental footprints are considerably more benign than their Mass Production counterparts. Significantly, each of the case-studies shows the interconnections between environmental, economic and social sustainability – they represent graphic examples of paradigmatic change.

Each is an exemplar of the possibilities opened by the new heartland technology of ICTs for beneficially transforming economic, social and environmental sustainability. Similar opportunities are available across a range of economic and social activities, as we saw in the thumbnail sketches in Chapter 6. But will these new opportunities for sustainable growth be realized? What factors will impede or encourage their development and adoption?

It is to this agenda that we now turn in the concluding chapters.

8
What's To Be Done?

In the early 1990s, I was deeply involved in the Industrial Strategy Project (ISP), an action research programme to develop an Industrial Policy for a post-Apartheid South Africa.[1] Over the course of three years, a group of nearly fifty researchers conducted detailed studies of sixteen economic sectors and four cross-cutting policy issues (human resource development and industrial relations; market structure and corporate concentration; trade policy; and regional economic strategies). This culminated in a comprehensive industrial strategy which informed the first generation of post-Apartheid Industrial Policy.

The Industrial Strategy Project made a major positive contribution in the post-Apartheid era. The detailed research conducted in the programme provided a picture of the character and international competitiveness of the South African economy. The contribution to capability-building was especially important. Many of our team subsequently became ministers and senior civil servants. And we were able to identify suites of policies which, had they been implemented, would have materially helped to construct a more just and dynamic economy, strengthening economic, social and environmental sustainability. However, policy implementation was execrable and, in later years, state coffers were looted across the range of governance levels. (I am happy to say that – with one exception – to the best of my knowledge, none of this malfeasance involved members of the ISP team!)

I learned four important lessons from my participation in the Industrial Strategy Project that are relevant to the policy agenda which I set out in this chapter. First, there is the need to clearly understand the nature of the challenge, and to answer the question of *why* we need to take action? From this, follows the second key challenge – the need for a Vision; given the character of the ICT heartland technology, *what* might a more sustainable world look like? Third, *how* can these outcomes be delivered? And then, fourth, *who* will drive the change agenda?

I addressed the *why* question in the concluding section of Chapter 6. I offered a number of examples of the potential negative impact of ICTs on sustainability – cybercrime, automated weaponry, the invasion of privacy and the impact on employment. These examples show how imperative it is to provide directionality to the trajectory of the unfolding ICT techno-economic paradigm. But which fork in the road will we take? *What* might an ICT-enabled more sustainable world look like? For, as the Head of Research and Development at the giant Philips transnational corporation programme advised the South African Industrial Strategy Team in 1993, 'If you don't know where you are going, you will probably land up somewhere else.' But having a vision is not enough. There remains the critical question of *how* we will be able to steer the paradigm in the right direction.

In this chapter, I will begin briefly with the *what* question, and then outline five policy agendas which can transport us in the desired direction to deliver a more sustainable world (the *how*). *Who* might drive this directionality will be the subject matter of the final concluding chapter.

8.1 The What – Visioning a More Sustainable Future

What might a more sustainable future look like? This is an easier question to ask than to answer. There is no Darwinian inevitability determining the complexion of the new ICT techno-economic paradigm, and the future can take a number of forms. Moreover, we peer into this murky future through translucent binoculars. And, even worse, we are peering through what often seems to be the incorrect end of the binoculars. Despite these limitations, it is possible to envision a more environmentally, economically and socially sustainable world, based on the opportunities opened up by the new ICT paradigm and documented in the two previous chapters.

A more sustainable environment

The relationship between humans and the natural environment will experience a fundamental transition. Instead of the environment being seen as a resource to be exploited, humankind will recognize our symbiotic interaction with nature, and that environmental sustainability and social and economic sustainability go hand-in-hand. A green agenda will be seen not as a cost to society, but as an opportunity to add value and improve our quality of life.

A more sustainable environment will emerge in the short, medium and long term. In the short term, there will be a significant reduction in waste, pollution and habitat destruction. These trends will be sustained over time and will be driven by changes in technology, in the economy, in the organization of society and in norms and behaviour. Societies will transition from a linear Take–Make–Use–Waste world to a Circular Economy with minimum disruptive environmental impact.

How will these sustainability outcomes be measured? As we saw in Chapter 4, an international panel of earth scientists investigating the biosphere's Planetary Boundaries identified six achievements which will reflect significant progress in rebuilding environmental sustainability. First, the emission of greenhouse gases such as carbon dioxide and methane, which are driving climate change and climate chaos, will be significantly reduced. Second, other environmentally threatening emissions which are close to exceeding Planetary Boundaries will be significantly curtailed or reversed. These include chemical pollutants, and nitrogen, phosphorous and chemical residues. Third, the loss of global habitats on earth (primarily forest loss), at sea and in the atmosphere will be halted, and in some cases be reversed. Fourth, the loss in biodiversity in insects and plant life will be halted, and in some cases be reversed. Fifth, adequate supplies of water will support environmentally sustainable and distributed production and consumption. And, finally, plastics-based production and consumption will largely be replaced by other environmentally sustainable inputs.

A more sustainable economy

As we saw in previous chapters, after the mid-1970s the economy in most high-income countries suffered from a number of accelerating problems, including a decline in economic, productivity and investment growth, increasing economic polarization and growing economic volatility. A more sustainable economy will involve a reversal of these trends. A new form of economic growth, placing greater value on the environment and social solidarity, will be reinforced by a revival of investment, productivity and economic growth. The growth path will be less volatile and less vulnerable to periodic recessions. The separation of production from consumption – both globally and within countries and regions – will be reduced. More flexible production systems will be less scale-intensive, and goods and services will be more tailored to the needs of individual consumers and more suitable for shared consumption. Investment will increasingly be directed towards the greening of production and consumption.

Production and consumption will be brought closer together. This will be reflected both within countries and, especially, in economic relations between countries. Whilst the global flow of ideas and knowledge will continue to increase, global supply chains will reduce in intensity and be less extensive. Regional supply chains (for example in the division of labour between adjacent countries) will take up some of the reduction in globally stretched intercontinental supply chains. Trade between countries will be more balanced, and the share of low-income economies in global output will increase.

A more sustainable society

A more socially sustainable world will involve changes in lifestyles, changes in the distribution of power and greater civic participation. These changes will not only allow for more cohesive patterns of living and social interaction, but will also result from and support changes required to deliver economic and environmental sustainability.

Beginning with lifestyles, each techno-economic paradigm has a distinctive lifestyle which supports consumption and social interactions and has impacts on the environment. Changes in techno-economic paradigms are thus reflected in major changes in lifestyles. For example, Perez contrasts the different lifestyles in Mass Production with those which dominated in the preceding techno-economic paradigm. Transport by trains, horses, carriages, stage-coaches, ships and bicycles was succeeded by automobiles, buses, trucks, planes and motorcycles. Mass media, radios, movies and TV took the place of local newspapers. In the home, central heating replaced coal fires, and appliances such as washing machines supplanted human labour. Fridges, freezers and plastic packaging meant that food could be stored and did not have to be purchased and cooked at regular intervals. And residence moved from town centres to the suburbs. In the later years of the Mass Production paradigm, these various elements combined to provide women with the increasing freedom to be liberated from the home – the women's movement was given a new impetus.

Perez provides a compelling vision of what the dominant lifestyles in the ICT techno-economic paradigm might look like, and here it is worth quoting her at some length:

> This new way of life is marked by the desire to reduce pollution and toxicity, to protect the environment and to promote health, to purchase experiences over products and to adopt sharing or rented services rather than permanent ownership of goods, and to aspire to 'networked' creative and collaborative work rather than joining pyramidal hierarchies. Such new practices and new values can already be observed among the educated, the wealthy and the young. Good health is a central aspiration, reflected in the rapidly growing market for organic, locally-sourced fresh foods, the surging popularity of cycling as a mode of city transport, and the increasing abundance of exercise apps, personal trainers, physiotherapists, and all other aspects of preventive self-care. Solar panels, 'living' roofs and environmentally-friendly architecture are showpieces for the elite, and no longer reserved for those 'living off the grid'; electric/hybrid cars and energy-efficient appliances are sold at the top of their respective ranges, while those who can't afford the new technology are seen to make do with 'old-fashioned' polluters.[2]

These changes in lifestyles will be accompanied by the reversal of the trend towards increasing inequality. The distribution of both income and wealth will become more equal, and the power of the plutocracy and very large corporations to shape public perceptions and popular attitudes in ways which favour the power of the wealthy will be curbed. A more socially sustainable society will require and result in the replenishment of government revenues. This will allow for a reversal of austerity policies, a rebuilding of social expenditures, investments in skills and training, and the building of the infrastructure required to facilitate the full deployment of the ICT techno-economic paradigm. Increased government revenues will support the development of innovations which promote environmental and social sustainability.

Governance structures will be reformed at three levels. At the global level, inter-country agreements will tackle problems which cannot be addressed by individual countries. At the national level, governments will play a lead role in the promotion and enabling of the new more sustainable techno-economic paradigm. Below the national level, much more power will be given to local governments. Civil society organizations will play a more active role in the allocation of resources and the delivery of services, particularly at a local level. 'Localism' will flourish in production, consumption and lifestyles.

Finally, global migration which results from political conflict, the lack of opportunities and climate change will be reduced. Accelerated economic development in low-income economies will not only create employment for many more people but also provide opportunities for the most talented and creative. This will reduce the economic and social costs of the brain-drain to high-income countries.

8.2 The How – What Actions Will Deliver a More Sustainable World?

So much for the *'what'*. The Vision is 'easy'. But *'how'* are we to impart directionality to the evolving ICT? Five major synchronized sets of responses can help us to rebuild a more sustainable world. We need to:

- regulate and change behaviour in the financial sector
- redistribute wealth and incomes and reduce the power of giant corporations
- implement a Smart Green New Deal
- strengthen global and local governance
- promote global development

Each of these policy agendas can be met through a multiplicity of detailed interventions and changes in behaviour. As David Fleming (a green activist) observed, 'Large-scale problems do not [only] require large-scale solutions: they require small-scale solutions within a large-scale framework.'[3] Moreover, context is important, in terms of both location and time. Responses will need to vary and to change over time to reflect these contextual factors. Therefore, all we can do here is to set out the major areas in which action is required. As we will see in the concluding chapter, a more sustainable world can only be realized if complementary policies are adopted which span all the three dimensions of sustainability. Moreover, there is a hierarchy and a sequence if directionality is to be achieved.

Regulating and changing behaviour in the financial sector

The Great Crash of 1929 and the subsequent Great Depression of the 1930s led to the ruination of a great many individual investors. They lost faith in the financial sector and, as a result, between 1930 and 1933 there were a series of major 'bank-runs' in the US as depositors sought to reclaim their money before the banks might collapse. In 1933, the Glass–Steagall Act responded to the speculative lending boom of the 1920s and the subsequent panic of the Great Stock Market Crash of 1929 by forcing the separation of investment banking (that is, funds for investment and speculation) from retail banking (funds for everyday living). Together with other measures, the Glass–Steagall provisions stabilized the financial sector and facilitated the recovery of the US and other large economies. Thereafter, banks directed their loans towards the productive sector rather than to investments in speculative assets. Similar regulations were introduced across the spectrum of the high-income economies. This regulation of the financial sector underwrote the deployment of the Mass Production paradigm in the Golden Age between 1950 and the mid-1970s.

In the early 1980s, pressure exerted by the plutocracy and the financial sector led to the loosening of the regulatory strings on the financial sector. Margaret Thatcher's 'Big Bang' reforms of the stock market in the UK removed the barriers between speculative banking and retail banking. A similar relaxation of regulation occurred in the US, and the Glass–Steagall Act was repealed. This loosening of regulations coincided with the innovation of electronic technologies which facilitated rapid speculative trading and reduced the transparency of financial transactions. As we saw in previous chapters, it also coincided with massive injections of liquidity into the economy through Quantitative Easing (QE) policies. QE was designed to prop up falling demand as the Mass Production paradigm began to atrophy. But this objective failed. Instead, in tandem with the loosening of controls over banking and the development of electronic banking, QE provided the fuel which ignited the blaze of financial speculation which gathered pace after the turn of the millennium.

These developments led to the financial crisis in 2008. Reflecting the political power of the banking sector, policy makers failed to grasp the nettle and introduce structural reforms to rein in speculative financial capital and to reduce financial liquidity. Instead, the policy response was to stick a plaster over a festering sore. For example, the Obama Administration, which took office in 2008, appointed the same cadre of policy makers who had ushered in the crisis in the first place. Whilst the Dodd–Frank Act of 2010 did reinstitute some controls over the banks, these controls were light-touch. Their primary purpose was to protect the big banks from default – 'the banks are too big to be allowed to fail'. In 2018, the Trump Administration loosened controls further, this time over 'smaller banks' – those with assets of less than $250 billion.

Therefore, if the major global economies are to transition to a more sustainable growth trajectory, structural reforms involving greater regulation of the financial sector are necessary. The first requirement is to reduce the size of the very large banks. The need to protect the economy from default by banks which 'are too large to fail' undermines the capacity to regulate their speculative activities. Second, controls must be imposed to limit financial speculation. This can be achieved, *inter alia*, by ensuring the separation of retail and speculative banking; limiting the capacity of the 'shadow banking sector' (such as hedge funds) to promote risky lending; controlling the expansion of cryptocurrencies such as Bitcoins which, unlike national currencies, are not related to the size of the productive economy; regulating the use of high-frequency and automated trading in shares, commodities and currencies; introducing a financial transactions tax targeted at short-term cross-border money transfers to inhibit currency speculation; and increasing transparency into financial transactions to avoid the 'CDO fiasco' of the 2008 Financial Crisis. (Collateralized Debt Obligations bundle worthless financial assets with sound financial assets. Purchasers of CDOs have no measure of the true worth of their investments, with the result that large flows of finance have been directed to financial packages that are essentially worthless.)

The overall objective of these reforms in the financial sector is to reorient the trajectory of lending from speculation and short-term lending to the support of the productive sector's transition to the new techno-economic paradigm.

Reducing the concentration of individual and corporate power

From the early 1980s, income and wealth inequality grew rapidly and sharply in all of the major economies, and particularly in the US and the UK. As we saw in Chapter 3, the gains accruing to the plutocracy were used to promote and support a neo-liberal policy agenda. This resulted in social exclusion, growing pockets of poverty and the erosion of welfare expenditures. The neo-liberal policy agenda also undermined the sustainability of economic growth by favouring financial speculation over productive investment, and through the neglect of investments in the infrastructure required to support economic growth. Further, by undermining the legitimacy of government interventions in the economy, the neo-liberal agenda failed to place adequate controls over climate and other environmentally damaging emissions.

The concentration in the ownership of wealth and income at the individual level was mirrored and underwritten by the growth of concentration in the corporate sector. Many economic sectors became increasingly dominated by a handful of large firms. For example, four trading firms – ADM, Bunge, Cargill and Louis Dreyfus, known as the ABCD group – account for between 75 and 90 per cent of global grain trade.[4] In the retail sector in most high-income economies, the six largest retail chains account for more than 70 per cent of total sector sales. Similar trends towards concentration and monopoly power are to be found in the development of the core technologies of the ICT techno-economic paradigm. Five large firms control key gateways to the diffusion of the new technologies. They are referred to as the 'FAAMGs' – that is, Facebook, Apple, Amazon, Microsoft and Google (whose holding company is now known as 'Alphabet'). Some indications of their size are shown in Box 8.1.[5]

Stemming the adverse consequences of the growing concentration

Box 8.1 Market Dominance by the FAAMGs (Facebook, Apple, Amazon, Microsoft and Google)

- Facebook's revenues in 2019 were $71 billion, an increase of more than 27 per cent over the preceding year. It controlled more than 70 per cent of the social media market. Facebook also owns WhatsApp (with more than 1.2 billion global users) and Instagram (with more than 1 billion users worldwide). Together, Google and Facebook accounted for 59 per cent of total digital advertising revenue in the US, and for 63 per cent in the UK.
- Apple's market capitalization in 2019 was equivalent to more than 1 per cent of total global GDP, and more than 5 per cent of US GDP. Its revenues of $260 billion exceeded the GDP of 183 countries, including Turkey, the Netherlands, Saudi Arabia, Argentina and Sweden.
- Amazon's growth has been, and continues to be, spectacular, with total revenue rising from $136 billion in 2016 to $281 billion in 2019. In the US, more than half of all e-commerce is transacted through Amazon.
- Microsoft dominates the operating system of personal computers (88 per cent of the total market), employs more than 144,000 people worldwide and had total revenue in 2019 of $125 billion, with a net income of $39 billion.
- Through its subsidiaries (such as Google X, Google Ventures, Google Capital, Calico and Life Sciences), Alphabet has a large and often dominating presence in key emerging sectors such as the internet, Artificial Intelligence, machine-learning, life sciences, investment capital and research. In 2019, Alphabet employed more than 103,000 people worldwide and its annual revenues exceeded $162 billion, an increase of one-fifth over 2018. Google accounted for more than 80 per cent of searches on the internet.

of income, wealth and corporate power is hence imperative for the remaking of sustainability. A number of policies can contribute to achieving this end. First, inequalities in wealth need to be reduced. Wealth is not just a source of income inequality today, but also a source of intergenerational income as death duties are often negligible. Second, and related to the distribution of wealth, measures are required to address inequalities in the *'predistribution of income'* – that is, the inequality in earned income (including bonuses) before taxes. The ratio between CEO and average worker remuneration in the US grew from 20:1 in 1965 to 58:1 in 1989, and to 312:1 in 2017.[6] In the UK, the ratio grew from 47:1 in 1998 to 133:1 in 2018.[7] Third, measures are required to promote the *'redistribution'* of *post-tax* incomes, such as salaries, bonuses and dividends. As we saw in Chapter 4, the tax rate on the highest incomes has fallen from more than 90 per cent in the post-war period to levels which, after exemptions of various sorts, are often less than 15 per cent.

Fourth, it will be important to challenge the drift to declining corporate taxes. As we saw in Chapter 2, there has been a 'war of incentives' by governments designed to attract investment (even though the evidence suggests that it is business opportunities rather than tax rates which are the primary factor incentivizing corporate investment). Corporate tax rates in the UK, for example, fell from 27 per cent in 2010 to 17 per cent in 2019. Moreover, giant global companies reduce their tax payments through complex financial arrangements between affiliates in different countries. The net designed to avoid what the OECD calls 'Base Erosion and Profit Shifting' needs to have a fine mesh to catch the full range of tax-avoiding malpractices. And, since digital commerce companies such as Amazon and Google manage to avoid taxes through elaborate transfer pricing schemes, and where they do pay taxes these are in countries where they have residence rather than where they do business, a digital sales tax should be imposed on their turnover in all countries where they operate.

A further element in measures designed to limit inequality arising from the operations of the corporate sector is to remove the incentives favouring shareholder interests (that is, owners of firms) over stakeholder interests (that is, not only owners but also labour, consumers, communities and the environment). As we saw in Chapter 2, privileging the interests of shareholders and management led to the widespread looting of company coffers, the growth in corporate debt, and shortening time horizons in innovation and investment decisions.

Finally, there is the need to strengthen and implement policies to reduce the concentration of ownership and market share in the corporate sector. This will include measures to contain the size of 'too large to fail' banks, and the 'too large to care' giant FAAMG software platform firms. But the growth of market concentration in the Mass Production paradigm is not limited to the ICT sector. It has grown pervasively across sectors. However, perhaps the most important arena of concentration which needs to be addressed is the concentration of ownership in opinion-forming traditional media and in social media. As we saw in Chapter 3, the capacity to shape public opinion is the primary source of power that the plutocracy possesses to orient the social, the political and the economic systems to meet its interests rather than those of society and the environment at large.

A Smart Green New Deal

It makes a great deal of sense to privilege a response to environmental sustainability as one of the primary drivers for the full deployment of the ICT techno-economic paradigm. First, the environmental crisis poses existential threats in a way which is not true for the social and economic arenas. Responding to it cannot be deferred. Second, the remaking of environmental sustainability will simultaneously contribute to an enhancement of social and economic sustainability. Third, not only do the new ICT heartland technologies provide bountiful opportunities for rebuilding environmental sustainability, but in so doing they promote the development and deployment of the new technologies in other areas of economy and society.

This calls for a New Deal focusing on the greening of production and consumption. But it is not just a New Deal which is required in the transition to a more sustainable world. It is one which involves a 'Smart New Deal' which takes full advantage of the transformative potential of the new heartland ICT technology. Before I outline what this Smart Green New Deal may involve, it is first necessary to reframe the discourse from a focus on the costs of the green agenda to the benefits which it offers.

A pervasive theme in the opposition to action on the environment is the argument that the proposed changes are unaffordable. Changing production processes requires new equipment and the retraining of existing staff. Decarbonizing transport and energy generation will require substantial investment, as will improving insulation in millions of houses. Moreover, the phasing-out of polluting industries will lead to considerable job loss and the disruption of many communities. For example, it is estimated that if the UK is to meet its objective of phasing out oil and gas energy generation by 2030, this will involve the loss of 280,000 jobs.[8] The automobile industry which dominates the German industrial sector currently employs 830,000. More than 250,000 of these jobs are likely to be lost by 2030 due to the switch to electrically powered vehicles.[9]

However, the costs of inaction may be much greater than the resources required to adapt to and to mitigate climate change. Environmental degradation and climate change place large costs on governments. The US Federal Accounting Office estimated the budgetary costs of climate change natural disasters at $350 billion between 2009 and 2018, with the annual costs projected to rise to $50 billion by 2050.[10] Individual industries, too, will be heavily affected by inaction. The global tourist sector, valued at $8.8 trillion and employing 319 million people in 2018, is substantially threatened by climate change.

Further, seen through reframed lenses, many of the 'costs of the green economy' are in fact opportunities for value addition and growth. The greening of production creates new avenues for investment, and provides jobs and incomes for many. The wind-power generating industry in Brazil created more than 90,000 jobs between 2012 and 2016.[11] In the UK, a study in 2019 assessing the costs and benefits of decarbonizing the economy estimated that every £1 spent on a green agenda would deliver £2 of benefits. A programme to reduce energy waste, to decarbonize heating, to decarbonize electricity generation and to balance the supply and demand for energy would deliver net benefits of £800 billion and create 850,000 new jobs by 2030.[12]

The Great Depression of the 1930s was overcome in large part as a result of Roosevelt's New Deal Program. The New Deal injected very large sums of government finance into the economy in a concerted 'big push' to revive the economy. It was accompanied by an evocative clarion call – 'The only thing we have to fear is fear itself.' In 1961, incoming President John Kennedy committed the US to land (and return!) a person on the moon before the end of the decade. At the time, this seemed a monumental, and probably insuperable, task. But large-scale coordinated investments in research across the spectrum of public and private institutions led to a successful moon-mission in 1969. This approach towards big problems – referred to by Mazzucato as a Mission Oriented approach[13] – is now necessary to drive a New Deal fit for the twenty-first century. What better than a Smart Green New Deal which promotes environmental renewal and which simultaneously supports the remaking of economic and social sustainability?

In Chapter 4, I chronicled the evolution of the environmentally damaging 'Take, Make, Use and Waste' trajectory in the Mass Production paradigm which has had devastating consequences for environmental sustainability, with collateral damages inflicted on social and economic sustainability. There is an alternative approach to production and consumption in the form of the Circular Economy. As its name implies, the Circular Economy is a 'closed-loop' system. In contrast to the linearity of 'Take, Make, Use and Waste', the Circular Economy is self-contained in environmental terms. It seeks to minimize its consumption of natural resources and to eliminate the jettisoning of waste materials into the environment. The Amsterdam Economic Board, a coalition of private-sector CEOs, city officials and civil society organizations identifies ten levels of circularity required to deliver the Circular Economy (Figure 8.1). This requires changes in norms and behaviour, changes in design philosophy, the repair and

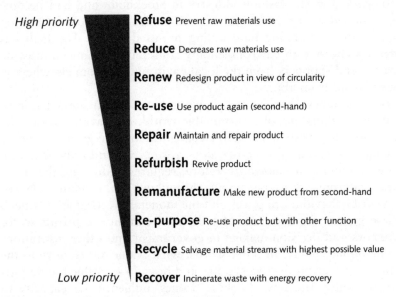

Figure 8.1 Levels of circularity: the 10 Rs
Source: Amsterdam Economic Board

re-use of products, the recycling of waste and the use of waste for energy regeneration.

Three sets of actions will promote the transition to a Circular Economy. The first is to incentivize changes in behaviour. The second is to build the infrastructure required to change behaviour, and the third is to foster new and more appropriate innovation paths.

Incentivizing changes in behaviour

The behaviour of individuals, firms and institutions is shaped by a combination of values, incentives (the carrot) and regulations backed by sanctions (the stick). The Swedish town of Eskilstuna, 1 hour from Stockholm, provides a good example of how norms and values can promote a more environmentally sustainable lifestyle. In 2019, this ex-steel-making town had an unemployment rate double the national average, and 10 per cent of its population were refugees. The town council developed a vision to reposition the town as a model Circular Economy. It invested in efficient energy generation schemes and in low-carbon public transport. For example, waste collection required the public to sort their garbage into seven different types of materials. The community responded with enthusiasm. Anna Bergström who had worked in the fashion industry in Stockholm and had become disillusioned with the harmful environmental impact of fast fashion established a shopping mall selling pre-used goods. The mall has struck a chord with environmentally conscious consumers, drawing visitors and shoppers from the local environment, from elsewhere in Sweden and from abroad.

But voluntary changes in behaviour have only a limited role to play in the remaking of a sustainable world. As David Mackay, the late Chief Scientist to the UK Department of Energy and Climate Change, observed, 'if everyone does a little, we will only achieve a little'.[14] Significant change, therefore, requires addressing the structural inducements to behaviour throughout the economy. A key driver of behaviour are prices and the monetary recording of 'value'. These govern the decisions of individual consumers, private-sector investors and decision-makers in government and other institutions in the public sphere. In other words, what 'value' do we give to the inputs into our productive systems and how do we value the outputs which result? And how do these 'values' influence our capacity to remake a more sustainable world?

The first and perhaps most difficult set of 'prices' to change are those which are grouped together to measure 'Gross Domestic Product' (GDP) and per-capita incomes. These measures are used to define 'economic growth' and play an overwhelmingly important role in public policy discussion. The Nobel Laureate credited with the invention of the GDP measure in the 1930s, Simon Kuznets, warned against the use of this monetary measure as an indicator of welfare. But his warnings were not heeded. For very many policy makers, corporations and citizens, changes in GDP (economic growth), welfare and progress are considered interchangeable.

There are a number of problems with using GDP as an indication of welfare. For one thing, it takes no account of the distribution of rewards – £100 means a great deal more to someone on the breadline than it does to Mark Zuckerberg, the billionaire CEO of Facebook (which played such a prominent role in the rise of populism in the US, the UK and elsewhere). For another, there is the issue of what is included and what is not included in the measurement of GDP. Starting with inclusion, what is the real societal value of chemical weapons or of coal-fired power plants which drive climate change? GDP measures these destructive and sustainability-damaging industries as making a positive contribution to output. Clearly, it would make more sense to subtract them from the calculation of GDP. Then there is the issue of what is not included in the measurement of GDP. For example, the work which homemakers (who are disproportionately women) undertake in the home is not measured as a contribution to GDP.

A second major valuation issue concerns the price of inputs into production. This sends a signal to producers in the economy. If an input is costly, producers will economize on its use; conversely, if input prices are cheap, the inputs will be used relatively abundantly. Critically, the prices of many inputs into production do not reflect their real costs, since many of the environmental and social costs of production are not included in the cost-structure of producers. For example, many polluting industries are not required to cover the costs of cleaning up their emissions. Perhaps the most sustainability-challenging set of costs not included in production prices are the costs of climate change resulting from the use of fossil fuels. The IMF estimated that, in 2015, the combined cost of annual subsidies by governments to the fossil-fuel industry and the cost of the environmental damages resulting from the use of fossil fuels was $4.7 trillion, equivalent to 6.5% of global GDP.[15]

There are a range of taxes which affect the incentives governing the environmental impact of production and consumption. Figure 8.2 shows the breakdown of tax revenue in the UK. The major contributor, perhaps unsurprisingly, is income tax – that is, the taxes paid by all citizens on their earnings (31 per cent of total receipts). The second largest contributor is a tax on labour supposedly directed towards pensions and social security provision – National Insurance Contributions (22 per cent). These taxes on labour are more than double the total tax on corporate profits (9 per cent), more than four times the tax on petroleum (5 per cent) and more than fifteen times higher than the combination of various environmental taxes (air passenger taxes, landfill taxes and climate change levies such as a carbon tax) (1.4 per cent). The key policy takeaway from these numbers is that the UK (and most other countries) levy tax employment at far higher levels than either corporate profits or environmentally damaging activities.

Beyond voluntary changes in behaviour and changes induced by relative prices, behaviour is also modified by government regulations. Whilst prices influence behaviour at the margin – they determine how much of one input may be used at the cost of another – regulations are mandatory. In the case of regulations, there is no discretion in the degree of performance and, typically, there are sanctions for non-compliance. Food imports containing pesticide residues or antibiotics are excluded from the market. Hazardous chemicals are

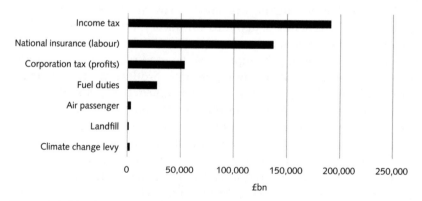

Figure 8.2 Total UK tax receipts, 2018–2019 (£bn)

Source: data from HMRC, *Tax and NIC Receipts: Monthly and Annual Historical Records, October 2019*

prohibited in the production of electronic components. Firms which emit toxic chemicals into the environment are fined. Clearly, in many cases, the extent and implementation of sustainability regulations is sub-optimal. If they were adequate, we would not find ourselves descending so deeply into an unsustainable world.

In the light of these various factors inducing individual, institutional and corporate practices, what are the key policy agendas which have a positive role to play in the remaking of an environmentally sustainable world?

First, the measurement of welfare has to change. This will not be easy since Gross Domestic Product and its attendant measures of welfare are deeply entrenched in societal norms and practices. However, there are other measures that can be used to supplement GDP and modify our estimates of 'welfare' and 'progress'. For example, the Human Development Index developed by the United Nations Development Programme is a composite measure of life-expectancy at birth, adult literacy and per-capita incomes. Another example is the Gross National Happiness measure developed in Bhutan, which includes equality, environmental conservation, the preservation and promotion of local culture, and the quality of governance. Beyond composite measures, there is a variety of individual indicators measuring welfare, of the sort identified by Wilkinson and Pickett and reported in Chapter 3.

Second, the structure of taxation has to change. In a world in which there are growing concerns about the dangers of mass unemployment in the era of robotization and Artificial Intelligence, it is clearly irrational to increase the cost of labour beyond the salaries paid to employees. Similarly, in a context in which the Take–Make–Use–Waste culture of Mass Production has led to major negative impacts on the environment, it is also counter-productive that the real cost of material inputs and of environmental damage are not paid by producers and users. Hence, a fundamental change in the structure of taxation is required. It needs to reduce the burden of tax on employment; it needs to tax material inputs, especially carbon-based fossil fuels; and it needs to tax the displacement of harmful materials such as carbon dioxide, particulates, pesticides and waste on to the environment.

Third, these price changes designed to promote the dematerialization of the economy and society must be supported through a combination of changes in attitudes and lifestyles. Consumers in the high-income economies need to consume less and to forgo the purchase of unnecessary and single-use products. The 'good life' needs to be defined in terms of services and leisure, rather than material products. Consumers can be provided with incentives to alter their behaviour. For example, H&M in Sweden offers a discount to customers handing in used clothes.

Fourth, the corporate sector has to change its practices. In response to consumer pressure and government regulations, supermarkets have reduced their use of plastic packaging. Firms such as Nestlé have committed to reducing their offtake of clean water, and Unilever has set itself stringent targets to reduce packaging. Since an increasing number of consumer goods are controlled by software rather than mechanical technologies, improvements in products can be delivered by changing the controlling software over the internet. As we saw earlier, this trajectory is already under way. The performance of mobile phones is regularly improved through software updates, and Tesla, Volkswagen and other firms are applying the same principles in the automobile sector.

Fifth, the transition from retail stores to e-commerce has done much to strip the costs out of the production and distribution cycle, and to reduce prices to final consumers. To some extent, it also reduces the environmental costs of consumers driving to shopping malls. However, there is a fine environmental balance in this transition. The flow of vehicles delivering single Amazon and other e-commerce purchases, often on multiple occasions in a single day, significantly increases the environmental footprint of consumption. This is exacerbated by the overpackaging required to protect e-commerce purchases.

Finally, regulations have a critical role to play in promoting sustainability. For example, with respect to environmental sustainability, government regulations in the EU, the US and China force automobile producers to improve the fuel-efficiency of their vehicles by setting increasingly demanding performance targets. These regulations have played the major role in the development of more fuel-efficient internal combustion engine cars, and are currently driving the surprisingly rapid diffusion of electric cars. An emerging arena requiring urgent regulatory attention concerns the need to control deep-sea mining, where at present there are almost no controls over the extraction of oil and other materials from the ocean beds.

Infrastructure to support the Circular Economy

Each techno-economic paradigm requires distinctive infrastructure to support the diffusion of its heartland technology. For example, the first growth surge after the Industrial Revolution depended on canals, and subsequent surges required railways and centralized electricity grids. Automobilization was at the heart of the Mass Production paradigm and required a network of roads and highways and an extensive network of petrol filling stations. In contrast to Mass Production, the key infrastructure required to support the ICT paradigm is an information highway. This involves ubiquitous, high-speed, high band-width and low-cost internet connectivity. The deployment of IoTs – a primary driver of the ICT paradigm – requires the rapid building of 5G (and, in future, 6G) mobile phone networks. The primary energy source for this knowledge-intensive paradigm is cheap and ubiquitous energy. But, unlike fossil-fuel energy, the energy required to fuel the ICT paradigm cannot be environmentally damaging.

So, what steps are required to facilitate the diffusion of a green infrastructure suitable to promote a Green New Deal? First, the energy generation sector will need to decarbonize. This means a halt to investments in new carbon-intensive generating capacity, particularly coal-fired power stations. But this will not be adequate, since many installed greenhouse-gas emitting power stations have a long functional life in front of them. Hence, it will also require the decommissioning of many existing power plants. Fortunately, in a growing number of environments, renewable energy has lower 'total operating costs' (that is, repaying for the cost of installation as well as the recurrent operating costs) than ongoing operating costs in thermal plants. This means that scrapping well-functioning coal plants and replacing them with renewables can reduce the price of energy.

Second, why bother to generate energy renewably if you don't need the energy in the first place? In many cases, particularly in the residential sphere and in manufacturing, there is extensive scope for improved insulation. Moreover, in general, the costs of insulation are much lower than the costs of energy generation.

Third, the transport network must be reformed. Vehicles must be powered by renewably produced electric energy, rather than by petroleum-based internal-combustion engines. Air travel must be reduced, or be powered by renewable energy. This will require the development of electrically powered aircraft and the use of bio-fuels and hydrogen as sources of motive power. The development of high-speed long-distance rail will have an important part to play in reducing air transport. Shipping will need to make the transition to electric or hydrogen power. Shared personal transport must increasingly substitute for privately owned vehicles. This will involve a combination of improved and more accessible public transport systems (buses and trains) and 'uber-like' shared cars (perhaps involving driverless vehicles). It will also result from bringing production and consumption closer together, not just through a reduction in the reliance on global supply chains which span continents, but also within countries. Commuting to work over long distances can be reduced through more remote working, and descaled production plants in manufacturing.

Innovation to support the Green New Deal

In Chapter 2, we observed that, following a historically unprecedented spurt in economic growth after World War 2, there was a steady decline in growth rates in the major industrial economies after the early 1970s. A major cause of the reversal in growth trajectory was a fall in the rate of investment. But even more important than the quantity of investment was a decline in its 'quality' – that is, the productivity of investment. The primary driver of productivity is innovation – a combination of advances in production processes (for example, automation and robotization), new forms of organizing production (for example, global supply chains), new products (for example, mobile phones) and new services (for example, social media).

The key innovation challenges that are required are those which reflect and reinforce the sustainable directionality of the new paradigm. Meeting the challenge of climate change requires a big vision. This will include the development of radically new innovations. For example, there are a variety of potential technologies under development that can 'capture' carbon emissions. Some even aim to 'harvest' carbon dioxide from the atmosphere for use as an input in other sectors, such as in greenhouses growing soft fruit and vegetables in 'vertical farms' cited in multi-storeyed buildings in urban areas. These radical innovations require large resources and cannot be developed overnight. They are thus less attractive to the private sector. However, they also cannot be developed by the government sector alone. Hence, what is required is a Mission-Oriented innovation programme involving a wide range of institutions in the public, private and civil society sectors.

However, climate change is not the only big agenda that needs addressing through a Mission-Oriented research and innovation strategy. There are a range of large challenges which require similar levels of coordination and public–private cooperation, and which have a role to play in rebuilding a socially sustainable world. These include major public health challenges, such as the push for the testing, treatment and vaccination of new and threatening zoonotic viruses such as Covid-19 and a variety of neglected tropical diseases. The global push for a response to the Covid-19 virus both illuminates the need for Mission-Oriented research programmes and shows the capacity of diverse actors – including governments, the corporate sector and research institutions – to respond collectively to major challenges undermining sustainable livelihoods.

Strengthening global and local governance

The Mass Production paradigm saw the introduction of a system of top-down command and control. At the firm level, Henry Ford's pioneering development of mass production was founded on hierarchy. As he observed, he paid his labour force to work, not to think. But increasing scale, the centralization of power and top-down command and control were also reflected in the governance structures of Mass Production. Central government collected tax revenues, and passed funds down to various tiers of local government. The task of local government was to execute the strategic visions emanating from the centre. National programmes, with standardized procedures and evaluative methods, were rolled out across the country. Political control over local communities was increasingly externalized and standardized. Instead of local needs being supported by local action, services were delivered by national institutions. For all of these reasons, Mass Production increasingly resulted in the substitution of isolation and anomie for social solidarity. As we saw in Chapter 3, combined with the reduction in the centralized delivery of services as a result of austerity policies, this weakening social fabric was one of the major factors which led to social decay and the growth of populism.

In the context of growing local needs and falling central provision, locally driven initiatives have sprung up in many countries. This has led to a rising tide of municipalism across the globe. For example, in Porto Alegre in Brazil, a Participatory Budgeting programme was introduced in the early 1980s.[16] Local communities elected representatives. Meetings were organized at regular intervals to consider proposals made by citizens. The community voted on these proposals and the local municipality implemented these decisions. Citizen participation increased over the decades, and the share of the total budget controlled by the Participatory Budgeting scheme increased from 17 per cent in 1992 to 21 per cent in 1999. Sparked by the Porto Alegre experience, Participatory Budgeting schemes spread to more than 250 municipalities in Brazil, and then globally. There are now in excess of 1,500 such programmes around the world.

Another example of local initiatives springing up to fill the gap in provision caused by neo-liberal austerity policies is in Cleveland in the US.[17] The local economy was devastated by deindustrialization as globalization led to the outsourcing of jobs. Cleveland lost more than half of its population and most of its large local companies. Local 'anchor institutions' such as the hospitals and universities, which were by their nature immobile, were spending around $3 billion annually, much of it directed to purchases outside of the local economy. These anchor institutions pooled and redirected their purchasing to local companies, providing a significant boost to the local economy. Cleveland's experience spread across the US. For example, the Francisco Catholic Healthcare West in San Francisco lent millions of dollars to non-profit local suppliers, and the University of Pennsylvania redirected 10 per cent of its expenditure to local firms.

Drawing on this American experience, the local administration in Preston in the UK led an initiative in which a number of anchor institutions pooled their purchasing of inputs to promote local suppliers. Between 2012–13 and 2016–17, procurement within Preston increased by £78 million, expanding from 5 per cent to 18 per cent of total spend by the anchor institutions. During the same period, their expenditure in the wider, local Lancashire region grew by £200 million, from 39 per cent to 79 per cent of total spend.

The importance of local governance was highlighted during the Covid-19 pandemic. After the first wave of the pandemic struck, it became increasingly clear that a primary challenge was to limit the spread of the disease by tracking all those who had been unknowingly exposed to the virus. This could only be achieved by testing for infection, and then rapidly contacting those who might have been infected and requiring them to self-isolate for the period in which they might be infectious. After initial success in supressing the overall transmission rate, the next challenge was to cope with localized flare-ups of the disease. In both of these phases, it became clear that decentralized systems of track-and-trace (as practised in Germany, for example) were far more effective than the centralized programmes adopted in countries such as the UK. Moreover, the moral pressure required to persuade people to self-isolate even when they did not feel ill was more effective when the local community was involved. Instructions from central authorities were more likely to be ignored.

The transition from the centrifugal trajectory of Mass Production to the centripetal directionality in the ICT techno-economic paradigm provides an economic platform for enhanced local governance. Building on this economic and technological foundation, changes in the structure of governance can contribute to the rebuilding of environmental, economic and social sustainability. One key step is the devolution of much financial expenditure from the national to the local level. This applies to devolving funds not only to large cities but across the spectrum of national governance, including to small towns and local communities. Decisions on how local expenditure is allocated should be decided in part by Participatory Budgeting schemes. The design and delivery of social provision should increasingly be bottom-up and locally focused – subject, of course, to supervision on meeting minimum common standards.

In order to promote local clusters of growth and to take advantage of the decentralizing capacity of the new ICT techno-economic paradigm, local expenditure should be focused on enhancing local economic capabilities. Some examples illustrate the scope for building local economies. Programmes can be introduced which provide access to flexible technologies such as 3D additive manufacturing, and which build the skill base required to make efficient use of these new technologies. ICT-enabled 'maker spaces' (flexible accommodation providing opportunities for collaborative activities), business incubators and financial incentives can support local spin-offs from universities and technical institutions. Judicious pooling of purchasing decisions to locally based producers by anchor institutions can play an important role in promoting local clusters of production.

Particular emphasis should be given to the development of what is referred to as the Smart City infrastructure. This seeks to link a variety of urban facilities – such as transport, lighting and public services – through the widespread use of IoTs. This will not only strengthen the competitiveness of the local economy, but also make a major contribution to the greening of production and consumption. Contrary to the trajectory of past decades, less effort should be placed on a transport infrastructure designed to strengthen links with external economies (for example, airports and trunk roads), and more emphasis placed on the infrastructure facilitating logistics within the local economy.

There are two major caveats in this policy agenda designed to strengthen local economies and to contribute to a remaking of a sustainable world. The first is that the objective is to switch from a centrifugal outward-oriented *trajectory* to a centripetal inward-oriented *trajectory*. This transition cannot be absolute and must be governed by attention to cost, but cost seen in a dynamic environmental and social context. The dynamic context is one which recognizes that, with support, local suppliers have the capacity to improve their relative offering over time.

Second, at the same time that these trends towards localization are taking place, there is a simultaneous requirement to enhance the power of some key decisions which are made and enforced at the national and global levels. Governments need to provide a vision and to intervene decisively to drive a Green New Deal and to replenish state coffers through increased taxation. But action is also required at the transnational level. A great number of firms that operate globally have used their geographically diversified activities to avoid (and in many cases to evade) taxation. The deployment of the new ICT techno-economic paradigm will require more, rather than less, fiscal revenue, and the taxes required to fill government coffers can only effectively be collected at the national level and through global agreements and global actions. Other important arenas for supranational intervention include agreements to limit environmental destruction; stemming the flow of hazardous migration; controlling anti-competitive practices in the corporate sector; controlling politically damaging fake news in social media; regulating the financial sector; and fighting against communicable diseases.

But supra-national action necessarily also requires targeted support for low- and middle-income economies, to which our attention now turns.

Promoting global development

The analysis in previous chapters of the crises in economic, social and environmental sustainability focused on the high-income countries. There are two reasons for this restricted vision. Despite the rapid growth of output and capabilities in formerly low-income countries such as China and India, the high-income countries continue to dominate global production and innovation, accounting for more than 60 per cent of global output and consumption. Moreover, the economic and social structures in many middle- and low-income economies are qualitatively different from those in the high-income countries. Large numbers of their populations live outside of the cash and formal economy, and many engage in subsistence agriculture. Moreover, there is enormous diversity in what is quaintly referred to as 'The Rest of the World' in the measurement of global output and trade. Conditions in low-income countries such as Malawi are vastly different from those in middle-income countries such as China.

Nevertheless, there are a number of reasons why the middle- and low-income countries cannot be excluded from sustainability policy agendas in the high-income countries. Most importantly, the remaking of *global* environmental sustainability requires the introduction of substantial greening programmes in middle- and lower-income countries. Nowhere is this more evident than in the case of the use of fossil fuels in general, and coal in particular. The challenge is most acutely felt in the case of China and India, which together account for more than one-third of the global population. Both are committed to the growth of renewable energy. Yet both are actively investing in coal-powered energy generation. China is building a new coal-powered power station every two weeks, and, through its aid programme, in 2019 was financing the construction of more than 300 coal-powered plants in other countries.[18] However, if global environmental sustainability is to be rebuilt, the need for a greening agenda in middle- and low-income economies cannot be restricted to a reduction in the use of fossil fuels. It must address the full range of production and consumption patterns. The opportunities opened up by the Smart Green New Deal agenda across the spectrum of economic and social life applies as much to middle- and low-income economies as they do to high-income economies. A growing number of countries, such as Costa Rica in Latin America, Ethiopia in Africa and Bhutan in Asia, recognize these opportunities.

Costa Rica, for example, is likely to become the first country in the world to achieve zero net carbon dioxide emissions.

Ethics and values are important components of lifestyles and the sustainability agenda, and the elimination of global poverty is an important ethical concern to many citizens in high-income countries. Not only do lower-income economies account for more than 80 per cent of the global population, but the unmet 'absolute' (that is, basic) needs of their populations dwarf those in richer countries. Many of their citizens live at or near the level required to guarantee basic subsistence. An extra $10 of income for the world's poorest citizens is manifestly more valuable than the same income accruing to those living at the top of the global income pyramid. Thus, unlike the high-income countries which already have the capacity to meet their populations' basic needs, rapid growth in output is an essential requirement in developing economies. The primary moral responsibility for a reduction in the consumption of global raw materials and global emissions must therefore lie with the high-income countries.

Furthermore, economic growth in the high-income economies depends on the sustainability of economic growth in middle- and low-income countries. Although the ICT techno-economic paradigm will draw production and consumption closer together, it is currently the fact that low- and middle-income countries will continue to play an important role in global supply chains. Moreover, in a context of capitalism's endemic problem with underconsumption, middle- and low-income economies are also an important market for the output of high-income economies, particularly for machinery, new technologies and specialized services.

Global migration is another reason why developments in low- and middle-income economies should not be excluded from the policy agenda in high-income countries. On the one hand, the migration of highly skilled workers such as doctors, nurses, engineers and ICT specialists has had a major positive impact on social sustainability and economic growth in the high-income world. On the other hand, the rapid increase in the number of unskilled migrants and refugees resulting from a combination of climate change, conflict and poverty has had a significant impact in undermining social sustainability in the destination high-income countries.

Thus, there are clear reasons why it is in the interests of the high-income countries for sustainability to be built in low- and middle-income economies. However, the specificity and the diversity of their economic and social structures and their growth trajectories require dedicated examination which is beyond the remit of this book. Therefore, the policy proposals which follow, with respect to low- and middle-income countries, are limited to those areas relevant to the remaking of economic, social and environmental sustainability in the global economy and in high-income economies.

First and foremost, the primary challenge is to reduce greenhouse-gas emissions. This involves a combination of initiatives which are similar in many respects to changes required in the high-income countries. There is considerable scope for more efficient energy use in low- and middle-income countries. This cuts across virtually all activities in production (for example, production processes in industry and the burning of crop residues in agriculture), logistics (for example, fuel-inefficient transport systems) and consumption (for example, wood-burning cooking stoves). As in the case of high-income countries, the electrification of vehicles will lead to a significant reduction of greenhouse-gas and health-harming emissions. China has become a leading innovator in the development of electric cars and has also been one of the first countries to pioneer fuelled buses in public transport. The impact of substituting electric for gasoline-powered three-wheeled taxis in some Indian cities is a concrete example of the substantial health and environmental benefits that can be reaped, not just locally but also globally.

However, beyond fostering greater energy efficiency in low- and middle-income economies, there is considerable scope for generating low-cost energy through renewables such as solar power, wind power and bio-fuels. Because of their geography and the relative absence of centralized energy grids, these opportunities are particularly bountiful in many middle- and low-income economies. This drive for greater fuel efficiency and a transition to renewable energy will have devastating impacts on some developing economies that depend on the extraction and export of fossil fuels (such as those in West Africa). They stand to lose very substantial sources of revenue and foreign exchange. Hence, alternative sources of income will need to be developed in these affected countries, both to ensure their participation in programmes to reduce the use of fossil fuels, and for pressing ethical and political reasons.

Finally, the destruction of global habitats such as forests and the seas will need to be limited by international agreement. This will require that new forms of economic activity be developed to provide alternative sources of income for those whose livelihoods – existing and potential – are adversely affected.

Fortunately, the new ICT techno-economic paradigm offers considerable scope for promoting sustainable development in low- and middle-income countries. As I showed in Chapter 7, ICT-facilitated technologies such as mobile telephony and minimal-tillage farming provide significant opportunities for a new pattern of development. Moreover, because these economies are latecomers, they are not held back by outdated systems. They have the opportunity to leapfrog inefficient and outdated technologies. As can be seen from the pioneering development of mobile banking and distributed household energy generation in East Africa, this is not merely wishful thinking.

All of these initiatives require financial support and a new skill base. Yet in many economies, particularly lower-income countries, these are precisely the inputs which are missing and which account for their deep levels of poverty and environmental degradation. So it will be imperative for the high-income economies (and some middle-income economies such as China) to provide support for sustainable growth in these lower-income countries. The crucial step which this requires is for those in the higher-income economies to recognize that supporting sustainable development at the global level is a necessary condition for the remaking of sustainability in their own countries.

8.3 The Elephant in the Room – Who Will Drive the Transition to a Sustainable World?

I began this chapter by observing that, left unchecked, there is a danger that the new ICT techno-economic paradigm may exacerbate the trend towards social, political and environmental unsustainability. This was followed by a vision of a more sustainable society, premised on the full deployment of the new ICT techno-economic paradigm. In the face of these two contrasting scenarios, directionality is key. A suite of policies were then outlined which have the capacity to impart this sustainability trajectory.

A vision and a policy agenda are all very well in theory. But under what circumstances can this policy agenda be implemented? Who are the major stakeholders, and which policies are of first-order importance? It is to these thorny problems that our attention now turns, in the final concluding chapter.

9
Who Will Do It? Making Change Happen

My experience in the design (and non-delivery) of Industrial Policy in South Africa recounted in the previous chapter is, of course, not unique, either to me or to South Africa. Across the spectrum of policy experience, we can witness a steady erosion of the belief that progress can be achieved by the design of policy alone. Even if policy design follows many person-years of background research (as we saw in the case of the Industrial Strategy Project), the identification of appropriate policies does not in itself lead to change. The key takeaway from this South African story is that, to make a meaningful contribution to change, policy must be seen not just as design, but also as process.[1]

Two personal experiences illustrate the importance of policy process, in which the *why*, the *what* and the *how* must necessarily be driven by the *who*. The first refers to my work in Cyprus in the late 1980s. I had been tasked by the United Nations Development Programme with leading a team providing assistance to the government on Technology Policy. Simultaneously, my colleague Robin Murray, who had developed an international reputation as the leader of the policy team in the Greater London Council during the mid-1980s, led a team focusing on Industrial Policy.

The two teams worked closely together in these complementary programmes. We interacted intensively with the civil service and the private sector and reported directly to the government through the President George Vassiliou. We had considerable traction with the civil service and the private sector since our large teams were visiting and discussing policies at regular intervals. Towards the end of this process, Robin was in the UK and I went to see the President. I summarized what we were proposing, and he responded enthusiastically: 'Call together a meeting of the Directors General of all the Ministries, tell them that I like your approach and policies and that they are to be the policy agenda which the Civil Service must implement.' I was flattered – the President, no less, had tasked me with the job of telling his civil service what to do.

I did as asked, and was too flushed with my importance to get a measure of the frosty response I was receiving from the assembly of Directors General. I returned to the UK with a glow in my heart. I couldn't wait to tell Robin how successful we had been. Arriving near midnight on a Friday, I found it hard to restrain myself from phoning Robin to give him the 'good news'. When I got through to him on Saturday morning and told him what had happened, the phone went silent ... 'What? What have you done? If the President wanted our agenda to be the policy of his government, it was his job to inform his civil servants, not ours ... [And then, in the politest way – Robin had as sensitive a tongue as anyone could wish for] Do you realize that you have just scuppered the whole programme?' What a way for me to learn an invaluable lesson.

More recently, I was part of team which had great success in Barcombe, the small village in Sussex where I live. This is a closely knit community of around 1,600 people living in an area of 7 square miles. Our village store is the centre of social interaction. It has a post office and sells basic products. Customers who want variety and lower cost need to drive 5 miles to the nearest town to find a supermarket. Not everyone in the village has a car, and there is a large community of elderly people, many of whom have lived in the village for decades. The problem was that the village shopkeeper, having run the store for sixteen years, wanted to retire. He had tried to sell the store as a going concern for some months, but without success. He announced that he was therefore going to seek planning permission to turn the premises into a residence. This would have been devastating for the community, and especially for the elderly.

We then set about raising the funds for the village to purchase the property and to rent out the store to anyone who wanted a reasonable and steady income. The upshot was that the community of 650 households raised a total of £388,000. Two local residents – one with a Master's degree in archaeology, and the other with a Master's degree in environmental management – now run an improved shop as a commercial venture. The store provides a post office to the community and a depot for medical prescriptions, dry cleaning and e-commerce returns. But the truly impressive part of this story concerns the voting rights in the company which owns the property. Although the minimum shareholding is £500 (which makes up the bulk of shareholders by number), a few of the more wealthy village inhabitants provided much larger sums – in one case, £50,000. The group of the largest contributors met and decided, without prompting, that all shareholders should have the same voting rights, irrespective of the size of their contributions. The true value of this community initiative surfaced during the Covid-19 pandemic in early 2020. The lockdown made it difficult to travel to the nearest supermarket, and many people, including the vulnerable aged, had little capacity to make this journey anyway. The turnover of the shop in the first three months of lockdown was double that of the previous year. A local shop and post office was a vital asset to the resilience of a village of 1,600 people, and this outcome could not have been achieved without the participation of more than one-third of all households.

These two examples address the same point. Successful outcomes require not just a rationale (*why* change?), a vision (*what* do we want?) and a how (*what* do we have to do in order to achieve the vision?), but also a process (*who* owns the agenda and is going to do it?). In the Cyprus case, failure came from change being driven by outsiders. In the Barcombe case, successful change occurred because the affected citizens recognized the need to change, because they participated in the conception of the vision, because they shared the benefits, and because they identified the steps necessary to deliver the vision.

9.1 Entrepreneurship: Turning Fantasy into Fact

One of the cardinal tenets of the school of Innovation Management is that the rocket science of invention is the easy link in the innovation chain.[2] The truly difficult phase in innovation is transforming new and good ideas into commercial products. Schumpeter, the great Austrian economist, referred to this difficult part of the journey as entrepreneurship. The primary functions of an entrepreneur are to develop a vision, and to ensure that all the necessary inputs are available, that they are of adequate quality and appropriately priced, that a market exists for the final product, and that there is an effective way for delivering the product to final consumers and coping with the discarded materials after use. Crucially, finance has to be obtained for the whole venture and all stages have to have regulatory approval. Each of these links in the innovation chain requires collective endeavour by teams of people, generally working in different locations. Most commonly, the members of these cooperating teams also work in different institutions – some in supplier and customer firms, some in research establishments and others in civil society and government.

Each of these components of corporate entrepreneurship apply equally in the development and implementation of public policy. However, in most cases, the 'policy chain' is much more complex and challenging than the 'corporate innovation chain'. More interest groups are involved. Moreover, unlike the 'market' where a single indicator (monetary profit) is a relatively unambiguous indicator of successful innovation, policy outcomes are much more complex and are characteristically contested, even after implementation. The bigger the policy agenda, the more complex are the alliances for cooperative action, and the greater the arenas for contestation. And what could be bigger and more complex than the transition to a new socio-technical paradigm, particularly when this involves unavoidable changes in norms and lifestyles and shifting balances of political and economic power?

The transition in techno-economic paradigms is both aided and hampered by a complex combination of enablers and blinkers and fetters. On the positive side, the new heartland technology provides the opportunity for corporate profitability, revived economic growth, a more cohesive society and an improved environment. On the negative side are the blinkers (the personal and social mechanisms which act to prevent people from seeing the need for change and visioning the direction of change) and the fetters (the reactionary forces which seek to prevent change, either because change runs against their interests or because it disturbs their worldview). We will return to the role played by these enabling and blocking societal forces later in this chapter. But, before this, we need to identify who might be the primary drivers of change to provide a sustainability trajectory to the new ICT techno-economic paradigm?

9.2 The Private Sector Provides the Motive Power, the State is at the Steering Wheel (and Sometimes Pays for the Petrol)

The degree of autonomy given to private investors has been, and continues to be, one of the cornerstones of economic and political debate. At the one extreme are the proponents of 'free enterprise'. They march under the banner of a (selective) quote from the famous eighteenth-century moral philosopher Adam Smith:

> every individual, therefore, endeavours as much as he can both to employ his capital in the support of domestic industry, and so to direct that industry that its produce may be of the greatest value ... He generally, indeed, neither intends to promote the public interest, nor knows how much he is promoting it ... [B]y directing that industry in such a manner as its produce may be of the greatest value, he intends only his own gain, and he is in this, as in many other cases, led by an invisible hand to promote an end which was no part of his intention ... By pursuing his own interest he frequently promotes that of the society more effectually than when he really intends to promote it.[3]

Belief in an 'invisible hand' which translates individual greed into social good leads to a hands-off role for government in the transition to a new techno-economic paradigm. However, the market alone will not deliver the transition to a more sustainable world. To the contrary, as we have seen in earlier chapters, the neo-liberal free-market agenda undermined economic and productivity growth and contributed significantly to rising inequality, increasing social decay, the emergence of populist governments and the despoliation of the environment.

At the other extreme are the proponents of a command economy. Here the state not only regulates economic activity extensively but also is a major owner of productive enterprises. In its extreme manifestation, this ideology formed the core of Soviet communism after the 1930s and is still alive in contemporary Cuba. The command economy was demonstrably successful in meeting basic needs and in mobilizing economic resources to meet external military threats (as in the case of Russia's ability to repel the German invasion in World War 2, and Cuba's capacity to resist invasion from the US during the Bay of Pigs and in subsequent decades). But it is clear that the command economy provides little incentive to innovate, to meet consumer needs and to compete with more market-oriented economies on the global stage. Moreover, growth in the Soviet Union had severely negative environmental impacts.

Hence, it is evident that both extremes in this markets–states stand-off are sub-optimal. Some mix of responsibilities is required to deliver a more sustainable world. So, what is the optimal balance between free enterprise and state control in the transition to a more sustainable world? The answer is that there is no single answer, there is no 'one best way'. There is a variety of mixes in the roles to be played and the specific actions to be taken by states and markets in the roll-out of a sustainability-enhancing ICT techno-economic paradigm. However, whatever the mix, two core factors will determine successful outcomes.

The first is that it is unquestionably the case that the private sector has been, is currently and will primarily be responsible for the bulk of innovation in the economy. As we saw in Chapters 2 and 4, the 'Schumpeterian innovation motor' is the primary driver of economic growth. Capitalists search for new ways of doing things and new products and services as a way of escaping from competition. The challenge is to capitalize on the innovative dynamism of the private sector and to ensure that it delivers a more sustainable world. But, as we will see, this does not mean that the private sector is the only source of innovation, or that it can address large innovation challenges without state support.

The second ground-rule is that the private sector does not operate in a vacuum. Property laws define rights to ownership, competition laws define what sorts of firms can operate and how they can compete, regulations determine what products and what processes are permissible, infrastructure makes production and exchange possible, costly private innovation requires state financial support and a skilled labour force, and the prices of the inputs into production determine the character of new innovations. And, crucially, the structure of the tax system determines the relative cost structure and the relative profitability of alternative projects and innovations. All of these scene-setting parameters which affect the direction of economic growth are defined by government policy in its various forms. Thus, although the private sector may be the main motor of innovation, the direction of travel is steered by government. In the words of Frank Thorpe, the Managing Director of the UK arm of the Chinese electric car manufacturer BYD – 'You need ambition from government as well as intent from manufacturers.'[4]

Beyond the private sector

Bearing in mind the enormity of the challenge of transitioning to a new socio-techno-economic paradigm, it is not surprising that a variety of non-private-sector actors have important roles to play in the remaking of a more sustainable world. Four key parties can be identified.

Institutions of global governance operate at the 'highest' level of action. These include agreements such as conventions on climate change, institutions such as the World Trade Organization, the International Monetary Fund, the Bank for International Settlements, the World Intellectual Property Organization, the United Nations and the International Labour Organisation, and groups of countries such as the European Union and the ASEAN community in Southeast Asia. These transnational institutions contribute to the shaping of economic and societal progress. In some cases, these international agreements are backed by sanctions. For example, 'unfair trading practices' are punished with punitive tariffs in disputes settled by the World Trade Organization. Companies guilty of 'unfair competitive actions' have to pay fines to inter-government organizations such as the European Union. But in other cases – for example, the conventions on climate change and the UN Convention on the Law of the Sea – compliance is voluntary. It is striking that those conventions backed by sanctions primarily reinforce the search for profit and economic growth. Those with 'softer' voluntary agreements address environmental and social sustainability.

Below this transnational level stand national governments. Over the last two to three decades, the power of nation states has been eroded by transnational agreements. Nevertheless, there remains considerable space for the governments of individual countries to take actions which will affect the speed and character of the transition to a more sustainable world. Naturally, the larger the economy, the greater the power for autonomous action. Countries such as the US and China, or groups of countries such as the European Union, have the capacity to create rules which others have to follow (a hard lesson which post-Brexit Britain will surely discover). For example, the US exerts pressure on trading partners to open their economies to transnational corporations, particularly in areas where American firms are dominant. In other cases, large economies have the capacity to flout agreed rules and conventions – for example, China building artificial islands in the South China Sea.

At the 'lowest' level of governance are local and municipal authorities. Their absolute size will, of course, vary across countries. The state of Uttar Pradesh in India has a population of more than 225 million, making it the fourth largest 'country' in the world; Guangdon Province in China consists of more than 120 million people, exceeding the total population of the Philippines. But even within these regions, many elements of power and decision-making are devolved to the local level. And whilst the degree of this devolution of power clearly varies across countries and regions, as we saw in the previous chapter, some of the key steps necessary to build a more sustainable world require the enhanced participation of the various tiers of sub-national devolved governance.

Fourth, non-private-sector civil society organizations play a critical role in the shaping of the economy and society. Some of these organizations are large and transnational – for example, Greenpeace campaigns on the global environment, the Global Alliance on Tax Justice campaigns on global tax, and Fairtrade campaigns on basic incomes and working conditions for global producers. But many civil society organizations – indeed the bulk of them – participate at the local level. They promote local environmental issues, care for the excluded, organize foodbanks and lobby for living wages for local workers. These civil society organizations operate in two distinct and often complementary ways. On the one hand, they seek to influence public opinion, to pressure governments and corporations to act in particular directions and to change individual behaviour. For example, public pressure forced large companies to withdraw advertising from Facebook in 2020 in order to limit its dissemination of racist and inflammatory postings, including those posted by the US President. On the other hand, they are also focal points for sustainability activities, such as providing support for marginal communities, assisting informal and small-scale producers and engaging in practical projects to improve the physical environment (and saving village stores!).

9.3 Building Coalitions for Change

Whilst powerful parties can over-ride the concerns and interests of weaker parties, in most cases meaningful change necessitates cooperation between a diverse set of economic, political and social actors. The bigger the change agenda, the greater the need for alliances. Similarly, the bigger the change agenda, the more complex alliances become.

Imposing a sustainability directionality in the deployment of the ICT techno-economic paradigm is a change of substantial magnitude. It is the biggest agenda of our time. So what factors constrain the capacity to cooperate and to make alliances in building a more sustainable world?

- Some changes result in win–win outcomes – everyone stands to gain. But other changes lead to win–lose outcomes – some gain, and others lose. The big structural changes involved in paradigm transition are invariably of the latter variety.
- The complexity and magnitude of the challenge in providing directionality to the transition in the techno-economic paradigm involve parties and institutions from across the range of social and economic activity. Each of these participants has distinct objectives and ways of working. For example, the corporate sector measures success in terms of money and profitability; trades unions seek to maintain employment in existing activities; governments seek to be re-elected, generally within time-frames which are too short for significant structural change; civil society organizations seek to maximize social solidarity, measuring success in terms of social outcomes; environmental interest groups are concerned to minimize the environmental footprint of human activity.
- 'Time preference' is a critical element in these trade-offs, particularly with regard to the remaking of environmental sustainability. That is, to what extent should the present generation benefit at the cost of future generations? Or, vice versa, to what extent should the present generation pay the costs of providing a sustainable and comfortable life for future generations? And how do future generations get their voices heard in a social context of 'I want everything, now'?

- Some of the obstacles to cooperation reflect attitudes, norms and values. Like blinkers – the leather pads surrounding horses' eyes – they prevent people from seeing the need for change, the significance of the required changes and the necessity for rapid responses. Other obstacles to cooperation act as fetters, such as the conscious behaviour of opponents manipulating public opinion and seeking to prevent people and institutions from taking action.

There are a number of responses which can reduce or remove these impediments to cooperation. First, a well-established principle in economic and political policy is that when change leads to the uneven distribution of benefits, the 'winners' (that is those who gain) need to compensate the 'losers' (those who pay the costs of change). There can be a significant number of losers in paradigm change. For example, as we saw in the previous chapter, if the UK is to meet its objective of phasing out oil and gas energy generation by 2030, this will involve the loss of 280,000 jobs. In Germany, the automobile industry dominates the industrial sector and currently employs 830,000. It is estimated that more than 250,000 of these jobs will be displaced by 2030 due to the switch to electrically powered vehicles. In the US, almost 1 million workers are employed in the auto components and assembly sectors. The Ford Motor Corporation, America's second-largest vehicle manufacturer, estimated that the production of electric cars would require only half of the capital investment required to produce internal combustion engine cars, and would employ 30 per cent fewer workers.[5]

But, at the same time, the greening of the economy provides manifold opportunities for new employment. Wholly new products and services will generate new jobs. The shift from single-use privately owned to repairable durable products will provide employment for skilled workers repairing used products. Insulating homes, protecting the environment, building the ICT infrastructure and many other activities relating to the successful deployment of the ICT paradigm will create abundant opportunities for employment. And, perhaps most important, ICTs provide the capacity to reduce costs, as is shown by the price competitiveness of renewable energy in Texas, the heart of the US oil and gas economy. ExxonMobil will generate 70 per cent of its future Texas energy production through renewables, and the CEO of one of the oil majors, Occidental, declared that 'We put the solar in to lower our carbon footprint but also to provide lower-cost electrical power.'[6] These cost savings in energy generation will provide some of the resources required to ease the costs of transition.

Hence, the policy challenge is to facilitate the process of structural change. This will require the capacity to appropriate some of the gains generated in the transition to the new paradigm and to redirect these funds to activities designed to compensate the losers. As in the New Deal during the Great Depression in the 1930s, displaced workers can be retrained, and new industries and firms can be supported. Nevertheless, there will always be people who cannot be retrained to work in radically different industries, and other measures of compensation will need to be developed. For example, to the extent that it will indeed be the case that the rapid deployment of ICTs will displace many millions of workers, this may reinforce the call for a Universal Basic Income for all.

Second, alliances between different parties may be limited to specific issues.[7] As we saw in the introduction to this chapter, more than one-third of the population of Barcombe (the village where I live) joined together to save our village shop. But this was a single-issue intervention and, after the deal was completed, this alliance of villagers dissolved (although the boost it provided to social solidarity enhanced the robustness of the village's response to the Covid-19 pandemic). In Lewes (the adjacent town), citizens ran a campaign to prevent the locality turning into a dormitory town for commuters. In the productive sector, small and medium-sized firms may join together to co-invest in a local renewable energy facility. Or a town, such as many in Denmark, Germany and the Netherlands, may set up a community-controlled renewable energy plant. In each of these cases, the cooperation may initially be focused on single issues, and then may grow into wider and more long-lived alliances. For example, the Transition Town movement promoting local environmental and social action originated in Totnes, a small town in Devon, England, and now involves a network of more than 1,000 towns globally. At the corporate level, two firms may cooperate on a single venture to promote greening and decentralized, flexible production, and this may transition into long-run cooperation on these and similar issues, bringing in many more partners.

Third, mixed-motive alliances are fragile. This may not matter as long as they share common objectives. For example, China has been one of the leading actors promoting investment in renewable energy.

This has been led by the central state, which has conflicting objectives. On the one hand, it has sought to reduce pollution in cities and to promote the growth of next-generation green industries. But, on the other hand, it has been concerned with energy security. The fragility of these mixed motives for change is illustrated in the recent boom in the construction of environmentally damaging coal-fired plants in China. This reflects the primacy of energy security over environmental sustainability. Hence, the governance of alliances is critical. Lessons can be learned from comparative experience across the world on how mixed-motive alliances can be managed.

Fourth, although the transition to a more sustainable techno-economic paradigm will require root-and-branch changes in attitudes, in institutional organization, in patterns of governance and in technology, change is cumulative. It can begin at a low level and then diffuse rapidly. Often, as we saw in Carlota Perez' description of lifestyles in the previous chapter, changes begin as niche experiments, perhaps in consumption preferences (for example, shifting to locally produced organic food), in behaviour in the home (turning the thermostat down) and in new equipment in the factory (shorter and fatter pipes waste less energy). But these niche changes then increase in scope and spread rapidly – reduced and plastics-free packaging in supermarkets; insulation, solar panels and heat pumps in the home; redesigned factory layouts.

Finally, there is no 'one best way' in the successful transition to a more sustainable world. The phrase 'one best way' can be traced back to the writings of the management theorist F. W. Taylor in the late nineteenth and early twentieth centuries. Taylor provided a system for breaking down work-flow into a variety of individual tasks, each of which was subject to measurement, redesign and intensification. More recently, as we saw in Chapter 3, the American political scientist Francis Fukuyama declared in 1992 that the world was entering a period reflecting 'the end of history'. All political systems would, he believed, converge into liberal democracies, mirroring the structure, the efficiency and the political alliances of America in the 1980s. How wrong could these two opinion-makers be? The 'efficient' US economy which came to depend on Fordist work organization is currently clearly unable to compete effectively on the global stage. The not-very-democratic Chinese economy has made amazing leaps, is challenging the US as an innovation leader and is driving the decarbonization of transport at an astonishing rate.

So, there is a variety of routes to a more sustainable world. Each of these will have to take many of the required actions outlined in the previous chapter, but they will do so in their own unique way. Each family, firm, institution and country starts from different points, operates in different conditions and has its own individual trajectory. The idea that efficiency in the enterprise – let alone the structure and operation of social and political processes – can be reduced to a single template is an absurdity. Equally absurd is the belief that a single party can impose and direct the synergistic changes which are required to impose a sustainability directionality on the transition in techno-economic paradigms.

9.4 Change Is Cumulative

All change, and especially substantial change, is cumulative. In 1981, I interviewed the head of Computervision, an American firm pioneering the development of Computer Aided Design. Their annual turnover was around $70 million, but it was widely believed that the market would exceed $1 billion by the end of the decade. (In fact, the industry grew to more than $1.4 billion by 1990.) I asked the CEO whether he was concerned that General Electric, then the largest industrial enterprise in America, with a post-tax profit of more than $1.5 billion, would see the opportunity for market growth and invest heavily in the development of the new technology. 'Ah', he answered, 'you see you can't make a baby in one month with nine women'.

In the face of the urgent need to rebuild sustainability, particularly environmental sustainability, there is the danger that the cumulative nature of change will hinder the transition to the ICT techno-economic paradigm. For cumulative change involves a series of small steps, and what is required is a series of big – in fact, very large – changes. So the trick is to develop change trajectories which combine a myriad of rapid small changes which are embedded in a larger vision of coordinated change. As Rob Hopkins, one of the founders of the Transition Town movement observed, 'If we try and do it on our own it will be too little, if we wait for government to do it it will be too late, but if we can gather together those around us – our street, our neighbourhood, our community – it might just be enough, and it might just be in time.'[8]

A small example of how rapid structural change can be achieved through a myriad of small incremental changes concerns the transition to flexible just-in-time production in Japanese factories during the 1970s and 1980s. The US competitors to Japanese automobile firms had assumed (their blinkered path dependency) that the rapidly growing market share of their Japanese competitors resulted from the innovation of costly flexible manufacturing systems. However, in reality, the efficiency gains were largely driven by new work processes which turned F. W. Taylor's 'one best way' on its head. In contrast to Henry Ford's Taylorist maxim that 'I pay workers to work, not to think', the Japanese firms introduced a system of *kaizen*, continuous improvement, in which each worker was expected to make suggestions for improvements in process and product. In Toyota, the pioneer of systemic change in production organization, the workforce contributed more than 2.5 million suggestions for improvement in 1985 alone. A trivial example illustrates the astonishing potential of sustained cumulative incremental change drawing on the knowledge of the labour force. It used to take eight hours to change the dies defining the shape of body parts stamped out of flat metal. This imposed prohibitive costs on changing product variety. So, if Toyota was to move to more flexible production patterns (the vision driving its corporate strategy), it needed to reduce this 'dead' time on the production line. Over the course of three years, aided by *kaizen*, incremental changes were introduced which reduced the downtime from eight hours to two minutes.[9]

In summary, change is an unfolding process rather than an end state. Different starting points and different end points necessitate unfolding journeys. In the words of the Chinese philosopher Lao Tsu (the founder of Taoism), 'The journey of a thousand miles begins with one step.' But it is also a journey which is in many respects inherently unknowable. As Deng Xiaoping, the president who guided China through substantial structural change during the 1980s, observed, it is necessary to 'cross the river by feeling for the stones'.

9.5 How to Jump Over Walls

And now for the really difficult part ... How can we develop the capacity to 'jump over walls'? What, if anything, will be the mobilizers for the deployment of the ICT techno-economic paradigm with a directionality which promotes economic, social and environmental sustainability? Three core enablers will deliver this outcome. First, paradigm change requires the adoption of complementary interventions which reflect the systemic character of techno-economic paradigms. Second, governments have the key role to play in imparting directionality to the character of the new paradigm. And, third, paradigm change can only succeed if the power of the reactionary forces which hold back progress (the fetters to change) are challenged and overcome.

Synergistic interventions

If sustainability is to be rebuilt, there is a necessary complementarity between changes in the economic, social and political domains, with complex interactions with the environment. Here are a few examples of the systemic character of the required changes. A Green New Deal cannot be implemented without governments having the financial capabilities to build the information highway infrastructure and to foster the skills required to develop, install and use new greening technologies. This will require that neo-liberal austerity policies will need to be overturned. Another example: reinvigorating economic growth requires long-term investment horizons, and this necessitates a curb on financial speculation through a combination of taxation and regulation. This cannot be achieved without confronting and overcoming the power of the financial sector and the plutocracy. And yet another example: bringing production and consumption closer together requires a combination of devolved governance, the development of new technologies and a restructuring of infrastructure and transport systems. It also requires changes in regional government policies – as, for example, in the Smart Cities programme. A final example: more environmentally efficient production processes and more environmentally sustainable products will require changes in the sticks and carrots which governments provide through regulations, taxes and subsidies. They will also require that governments have the necessary financial resources to provide incentives for change, and this will require fundamental changes in the balance of political power.

The central argument of this book is that these complementarities can only be understood through the techno-economic framework and the critical role played by ICTs in the current era. Unless the systemic interactions between the economy, society, politics and the environment are acknowledged in the change agenda, meaningful change cannot occur. A technocratic agenda for change – for example, the belief that the fix for the environmental crisis lies with 'new technology' – will be a failed agenda for change.[10]

Governments must act decisively and with vision

The transition between paradigms results from myriad actions by individuals and groups of social, political and economic actors. However, paradigm change is of such systemic magnitude that it requires decisive actions to build a consensus on the need for change, and to overcome the fettering power of vested interests. Unavoidably, this requires visionary leadership at the highest level. As we saw in previous chapters, Roosevelt's New Deal policies during the 1930s performed these functions. Attacking 'the fear of fear itself' – that is, the crisis of confidence in American society – he offered a vision of a new society and economy. The New Deal backed this vision with very substantial investments in infrastructure and skills development, equivalent to more than 5 per cent of US GDP between 1933 and the onset of World War 2. In pre-war Europe, the big visions which helped to revive the economies were less admirable. In Germany and Italy, fascist governments used re-armament as the tool for their 'big push'. This led to the adoption of a similar programme in the UK after 1936. In the nineteenth century, Bismark responded to the 'Great Depression' in Germany with a headline programme of 'State Socialism'. This involved major changes in the management of the economy and society – tariffs were introduced to protect domestic industry, and unemployment insurance, pensions and compensation for industrial accidents were introduced to cushion the impact of the Depression on the labour force.[11]

As I showed in previous chapters, government responses after the systemic Financial Crisis in 2008 failed to provide a visionary agenda for structural change. A return to 'normality', 'business as usual', pervaded the agenda. President Obama appointed to his advisory team the very people who had participated in the formulation and implementation of the economic policies which contributed to the Crisis in the first place. In Europe, policies were introduced which sought to revive the *status quo ex ante*. For example, Greece's debt had largely been incurred with the private banking sector. But, as its Economic Minister at the time, Yiannis Varoufakis, recounts, so clearly, instead of allowing the banks to suffer the consequences of their irresponsible lending, the first step of the EU negotiators was to transfer this private-sector debt to European governments.[12] In both North America and Europe, the opportunities to use this Financial Crisis as a springboard for systemic transformation were fluffed.

It is unavoidable, therefore, that governments must play the lead role in promoting the transition to a new and more sustainable order. They may be aided in this by transnational institutions such as the EU, the IMF, ASEAN, the World Bank and the United Nations, and intergovernmental agreements arising from global movements such as the International Panel on Climate Change. Politicians and the systems supporting them have to develop a synthetic vision of the future and to propose a path to reach that destination. One possible rallying call for the transition to a more sustainable world is the adoption of a Smart Green New Deal. But that option is not free from problems. The greening of production and society may be a priority, and it may be a central requirement for rebuilding sustainability. But in itself, as I tried to show in the previous chapter, it is not the only challenge which needs to be overcome in the transition to a more sustainable economy, society and environment.

Confronting reactionary power bases

Virtually all change results in a combination of losers and winners. The large agendas involved in paradigm change magnify these contrasting impacts. Take the case of the decarbonization of energy. As in virtually all cases of radical technical change, the prime knowledge-base for the development of these new technologies resulted from government research programmes and government funding of research in universities and the private sector. But thereafter it has been the private sector which has driven the increasingly rapid application of this knowledge-base to meet commercial business opportunities. Building on this accumulated and often publicly funded knowledge-base, a number of firms in Europe, China and elsewhere have innovated effectively in the solar and wind power sectors. In the future, technological innovation in the storage of intermittent renewable power will provide business opportunities for existing and new firms. Aided by a combination of technological developments and government regulations, the world's third-largest economic sector – the automobile industry – is investing massively in electric cars. They see electrification as the route to their future profitability. And Tesla – the pioneer of large-volume production of electric cars – is now one of the world's largest companies by share value. These are the winners in paradigm change.

But at the same time there are parties who lose from this transition away from fossil fuels, and many of these are economically and politically powerful actors. For example, the oil and gas industry is being heavily disrupted, and many of the largest firms are scrambling to unwind their near-exclusive dependence on fossil-fuel energy. Threatened by a combination of public pressure and the increasing efficiency of renewable energy and electric cars, the gigantic oil and gas companies are being deserted by financial investors and are in danger of being dragged under in the medium term by the weight of their stranded assets. In June 2020, Shell wrote down $22 billion of assets and BP reduced its asset value by $17.5 billion. Not all of the large automobile producers will be able to make the successful transition to producing electric cars. And, since electric cars not only involve radically new technologies but also have fewer moving parts, the automobile supplier industry will also suffer heavily from the transition away from petroleum-driven cars. The same developments can be observed in a myriad of other sectors. For example, as we saw in the case of precision farming in Chapter 7, nimble new entrants such as the Small Robot Company may increasingly undercut the historic power of gigantic transnational firms such as Massey Ferguson.

It is not surprising, therefore, that there are powerful opponents to paradigm change. Staying with the example of fossil fuels, despite forming an Oil and Gas Climate Initiative to 'limit harmful emissions' after the 2016 Paris climate agreement, the five largest oil and gas companies spend nearly $200 million annually lobbying to delay, control or block climate change policies.[13] On the broader political front, as I showed in Chapter 3, the plutocracy is lobbying intensively to limit taxes and other measures designed to redistribute wealth and income. It is also actively seeking to influence social attitudes through control over the traditional and the new social media.

Hence, power – economic, political and social – lies at the centre of paradigm shift. Providing a sustainability directionality to change cannot be achieved without confronting and overcoming the power of these fettering vested interests.

9.6 Sequencing and Priorities: The Two-Shot Stimulus to a Paradigm Change and the Rebuilding of a Sustainable World

The prioritization and sequencing of actions required to rebuild a more sustainable world are essential. If a scatter-gun approach is adopted, the wood of structural paradigm change will be obscured by the trees of an overly detailed set of policy responses. To elaborate a cliché, whilst this longest of journeys begins with the first steps, the initial steps need to be bold, decisive and stretching. Only after the direction of travel has been set and the journey has begun will it be possible to fall into a canter, implementing the myriad of interventions required to reach the desired goal of sustainability.

So what might these initial bold and decisive steps be? Two stand out in importance. The first is to confront and overcome the power of the plutocracy. The fruits of their dominance can be seen in their growing share of income and wealth since the early 1980s. But the roots to their power lie in their command over social values and the domination of government agendas which resulted in the ideology of neo-liberalism, the small state, austerity policies and regressive taxation. As I showed in earlier chapters, this led to economic slowdown (Chapter 2), inequality, social exclusion and populism (Chapter 3) and a deteriorating environment (Chapter 4). The challenge to the hegemony of the plutocracy will necessarily have to involve measures to redistribute income and wealth. It will also require confronting their capacity to shape values through their control of social and traditional media. Their lobbying power over policy processes – for example, the Super PACs in the US – will need to be curbed. And steps will need to be taken to break the growing concentration of ownership and control over markets in the economy, particularly by the gigantic 'platform' companies such as Facebook, Amazon, Apple, Microsoft and Google.

This necessity of confronting the power of the plutocracy is not a call for preserving Fukuyama's hegemonic 'liberal democracy'. Many of the most effective changes delivering sustainability – for example, a response to the Covid-19 pandemic and the introduction of electric cars – have been implemented most effectively by authoritarian states such as China and Singapore. Conversely, whilst many liberal democracies have proved to be slow-movers on the road to paradigm change, others such as Costa Rica are pioneering the transition to a

net-zero-carbon economy. To repeat an earlier observation, there is
no 'one best way'.

The second priority area for change is the transition to a smart
green economy. This can be achieved through a comprehensive
'big-push', mission-oriented agenda of the sort which helped to
revive the US economy in the 1930s, and which enabled the US to
put a person on the moon in a decade. As we saw in Chapter 8, a
Smart Green New Deal – that is, a greening agenda which exploits
the manifold potential of the ICT heartland technology – is essential
if we are to overcome the greatest sustainability challenge which has
confronted humankind and other species since the dawn of time.
But, at the same time, the smart component of the green agenda will
lead to and support the adoption of the heartland ICT throughout
the economy and society. Smart greening is thus not just an objective
in paradigm change, but is simultaneously also a vehicle for change.
The Smart Green New Deal may be the rallying call for change, but
it will necessarily require complementary interventions. As I showed
in the previous chapter, imparting a sustainability directionality to
paradigm change unavoidably requires the curbing of the speculative
power of the financial sector; redistributing of wealth, incomes and
economic power; devolving some powers from the centre to the
periphery of government; and promoting sustainable development in
the developing world.

The trigger for change

So, what might trigger these changes? In Chapter 5, I reviewed
historical experience with the evolution of techno-economic
paradigms since the onset of the Industrial Revolution. In each case,
the turning point from the development to the deployment phase of
each paradigm involved a crisis of one sort or another, typically in the
building up and bursting of a financial bubble. In some cases, it also
resulted in political convulsion as the power of the reactionary forces
holding back change was challenged. Most recently, the agonies of
paradigm transition were evidenced in the Great Depression of the
1930s and World War 2. Neither of these relatively recent events
(Depression and war) are a particularly attractive option for the
world as we make the transition to the full deployment phase of the
ICT techno-economic paradigm.

In Chapter 2, I documented the declining economic dynamism

of the high-income economies after the mid-1970s, rescued for a couple of decades by the deepening of globalization. This resulted in a growing fragility of the global economy, with a huge growth in debt, unevenness in economic and trade performance and declining rates of investment and growth. Linked to the increasing fragility of the economic system, we have witnessed burgeoning crises of social and environmental sustainability. In recounting these developments, I asked the question: 'What might lead the increasingly unbalanced and fragile economic system to fall over?' I answered that by distinguishing between endogenous triggers (for example, a financial crisis bigger and deeper than that of 2008) and exogenous triggers (for example, a massive volcanic eruption or ... a global pandemic).

We may still see the global economy convulsing as a consequence of its internal structural problems, as virtual currencies such as Bitcoins, over-inflated stock market prices and the global debt mountain bring the Ponzi financial sector to its knees. But, from the vantage of early 2021, there is no need to wait for this disruptive economic crisis as the trigger for structural change. The Covid-19 pandemic has wreaked havoc at a global level and has made a return to 'normal' and 'business as usual' impossible. And whilst the pandemic was not the cause of the linked crises in economic, social and environmental sustainability, it is a disruption of gigantic proportions which exposes the structural fissures in the Mass Production paradigm. The pandemic has both negative and positive impacts. On the one hand, in addition to its devastating impacts on the health of the global population, Covid-19 has exacerbated the erosion of economic and social sustainability. But, on the other hand, in exposing the frailty of Mass Production's global supply chains, by illustrating the opportunities for new patterns of work and residence, by evidencing how damaging emissions can be reduced and by successfully illustrating the potential for collaboration across borders and between the public and private sector, it has shone light on the dark road to recovery.

Now, as the world seeks to cope with the devastating impact of Covid-19, the failure of vision which followed the Global Financial Crisis of 2008 must not be repeated. The rate of economic decline in the first quarter of 2020 was greater than that of the Great Crash of 1929. So great was this disturbance that it resulted in big shifts in the policy arena. In the UK, Margaret Thatcher's famous dictum 'There is no such thing as society' was explicitly challenged by Boris Johnson, the leader of the same Conservative Party. In the US and Brazil, the pandemic diminished the legitimacy of populist governments resisting structural change. Critically, Covid-19 re-legitimized the role of government. Conservative governments previously wedded to austerity policies have introduced basic income support programmes of a magnitude that their left-wing opponents could only dream of. In October 2020, even the IMF – the flag bearer for austerity policies during the neo-liberal era – declared that the austerity era was over.[14] The health response to the pandemic has shown the importance of big mission-oriented research programmes. And countries with public health systems responded much more effectively to the pandemic than those with health systems dominated by private provision.

So, change is not just possible, but already under way. And as the polymath Jared Diamond has observed, there are numerous positive examples to draw on. In 1973, the International Convention for the Prevention of Pollution from Ships reduced pollution of the world's oceans. Changes were enforced in the design of ships to separate oil tanks from water tanks and to require double-hulled tankers for oil-transport. Smallpox, one of the greatest killers known to humans, has been eliminated, as has polio. Joint action by governments reduced the hole in the ozone layer caused by refrigeration propellants. And, a mere five years ago, who would have predicted such a rapidly growing momentum in the private sector to develop electric vehicles, to develop bacterial technologies to eat plastic and to decarbonize their supply chains?

Each of these developments prefigures the sorts of responses required to make a successful transition to a more sustainable ICT techno-economic paradigm. But there is no guarantee that this will be the outcome. For example, in late March 2020, Pershing Square Capital Management made profits of $2.6 billion (100 times its outlay) having bet that Covid-19 would lead to a crash in stock market prices.[15] It then immediately reinvested these squalid proceeds in snapping up the shares of distressed companies which it judged would revive in the future. Banks and hedge funds in the US and the UK distributed large dividends and bonuses to shareholders and senior management in March 2020 in anticipation that this largesse would soon be prohibited by cash-strapped governments providing support to ailing firms and retrenched workers. So, to return to a theme with which this book began: whilst the new ICT techno-economic paradigm offers the opportunity to rebuild a more sustainable world, it does not guarantee this outcome. What transpires is a consequence of agency and social action.

The task is daunting, but not insuperable. The challenge is to deepen, widen and hasten the implementation of assorted measures seeking to rebuild economic, social and environmental sustainability. Chapter 8 provides a suggested agenda for action. It is surely flawed in many respects, and undoubtedly omits important policies. But, whatever its weaknesses, this agenda calls for a systemic response to change and identifies the need for urgent action. Moreover, it recognizes that change is a process necessarily involving coalitions of stakeholders, and that the challenges confronting us present a moving target. Viewed creatively, the journey to remaking sustainability is an exciting one, full of positive surprises. As the unknown artist commented, 'If I knew what the picture looked like, why would I bother to paint it?'

The French philosopher, Jean-Paul Sartre observed insightfully that 'To choose not to choose is in fact to choose.'[16] However, at this crucial turning point in history, we need a greater sense of urgency – 'To choose not to act is in fact to choose.'

Notes

Acknowledgements

1 http://freemanchris.org/publications.
2 https://robinmurray.co.uk.
3 www.carlotaperez.org.

2 The Rise and Fall of the Mass Production Economy

1 UNCTAD World Investment Report, https://unctad.org/en/Pages/DIAE/World%20Investment%20Report/Annex-Tables.aspx.
2 https://transportationtodaynews.com/news/17049-u-s-infrastructure-needs-exceed-2-trillion-american-society-of-civil-engineers-says.
3 M. Pisu, B. Pels and N. Bottini (2015), *Improving Infrastructure in the UK*, ECO/WKP(2015)62, Paris: OECD.
4 Data on house prices from www.globalpropertyprice.com.
5 W. Lazonick (2010), 'The Fragility of the US Economy: The Financialized Corporation and the Disappearing Middle Class', www.theairnet.org/files/research/lazonick/Lazonick%20FUSE%2020101003.pdf.
6 M. Mazzucato (2020), *The Value of Everything: Making and Taking in the Global Economy*, London: Penguin Books.
7 W. Lazonick (2018), 'Innovative Enterprise and Sustainable Prosperity', paper presented to the Conference on Development Planning, Buenos Aires, July 2018.
8 M. Z. Farooki and R. Kaplinsky (2012), *The Impact of China on Global Commodity Prices: The Global Reshaping of the Resource Sector*, London: Routledge.
9 www.stlouisfed.org/open-vault/2020/april/snapshot-record-high-household-debt.
10 https://fred.stlouisfed.org/graph/?id=NCBDBIA027N.

11 https://fred.stlouisfed.org/series/FDHBFIN.
12 www.cfr.org/article/does-italy-threaten-new-european-debt-crisis.
13 https://en.wikipedia.org/wiki/2010_Flash_Crash.
14 *Forbes*, 11 November 2019.
15 *Financial Times*, 17 October 2018.

3 The Bumpy Ride to Social Decay

1 https://en.wikipedia.org/wiki/Society.
2 https://en.wikiquote.org/wiki/Jair_Bolsonaro.
3 F. Fukuyama (1989), 'The End of History?', *The National Interest*, 16: 3–18.
4 The data evidencing these trends in inequality is drawn from the *World Inequality Report* (https://wir2018.wid.world/files/download/ wir2018-summary-english.pdf). Other invaluable sources on inequality and poverty are the writings of Tomas Piketty, Branco Milanovic and Martin Ravallion.
5 https://d1tn3vj7xz9fdh.cloudfront.net/s3fs-public/file_attachments/ bp-reward-work-not-wealth-220118-en.pdf.
6 T. Piketty and T. Goldhammer (2014), *Capital in the 21st Century*, Cambridge, Mass: Harvard University Press.
7 D. Acemoglu and D. Autor (2011), 'Skills, Tasks and Technologies: Implications for Employment and Earnings', in *Handbook of Labor Economics*, IV, Amsterdam: Elsevier, pp. 1043–171.
8 D. B. Kline, 'Real U.S. Wages Are Essentially Back at 1974 Levels', The Motley Fool, www.fool.com/investing/2018/08/14/real-us-wages-are-essentially-back-at-1974-levels.aspx.
9 D. Vaughan-Whitehead (ed.) (2016), *Europe's Disappearing Middle Class? Evidence from the World of Work*, Cheltenham: Edward Elgar.
10 P. Townsend (1979), *Poverty in the United Kingdom: A Survey of Household Resources and Standards of Living*, Harmondsworth: Penguin Books.
11 R. B. Reich (1991), *The Work of Nations: Preparing Ourselves for 21st-Century Capitalism*, New York: Simon and Schuster.
12 http://robertreich.org/post/135202830270.
13 *Financial Times*, 23 September 2019.
14 www.tuc.org.uk/sites/default/files/the-gig-is-up.pdf.
15 www.ohchr.org/documents/issues/poverty/eom_gb_16nov2018.pdf.
16 This section leans heavily on R. Wilkinson and K. Pickett's two pathbreaking books *The Spirit Level: Why More Equal Societies Almost Always Do Better* (London: Allen Lane, 2009) and *The Inner Level* (Harmondsworth: Penguin Books, 2019).
17 Wilkinson and Pickett, *The Spirit Level* and *The Inner Level*.
18 www.washingtonpost.com/lifestyle/travel/air-rage-incidents-are-on-the-rise-first-class-sections-arent-helping/2017/01/23.

19 www.rte.ie/news/business/2018/1123/1012900-google-ireland-paid-171m-in-tax-last-year.
20 https://itep.org/amazon-in-its-prime-doubles-profits-pays-0-in-federal-income-taxes.
21 *Washington Post*, 8 August 2019.
22 www.euractiv.com/section/elections/news/how-france-successfully-countered-russian-interference-during-the-presidential-election.
23 www.politico.eu/article/russian-botnet-promotes-far-right-messages-in-german-election.
24 https://en.wikipedia.org/wiki/Cambridge_Analytica.
25 *The Guardian*, 12 July 2018.
26 'Trump is the Natural Consequence of Our Anti-Democracy Decade', *The Guardian*, 8 December 2019.

4 The Collapse of Environmental Sustainability

1 https://en.wikipedia.org/wiki/Chicxulub_crater.
2 https://en.wikipedia.org/wiki/Laki.
3 https://whatsyourimpact.org/greenhouse-gases/carbon-dioxide-emissions.
4 United Nations Environment Programme (2016), *Global Material Flows and Resource Productivity*. This is the source for all the data cited on resource extraction.
5 T. Jackson (2009), *Prosperity Without Growth: Foundations for the Economy of Tomorrow*, London: Taylor and Francis.
6 www.bbc.com/future/story/20160612-heres-the-truth-about-the-planned-obsolescence-of-tech.
7 https://en.wikipedia.org/wiki/Planned_obsolescence#Contrived_durability.
8 https://en.wikipedia.org/wiki/Electronics_right_to_repair.
9 www.bbc.com/future/story/20160612-heres-the-truth-about-the-planned-obsolescence-of-tech.
10 Downloadable at www.soilandhealth.org/wp-content/uploads/0303critic/030320wastemakers/wastemakers.pdf.
11 https://ec.europa.eu/energy/intelligent/projects/sites/iee-projecEnergy.
12 V. Silva, H. G. J. Mol, P. Zomer, M. Tienstra, C. J. Ritsema and V. Geissen (2018), 'Pesticide Residues in European Agricultural Soils – A Hidden Reality Unfolded', *Science of the Total Environment*, 653: 1532–45.
13 I. K. Wernick, R. Herman, S. Govind and J. H. Ausubel (1996), 'Materialization and Dematerialization: Measures and Trends', in J. H. Ausubel and H. D. Langford (eds.), Technological Trajectories and the Human Environment, Washington, DC: The National Academies Press.
14 https://en.wikipedia.org/wiki/Plastic_pollution#Decomposition_of_plastics.

15 *The Guardian*, 18 February 2019.
16 https://en.wikipedia.org/wiki/Microplastics.
17 www.anthropocene.info/anthropocene-timeline.php.
18 F. Sánchez-Bayo and K. A. G. Wyckhuys (2019), 'Worldwide Decline of the Entomofauna: A Review of its Drivers', *Biological Conservation*, 232: 8–27.
19 Ibid.
20 www.fao.org/news/story/en/item/1194910/icode.
21 www.bbc.co.uk/news/uk-england-35131751.
22 *The Guardian*, 12 June 2020.

5 Mass Production Runs Out of Steam

1 The neo-Schumpeterian theory of techno-economic paradigms informs the discussion in this chapter and provides the intellectual architecture for this book. Within this body of theory, I have drawn on the analytical framework developed by Chris Freeman, Carlota Perez and Francisco Louca: C. Freeman and F. Louca (2001), *As Time Goes By: From the Industrial Revolution to the Information Revolution*, Oxford University Press; C. Perez (2002), *Technological Revolutions and Financial Capital: The Dynamics of Bubbles and Golden Ages*, Cheltenham: Edward Elgar; C. Freeman and C. Perez (1988), 'Structural Crises of Adjustment', in Giovanni Dosi, Christopher Freeman, Richard Nelson, Gerald Silverberg and Luc Soete (eds.), *Technical Change and Economic Theory*, London: Frances Pinter. Other major variants of this analytical tradition are to be found in the socio-technical school, in particular the Multi-Level Perspective (MLP) and Deep Transition frameworks. For the former, see F. W. Geels (2005), *Technological Transitions and System Innovations: A Co-evolutionary and Socio-technical Analysis*, Cheltenham: Edward Elgar; and J. Grin, J. Rotmans and J. Schot (2010), *Transitions to Sustainable Development: New Directions in the Study of Long Term Transformative Change*, London and New York: Routledge. For the Deep Transition framework, see J. Schot and L. Kanger (2018), 'Deep Transitions: Emergence, Acceleration, Stabilization and Directionality', *Research Policy*, 47, 6: 1045–59; L. Kanger and J. Schot (2019), 'Deep Transitions: Theorizing the Long-Term Patterns of Socio-technical Change', *Environmental Innovations and Societal Transitions*, 32: 7–21.
2 J. A. Schumpeter (1911), *The Theory of Economic Development: An Inquiry into Profits, Capital, Credit, Interest and the Business Cycle*, Harvard Economic Studies 46, Cambridge, Mass.: Harvard University Press.
3 Freeman and Perez, 'Structural Crises of Adjustment'.
4 Two widely promoted approaches to meeting the challenges of contemporary economic disruption – 'The Fourth Industrial Revolution' and 'Industry 4' – conflate changes in technological systems and changes

in techno-economic paradigms. The bundle of technologies which they promote do not meet the four characteristics of heartland technologies. Moreover, their agendas fail to recognize adequately the systemic interactions between technology, macroeconomic policy, institutions, power relations, and norms and values.

5 Perez, *Technological Revolutions and Financial Capital*.

6 Ibid.

7 https://en.wikipedia.org/wiki/Canal#Industrial_Revolution.

8 www.saburchill.com/history/chapters/IR/033.html.

9 https://en.wikipedia.org/wiki/Ford_Model_T.

10 Ibid. I have updated the Wikipedia data from 2017 to 2020 prices, using US Bureau of Labor statistics.

11 J. K. Galbraith (1954), *The Great Crash, 1929*, New York: Houghton, Mifflin, Harcourt.

12 www.britannica.com/event/stock-market-crash-of-1929.

13 https://en.wikipedia.org/wiki/United_States_aircraft_production_during_World_War_II.

14 It is too much of a diversion to expand on this development here. But there is an extensive literature documenting these trends, including the classic texts by M. Piore and C. Sabel (1984), *The Second Industrial Divide* (New York: Basic Books), and M. Best (1990), *The New Competition* (Oxford: Polity).

15 https://en.wikipedia.org/wiki/World_Trade_Organization.

16 K. Hoffman and R. Kaplinsky (1988), *Driving Force: The Global Restructuring of Technology, Labor and Investment in the Automobile and Components Industries*, Boulder, Colo.: Westview Press.

17 www.marineinsight.com/maritime-history/the-history-of-containerization-in-the-shipping-industry.

18 D. Hummels, Jun Ishii and Kei-Mu Yi (2001), 'The Nature and Growth of Vertical Specialization in World Trade', *Journal of International Economics*, 54, 1: 75–96.

19 S. Ponte, G. Gereffi and G. Raj-Reichert (eds.) (2019), *Handbook on Global Value Chains*, London: Edward Elgar.

20 Y. Xing and N. Detert (2010), *How the iPhone Widens the United States Trade Deficit with the People's Republic of China*, ADBI Working Paper 257, Tokyo: Asian Development Bank Institute.

21 UNCTAD (2013), *Global Value Chains and Development: Investment and International Trade in the Global Economy*, Geneva: United Nations Conference for Trade and Development.

22 https://en.wikipedia.org/wiki/Interstate_Highway_System.

23 Perez, *Technological Revolutions and Financial Capital*.

24 www.encyclopedia.com/history/culture-magazines/1950s-tv-and-radio.

6 Information and Communication Technologies

1 A widely cited account of the development and potential of ICTs can be found in A. McAfee and E. Brynjolffson, *The Second Machine Age: Work, Progress, and Prosperity in a Time of Brilliant Technologies*, New York: W. W. Norton, 2014. See also the work of J. Rifkin – for example, *The Third Industrial Revolution*, London: Palgrave Macmillan, 2011 – and K. Schwab, *The Fourth Industrial Revolution*, London: Penguin, 2016.

2 P. Wohlleben (2016), *The Hidden Life of Trees: What They Feel, How They Communicate*, Vancouver: Greystone Books.

3 www.bankmycell.com/blog/how-many-phones-are-in-the-world.

4 https://techjury.net/stats-about/big-data-statistics/9.

5 https://en.wikipedia.org/wiki/Examples_of_data_mining.

6 https://images.techhive.com/assets/2017/04/10/cw-50th-anniversary-storage-trends.pdf.

7 https://en.wikipedia.org/wiki/Transistor_count.

8 www.zocalopublicsquare.org/2020/03/22/what-is-moores-law/ideas/essay.

9 www.cn-jif.com/main.asp; http://old.dongguantoday.com/Economic04.htm; www.economist.com/node/21552898.

10 *Financial Times*, 19 June 2019.

11 M. K. Leung, letter to *Financial Times*, 27 June 2019.

12 www.theguardian.com/technology/2019/sep/15/ex-google-worker-fears-killer-robots-cause-mass-atrocities.

13 C. B. Frey and M. A. Osborne (2017), 'The Future of Employment: How Susceptible Are Jobs to Computerization?' *Technological Forecasting and Social Change*, 114: 254–80. However, a more sober assessment of the employment impact of robotization and Artificial Intelligence by the OECD in 2017 challenged these startling estimates (www.theverge.com/2018/4/3/17192002/ai-job-loss-predictions-forecasts-automation-oecd-report). Using the criterion of a more than 70 per cent chance of automation displacing individual tasks, they estimated that around 14 per cent of jobs in the OECD economies would be lost. Although far lower than the worst-case predictions in the Oxford University report, the OECD estimate nevertheless involved the loss of 66 million jobs in the high-income economies, 13 million of which will be in the USA.

14 www.theverge.com/2018/4/3/17192002/ai-job-loss-predictions-forecasts-automation-oecd-report.

7 Transformative Change in Practice

1 E. Osongo and J. Schot (2017), *Inclusive Innovation and Rapid Sociotechnical Transitions: The Case of Mobile Money in Kenya*, SWPS 2017-07, Brighton: Science Policy Research Unit; and A. Demirgue-Kunt,

L. Klapper and D. Singer (2017), *Financial Inclusion and Inclusive Growth: A Review of Recent Empirical Evidence*, World Bank Policy Research Working Paper 8040, Washington, DC: World Bank.

2 https://en.wikipedia.org/wiki/Coal_mining.

3 B. K. Sovacool, K. Lovell and M. B. Ting (2018), 'Reconfiguration, Contestation, and Decline: Conceptualizing Mature Large Technical Systems', *Science, Technology, & Human Values*, 43, 6: 1066–97.

4 https://en.wikipedia.org/wiki/Myitsone_Dam#Economics.

5 T. Scudder (2005), *The Kariba Case Study*, Social Science Working Paper 1227, Pasadena: California Institute of Technology.

6 Renewable Energy Network, REN 21, www.ren21.net.

7 M. Lipton and J. Litchfield (2002), 'The Impact of Irrigation on Poverty', mimeo, p. 32 (pers. comm.).

8 'Wind Sweeps Coal from Top of Texas Power List', *Financial Times*, 13 January 2020.

9 www.irena.org/costs; https://about.bnef.com/blog/tumbling-costs-wind-solar-batteries-squeezing-fossil-fuels; https://about.bnef.com/new-energy-outlook/; www.ren21.net/future-of-renewables/global-futures-report.

10 F. Schumacher (1973), *Small is Beautiful*, London: Blond and Briggs.

11 https://mailchi.mp/118657fdd7bc/reconnecting-with-our-soil-5039 43?e=742106fed6.

12 https://greenlivingjournal.com/page.php?p=9108.

13 *Financial Times*, 4 July 2019.

14 https://mailchi.mp/118657fdd7bc/reconnecting-with-our-soil-5039 43?e=742106fed6.

15 C. Christensen (1997), *The Innovators Dilemma*, Boston: Harvard Business Review Press.

8 What's To Be Done?

1 A. Joffe, D. Kaplan, R. Kaplinsky and D. Lewis (1995), *Improving Manufacturing Performance: The Report of the Industrial Strategy Project*, University of Cape Town Press.

2 C. Perez and T. Murray Leach (2018), *A Smart Green 'European Way of Life': The Path for Growth, Jobs and Wellbeing, Beyond the Technological Revolution*, WP-2018-01, p. 16, www.beyondthetechrevolution.com.

3 www.flemingpolicycentre.org.uk/david-fleming-2.

4 *The Guardian*, 14 November 2019.

5 www.exchangewire.com/blog/2019/03/28/facebook-google-the-duopolys-dominance-increases.

6 www.theguardian.com/business/2018/aug/16/ceo-versus-worker-wage-american-companies-pay-gap-study-2018.

7 www.bloomberg.com/news/articles/2019-01-04/u-k-ceo-pay-to-top-average-worker-s-2019-income-by-lunchtime.

8 http://theconversation.com/labours-green-new-deal-is-among-the-most-radical-in-the-world-but-can-it-be-done-by-2030-123982.

9 *Financial Times*, 3 December 2019.

10 www.marketwatch.com/story/6-ways-to-prepare-your-finances-for-climate-change-2016-12-20.

11 K. Hochstetler, *Political Economies of Energy Transition: Wind and Solar Power in Brazil and South Africa*, Cambridge University Press, 2020.

12 http://theconversation.com/labours-green-new-deal-is-among-the-most-radical-in-the-world-but-can-it-be-done-by-2030-123982.

13 M. Mazzucato (2011), *The Entrepreneurial State*, London: Demos.

14 www.cam.ac.uk/news/solving-the-uk%E2%80%99s-energy-problems.

15 D. Coady, I. Parry, N. Nghia-Piotr Le and B. Shang, *Global Fossil Fuel Subsidies Remain Large: An Update Based on Country-Level Estimates*, Working Paper No. 19/89, Washington, DC: International Monetary Fund.

16 https://en.wikipedia.org/wiki/Participatory_budgeting.

17 https://neweconomics.opendemocracy.net/preston-model-modern-politics-municipal-socialism.

18 www.flemingpolicycentre.org.uk/david-fleming-2.

9 Who Will Do It? Making Change Happen

1 Two widely cited texts on the importance of developing Industrial Policy as a process are H. Mintzberg, J. B. Quinn and S. Ghoshal (1998), *The Strategy Process*, London: Prentice Hall; and D. Rodrik (2004), *Industrial Policy for the Twenty-First Century*, Cambridge, Mass.: John F. Kennedy School of Government, https://j.mp/2nRcNXi.

2 J. Tidd and J. Bessant (2014), *Strategic Innovation Management*, Oxford: Wiley.

3 A. Smith, *The Theory of Moral Sentiments*, London: T. Creech and J. Bell & Co., 1790, pp. 488–9.

4 *Financial Times*, 6 November 2019.

5 www.americanprogress.org/issues/economy/reports/2020/09/23/489894/electric-vehicles-win-american-workers.

6 *Financial Times*, 7 April 2020.

7 H. Schmitz (2015), 'Green Transformation: Is There a Fast Track?' in I. Scoones, M. Leach and P. Newell (eds.), *The Politics of Green Transformation: Pathways to Sustainability*, Oxford: Routledge.

8 R. Hopkins (2010), 'What Can Communities Do?' in R. Heinberg and D. Lerch (eds.), *The Post Carbon Reader: Managing the 21st Century's Sustainability Crises*, Healdsburg, Calif.: Watershed Media.

9 K. Hoffman and R. Kaplinsky (1988), *Driving Force: The Global Restructuring of Technology, Labor and Investment in the Automobile and Components Industries*, Boulder, Colo.: Westview Press.

10 The widely promoted agendas of the 'Fourth Industrial Revolution' and 'Industry 4' adopt this technocratic approach to system change, believing that the answer to societal challenges can be found in the adoption of ICTs and other new technologies, such as biotechnology.

11 T. Pierenkemper and R. Tilly (2004), *The German Economy during the Nineteenth Century*, Oxford and New York: Berghahn Books, pp. 136–44.

12 Y. Varoufakis (2017), *Adults in the Room: My Battle with Europe's Deep Establishment*, London: The Bodley Head.

13 *The Guardian*, 22 March 2019.

14 *Financial Times*, 17 October 2020.

15 *The Guardian*, 25 March 2020.

16 J.-P. Sartre, in a lecture given in 1946: 'Existentialism Is a Humanism', in Walter Kaufman (ed.) (1956), *Existentialism from Dostoyevsky to Sartre*, Cleveland: World Publishing Company.

Index

3D printing (additive manufacturing) 129–30, 134–5, 197

Acemoglu, D. 227n7
advertising 85–6, 106, 116, 138, 183, 210
air rage 48–9
Alphabet 23, 138, 183
Alston, P. 44, 53
Amazon Inc. 52, 128, 132, 182–4, 192, 221, 228
Anthropocene 71, 86, 89, 229
anxiety 47–8, 136
Apple 23, 82–3, 113, 182–3, 221
Artificial Intelligence 29, 131–3, 137, 142, 167–8, 183, 191, 231
austerity policies 8, 26–5, 51–4, 59, 179, 195–6, 217, 221, 224
Ausubel, J. H. 228n13
automated stock trading 29
automated weapons 142
automobiles
  electric vehicles 138
  number 87, 139, 178
automobilization 8, 107, 116, 123, 193
Autor, D. 42n7

Barcombe 204–5, 213
Big Data 131–3, 137, 167, 169, 231
bitcoins 29–30, 141–2, 181, 223
Best, M. 230n14
Bolsonaro, J. xi, 36, 90, 227
Brexit 36, 54–8, 142, 209
Brynjolffson, E. 231n1

bubble, financial 2, 7, 25, 32, 96, 99, 101–2, 222

Cambridge Analytica 56–7, 142
chemical residues 77, 87–8, 90, 97, 153, 162, 167–9, 171–2, 176, 189, 190–1
China
  conflict 32, 142, 210
  Covid-19 31–119
  employment 11, 43, 112, 135
  environment 201, 214, 219, 221
  growth 5–6, 10, 12, 40, 199
  inequality 37–9
  investment 12, 16, 20, 154, 156, 201–2, 213
  trade 9, 15, 24, 30, 64, 79, 113, 116
Christensen, C. 169, 232n15
Circular Economy xii, 176, 187–8, 193
civic participation xii, 35, 49–50, 117, 140–1, 145, 177, 179, 187, 195, 206, 210–11
Coady, D. 233n15
coal
  decommissioning 193
  emissions 74–6
  energy supply 69, 81, 118, 100–1, 123, 150–2, 159–60, 178, 189, 190
  fatalities 152–8
concentration, corporate 174, 182–6, 221
consumption
  green 188, 192, 198, 200–1
  pattern, balancing supply 2, 8, 16–20, 27, 39, 63, 66, 77–87, 104, 106, 114–18, 133–8, 142–6, 199, 214

consumption (*cont.*)
  proximity to production 161, 175, 177, 179, 194, 217
  tax 190
Covid-19
  causes 31, 92, 119
  economic growth 2, 6–8, 30, 43, 119, 136, 223
  governance and social solidarity 82, 196, 223–4
  global supply chains 31, 113
  vaccines 138, 195–7, 221
cybercrime 141–2, 173
Cyprus Industrial Strategy 203–4

dams 19, 45, 70, 73, 153–60
data capture, storage, transmission 126–8
debt 6, 8, 17, 21, 24–8, 32, 43, 95, 181–2, 184, 218–19, 223, 226–7
deindustrialization 8, 16, 30, 196
dematerialization 77–9, 139, 191–2
Demirgue-Kunt, A. 231n1
Detert, N. 230n20
digital logic 124–38
directionality 2, 43, 121,176–80, 194, 197, 211, 215–22
Dodd–Frank Act 181
Dosi, G. 229n1
Dudley, G. 229n1

economic growth
  Covid-19 crisis 2, 6–8, 30, 43, 119, 136, 223
  measurement 188–91
  revival 7, 18, 134–5, 177, 217
  slowdown 8–12, 95–6, 221
electric vehicles 86, 139, 186, 192–4, 201, 212, 224
electronic data interchange (EDI) 127
emissions
  carbon dioxide 68, 70–1, 74–5, 78–9, 87, 90–1, 153, 158, 176, 191, 194
  methane 69, 71, 74–5, 77, 87, 153, 201
employment 6, 15, 17, 25, 30, 39, 43–4, 51, 61–3, 99, 105–6, 135, 142–3, 149, 152, 164, 175, 179, 190–1
extinction
  megafauna 68
  species 92–3

Facebook 56–7, 140, 182–3, 189, 210, 221
financial crisis 2, 7, 12, 14, 20–9, 32, 43, 51–3, 59, 96, 99, 103–5, 119, 181, 218–23
financialization 21–1, 24, 22
flexible production systems 128–30, 134–5
Ford, Henry 103–9, 114, 124, 135, 142, 158, 166, 172, 178, 185, 212, 216
fossil fuels 73–7, 140, 150–3, 159, 189–93, 199–201, 220
Freeman, C. xii, 97–8, 102, 121
Frey, C. B. 227n13
Fukuyama, F. 36–7, 62, 115, 214, 221, 227n3

Galbraith, J. K. 230n11
Geels, F. W. 229n1
Geissen, V. 228n12
gender relations 116
Gereffi, G. 230n19
Ghoshal, S. 233n1
Glass–Steagall Act 180
Golden Age 2–3, 8–10, 14, 20, 31, 39, 43, 58, 63, 95, 99–101, 105–7, 114–15, 123, 130, 180
governance
  corporate 22
  global 37, 63–4, 107, 111, 117, 179, 198, 209
  local 179, 196–7, 210, 217
  national 36, 58, 97, 158, 174, 179, 198, 209
Govind, S. 228n13
Great Acceleration 3, 71, 76–7, 85, 89, 117
Great Depression (1930s) 8, 17, 20, 31, 53, 95, 101, 103, 106, 119, 152, 180, 186, 213, 218, 222
Great Recession (2008) 2, 7, 17–18, 25–7, 32, 95, 99, 177
Green New Deal 185–8, 194–5, 199, 217, 219
Grin, J. 229n1
Gutenberg printing press 126

heartland technology 3–4, 96–101, 121–7, 133, 141–5, 149–50, 161, 173–5, 185, 193, 206, 222
Herman, R. 228n13
Hochstetler, K. 233n11

Hoffman, K. 230n16
Holocene 67–71, 85, 89
Hopkins, R. 215, 233n8
Hummels, D. 230n18
hydroelectricity 75, 150–61, 172

industrial policy 15, 174–6, 203
inequality 3, 14, 16–17, 37, 37–51, 59,
        95, 99, 116, 119, 143, 154, 159,
        178, 182–4, 207, 221
infrastructure 8, 10, 12, 16–20, 27, 35,
        53, 59, 63, 69, 80, 106, 110, 113,
        116, 134–6, 145, 154, 158, 179,
        182, 188, 193, 197–8, 208, 217–18
International Monetary Fund (IMF) 26,
        33, 107, 112, 189, 209, 219, 224
Internet of Things (IoT) 130–1, 137,
        140–1, 193, 198
investment 7, 8, 10–20, 21–30, 35, 52,
        63–4, 80, 95, 99, 101, 104, 106,
        109, 114, 132, 151–62, 177–86,
        193–4, 212, 213, 217–18, 223
IPCC 91–2
Ishii, J. 230n18

Jackson, T. 228n5
Joffe, A. 232n1
John Deere 167–9

Kaplan, D. 232n1
Kaplinsky 230n16, 232n1, 233n9
Kemp, R. 229n1
Klapper, L. 232n1
Koch brothers 57–9

Lazonick, W. 22, 226n5, 226n7
Le, N. 233n15
Leach. M. 233n7
legitimacy (political) 35–6
Lewis, D. 232n1
liberal democracy 34–6, 61–3, 115, 118,
        221
lifestyles 2, 4, 97, 106, 115–17, 177–9,
        188, 191, 200, 208, 224
Lipton, M. 232n7
Litchfield, J. 232n7
Louca, F. 229n1
Lovell, K. 232n3
Lyons, G. 229n1

Marx, K. 81
Mazzucato, M. 22, 226n6, 186, 233n13
McAfee, A. 231n1
Microsoft 23, 83, 182, 183, 221
migrants 11, 55–6, 59–62, 112, 200
Milanovic, B. 112, 227n4
Mintzberg, H. 233n1
M-Kopa 148–9
mobile phones 82–3, 131, 139–48, 172,
        192, 194
Mol, H. G. J. 228n12
M-Pesa 145–9
Murdoch, R. 57
Murray, R. xii, 203–4
Murray Leach, T. 232n2

Nelson, R. 229n1
neo-liberalism 7–8, 15–24, 34, 37, 51–4,
        95, 112, 116–18, 182, 196, 217,
        221, 224
new deal
    green new deal 185–8, 194–5, 199, 217,
        219
    Roosevelt 17–18, 106, 185–6, 217
Newell, P. 233n7

obsolescence
    product 81–3
    systems 83
Osborne, M. A. 231n13
Osongo, E. 231n1

Packard, Vance 84–5
Parry, I. 233n15
participatory budgeting 196–7
Perez, C. xii, 97–102, 121–4, 177–8, 214,
        226n3, 229n1, 232n2
pesticides 87, 90, 153, 165–6, 171, 191
Phoebus Cartel 83–4
Pickett, K. 44–50, 191, 227n16
Pierenkemper, T. 234n11
Piketty, T. 39, 227n4
Piore, M. 230n14
planetary boundaries 89–90, 176
plastic 73, 84, 88–90, 97, 101, 129,
        176–8, 192, 214, 224
plutocracy 8, 37, 51, 54, 58–9, 63, 95,
        116, 118, 142, 178, 180, 182, 185,
        217, 220–1
Ponte, S. 230n19

populism 34, 59, 62, 95, 99, 189, 195, 221
poverty 24–5, 42–4, 51–4, 59, 116, 119,
    182, 200, 202, 222, 227n4
productivity
    agricultural 89, 153, 162–5, 171–2
    decline 7, 11, 13–14, 19, 22, 24, 95,
        103–9, 173, 194, 207
    increase 10, 69, 123, 134–6, 149
    profitability 22, 96–9, 107–11, 132–4,
        172–3, 206, 208, 211, 220
protectionism 30–31, 64, 105, 116–17

quantitative easing 20, 23–7, 181
Quinn, J. B. 233n1

Raj-Reichert, G. 230n19
Ravallion, M. 227n4
Reagan, R. 18, 23
Reich, R. 43, 58–9, 227n11
renewable energy 73–5, 81, 131, 139–40,
    145–51, 158–61, 193, 199, 201,
    212–13
Rifkin, J. 231n1
Ritsema, C. J. 228n12
Rodrik, D. 233n1
Rotmans, J. 229n1
rust belts 15, 25, 30, 116

Sabel, C. 230n14
Sánchez-Bayo, F. 229n18
Say's Law 16
Schmitz, H. 233n7
Schot, J. 229n1, 231n1
Schumacher, F. 232n10
Schumpeter, J. 81, 96–8, 121, 141, 205–6,
    208, 229n1
Schwab, K. 231n1
Scoones, I. 233n7
Scudder, T. 232n5
sensors, digital 126–7, 130, 137, 140
Shang, B. 233n15
shareholders 19, 21–3, 169, 184, 205, 224
Silva, H. G. 228n12
Silverberg, G. 229n1
Singer, D. 232n1
Small Robot Company 169–70, 220
smart city programme 197–8
Smith, A. 43, 81, 102–3, 207, 233n3
Soete, L. 229n1
Sovacool, B. 75, 232n3

suburbanization 2, 8, 18, 106, 115
supply chains 10, 15–16, 30–2, 64, 79,
    113, 119, 129, 134–6, 177, 194,
    200, 223–4

tax 15, 18–27, 35, 40, 52–63, 108, 112,
    181–4, 190, 210, 215–17, 220–8
Thatcher, M. 18, 34–5, 52, 180, 225
Tienstra, M. 228n12
Tilly, R. 234n11
Ting, M. B. 232n3
Townsend, P. 42, 227n10
Toyota Manufacturing System 109–10, 216
tractors, environmental impact 164–71
trade
    barriers, protectionism 30–1, 64, 105,
        116–17
    imbalances 16, 25, 30–1
    reduction in tariffs 14–15, 108, 112
Transition Town movement 213
Trump, D. xi, 23, 30, 36–7, 40, 51, 54–7,
    61, 64, 90, 118, 142, 181

unemployment 6, 17, 25, 43, 51, 61, 63,
    99, 105, 188, 191, 218
UNEP 75–6, 80

Varoufakis, Y. 218, 234n12
Vaughan-Whitehead, D. 227n9
volatility, economic 8, 29, 32, 95, 177

wages 9, 16, 39, 41, 44, 51, 63, 104, 112,
    210
Watson-Jones, S. 161, 164, 166–7, 169
welfare 18, 20, 24, 36, 46, 53–4, 58, 63,
    82, 114
Wernick, K. 228n13
Wilkinson. R, 44–50, 191, 227n16
Wohlleben, P. 231n2
Wolf, M. 33
World Bank 9–12, 112, 157–8, 219
World Trade Organization 64, 108, 209
Wyckhuys, K. A. G. 229n18

Xing, Y. 230n20

Yi, K-M. 230n18

Zomer, P. 228n12
zoonotic diseases 92, 119, 195